Bread and Roses

Bread and Roses
Gender and Class Under Capitalism

Andrea D'Atri

Translated by Nathaniel Flakin

PLUTO PRESS

First published by Ediciones IPS, Argentina 2004
English language edition first published 2021 by Pluto Press
345 Archway Road, London N6 5AA

www.plutobooks.com

Copyright © Andrea D'Atri and Ediciones IPS Argentina, 2013; Translation copyright © Nathaniel Flakin 2021

The right of Andrea D'Atri to be identified as the author of this work has been asserted in accordance with the Copyright, Designs and Patents Act 1988.

Work published within the framework of "Sur" Translation Support Program of the Ministry of Foreign Affairs and Worship of the Argentine Republic. Obra editada en el marco del Programa "Sur" de Apoyo a las Traducciones del Ministerio de Relaciones Exteriores y Culto de la República Argentina.

British Library Cataloguing in Publication Data
A catalogue record for this book is available from the British Library

ISBN   978 0 7453 4117 0   Hardback
ISBN   978 0 7453 4118 7   Paperback
ISBN   978 1 7868 0726 7   PDF eBook
ISBN   978 1 7868 0728 1   Kindle eBook
ISBN   978 1 7868 0727 4   EPUB eBook

This book is printed on paper suitable for recycling and made from fully managed and sustained forest sources. Logging, pulping and manufacturing processes are expected to conform to the environmental standards of the country of origin.

Typeset by Stanford DTP Services, Northampton, England

Simultaneously printed in the United Kingdom and United States of America

To Ana María Layño, my mother, for giving me the freedom to be a different woman than she was, and also a different woman than she would have wanted me to be.

Contents

Preface to the English Edition — ix
Acknowledgments — xiv
Biography — xv

Introduction — 1
   Gender and Class on International Women's Day — 1
   Oppression and Exploitation — 3
   Gender Unites Us, Class Divides Us — 4
   Capitalism and Patriarchy: A Well-Matched Marriage — 6
   Women's Struggle and Class Struggle — 8

1. Grain Riots and Civil Rights — 9
   Bread, Cannons, and Revolution — 9
   Female Citizens Demand Equality — 13
   Liberty, Fraternity, and Inequality of Class and Gender — 15

2. Bourgeois Women and Proletarian Women — 19
   Steam Engines, Looms, and Women — 19
   Women Workers Organize to Fight — 21
   A Government of the Working People of Paris — 25
   The Women Incendiaries and the Ladies with Parasols — 27

3. Between Philanthropy and Revolution — 31
   Voting Rights or Charity? — 31
   Reform or Revolution? — 34
   A Woman Living Between Two Eras — 39
   On the Need to Welcome Foreign Women — 46
   Petition to Reinstate Divorce — 49
   The Workers' Union — 52
   The *Tour de France* — 60

4. Imperialism, War, and Gender — 63
- Debates in the Second International — 63
- Women at War — 69
- Women and Nations — 71
- Freedom During Wartime, Oppression During Peacetime? — 75

5. Women in the First Workers' State in History — 82
- The Spark that Could Light the Flame — 82
- Bread, Peace, Freedom, and Women's Rights — 87
- Harrowing Contradictions — 90
- The Philosophy of a Priest, the Powers of a Gendarme — 94
- Comrade Kollontai — 97
- Oppositional Women — 103

6. From Vietnam to Paris, Bras to the Bonfire — 110
- Economic Boom and Baby Boom — 110
- Liberty, Equality, Sorority — 113
- Radical and Socialist Feminists Against Patriarchy — 116

7. Difference of Women, Differences Between Women — 122
- The Imperialist Offensive Sweeps Everything Away — 122
- Autonomous and Institutionalized Feminists in Latin America — 126
- Revaluing the Feminine — 129
- Integrated or Marginalized — 131
- Intersection of Differences — 133

8. Postmodernity, Postmarxism, Postfeminism — 138
- The 1990s: NGO-ization and Gender Technocracy — 138
- Performativity, Parody, and Radical Democracy — 140
- Consumerism, Individualism, and Skepticism — 145

By Way of Conclusion — 148

Appendix — 151
  Bread and Roses: International Manifesto (2020)
Bibliography — 168
Index — 175

Preface to the English Edition
15 Years of Bread and Roses

As I write the preface to this new edition of *Bread and Roses: Gender and Class Under Capitalism*, the Covid-19 pandemic is sweeping across the world, showing that dystopian fiction can become reality and everyday life can transform into soporific and surreal lethargy. Between the first edition in Spanish and this first edition in English, only 15 years have passed—but the distance between then and now is enormous, defined by the "before" and "after" of the coronavirus.

To understand this, it is perhaps worth remembering that this book was originally published in 2004 in Argentina; at that time in the United States, Mark Zuckerberg and his friends at Harvard were launching a website to connect the university's 20,000 students. Today, Facebook has over 2.3 billion users worldwide, besides owning WhatsApp, the leading messaging service, without which it is impossible to imagine this life in confinement, full of virtual classes, working from home, online entertainment, and video calls. In the midst of a global crisis and the dizzying events occurring every day, the year 2004 feels like it was more than a century ago.

Bread and Roses: Gender and Class Under Capitalism was later published in Venezuela in 2007, in Brazil in 2008, and in Mexico in 2010. In 2013, a new corrected and expanded edition was published in Argentina—that is the version that is presented here in English by Pluto Press. Although it was revised almost a decade after its initial publication, this text nonetheless pre-dates the international feminist wave of recent years and the great events the world is currently witnessing. This same version was translated and published in Italy in 2016, and in Germany and France in 2019.

* * *

When the first edition of *Bread and Roses: Gender and Class Under Capitalism* appeared in Argentina, we dared to propose that the relationship between the categories of gender and class be considered in the heat of history. We did this from the extreme South of our continent, and outside of academic circles. For this reason, although this book neither offers a detailed account of each of the infinite struggles of the international women's movement, nor covers all the theoretical debates that traverse the movement, it does have the merit of presenting the hypothesis—15 years ago—that there will be no gradual, evolutionary progress toward the expansion of political rights and democratic freedoms for women.

At a time when feminist struggles were not on the front pages, this book argued that advances and setbacks in the struggle against patriarchy, within the framework of the capitalist system, coincide with periods of reforms, revolutions, or reaction. The idea that women's struggles advance and retreat with the ups and downs of the class struggle runs through this book. And just as defeats of the masses meant that women and other oppressed sectors of society were silenced and forced to wait, revolutionary processes brought about unusual transformations, at an unexpected speed, of everyday life and social and political institutions.

This book does not contain an extensive discussion of the struggles for sexual liberation, about which we have written numerous articles. Nor is there an analysis of racism and the intricate web of oppressions that links gender and class with race, ethnicity, and nationality. Were we to rewrite this work today, having gone through great experiences of collective struggle and learnt a great deal, we would include an analysis of how capitalism organizes lives and bodies into hierarchies, shaping the working class in complex and heterogeneous ways. And without a doubt, the recent rebellions in the United States in the wake of the police murder of George Floyd and against the institutional racist violence of US imperialism—with Black women in the front lines of the mobilizations—would be a source of inspiration for such a new work on women's oppression and the perspectives for emancipation. The emergence of a new generation of people who are taking up the perspective of a socialist society in the heart of imperialism would similarly inspire.

* * *

But when we wrote *Bread and Roses: Gender and Class Under Capitalism*, we were swimming against the stream in Argentina at the time: the social movements and the resistance struggles against the economic and political crisis at the end of the twentieth century were accelerating their steps toward assimilation into the political regime, abandoning their most radical aspects. Since that first edition appeared in 2004, the neoliberal discourse of "expansion of rights" has become established as the only possible horizon for social movements, including feminism. And paradoxically, in the midst of this retreat by social movements—and starting as a small minority—we not only published this book, but also made an effort to build a material force that would be able to incarnate the ideas reflected in it.

That is why, despite the important shortcomings and omissions in its pages, and even despite the major events that took place after the revised edition appeared in 2013, this book retains a particular value that is not an individual achievement of its author. If I mostly write in the first person plural, this is because *Bread and Roses: Gender and Class Under Capitalism* is the result of an intense militant activity of swimming against the stream. Its pages originated in activism and struggles against exploitation and oppression; it was read and debated by young people fighting for the legalization of abortion, by women workers who took over their factories and got them running under workers' control in the midst of a capitalist crisis, and by students who were not content to see their anti-patriarchal hatred be converted into a mere slogan or a passing fad.

This book's journey, from hand to hand, allowed a small nucleus of revolutionary Marxist militants to set up the women's group **Pan y Rosas** (Bread and Roses), with a perspective that is class-based, anti-imperialist, anti-capitalist, and anti-racist—in other words, socialist and revolutionary. Today, more than 15 years later, as this book appears in English, that original nucleus has transformed itself into a tendency with thousands of women workers in the service sector and in industry, with precariously employed women, with women who do not earn wages, and with young students. Our tendency has developed in Brazil, Chile, Bolivia, Uruguay, Peru, Mexico, Venezuela, Costa Rica, Spain, France, Germany, and Italy.

Our tendency includes women workers from the multinational corporation PepsiCo in Argentina, who shut down production together with their male colleagues so the entire factory workforce could join the women's strike against femicides in 2016. **Pan y Rosas "Teresa Flores"** also includes some of the healthcare workers, teachers, and young people from the "Front Line" in Chile, who occupied the squares and streets in the final months of 2019 to repudiate the murderous Piñera government. In the Spanish State,

Pan y Rosas supports every single action of *Las Kellys*, a group of precarious cleaning workers at corporate hotel chains who are mostly immigrants from Africa and Latin America; these comrades have also written extensively about the debates on neoliberal feminism, the Right, and lesser-evilism in the imperialist European Union. Our comrades in Bolivia put their bodies at the front of the mobilizations that were repressed with blood and fire by the dictatorship of Jeanine Añez. In France, we are proud that the African immigrant women who went on strike against the company ONET, which exploits them as they clean the train stations in Paris, are our comrades; they are part of **Du Pain et Des Roses** alongside railway workers, bus drivers, and students. In Argentina, women shop stewards at the multinational corporation Mondelez (formerly Kraft Foods) who stopped the production lines to protest against a boss's sexual harassment of a worker are also part of **Pan y Rosas**. In Mexico, **Pan y Rosas** is on the front lines of the struggle against sexist violence, alongside mothers and friends demanding justice for the victims of femicides in Ciudad Juárez. In Brazil, our Black comrades from **Pão e Rosas** are leading, together with the revolutionary Black organization *Quilombo Vermelho*, the struggle against the precarious working conditions that especially affect Black women—in a clear demonstration of the unity that exists between class, gender, and race for capitalist exploitation. They also recently published a book about racism and capitalism.

These are some of the thousands of women workers and students, lesbians, trans people, Latinx, people of African descent, immigrants, and indigenous people who form part of the international feminist socialist tendency **Pan y Rosas**. Today, as I write this preface to the English edition, some of them are in the front lines of struggle against the coronavirus in hospitals in Europe, the United States, and Latin America.

The construction of this militant international tendency has inspired the successive editions of this book in different countries, and at the same time this book has been an elemental pillar of this process of organizing thousands of women. *Bread and Roses: Gender and Class Under Capitalism* has become a tool to generate debates and to strengthen convictions, without dogmatism, while always remaining intransigent with the ruling class, the institutions, and the ideologies that maintain, reproduce, and legitimize patriarchal capitalist exploitation and oppression.

* * *

Preface to the English Edition

The current pandemic, which is spreading across the planet and leaving a trail of infections and deaths, has provoked interesting and controversial debates about the world that will come. Will nothing be the same as before, or will everything return to "normalcy"? Will this mark the end of Western capitalist democracy and the emergence of new totalitarian regimes, with an unprecedented increase in racist and patriarchal violence? Or, on the contrary, will humanity create new forms of self-organization and reorganize society on the basis of egalitarian parameters?

Whatever happens, it will not depend on the coronavirus. It will depend, on the one hand, on the ruling classes and their governments who, in their zeal to protect capitalist profits, will attempt to load the costs of the crisis onto the shoulders of the working masses; and, on the other hand, it will be subject to the response that the masses are capable of giving in the face of these austerity plans. As long as the capitalists' reactionary forces are not opposed by a collective social subject, one that fights for its own solution to the crisis that threatens us today, while remaining independent of all the capitalists' political representatives and defending the perspective of a radical transformation, new and worse crises will occur in the future for millions of human beings.

This material force must be built. Young people in the United States, with Black people in the front lines, together with their Latinx siblings, fill us with hope that it is possible to move forward on this path. An anti-capitalist and revolutionary feminism cannot avoid this task, even less so as the new crisis we are entering highlights the deep contradiction between a parasitic class's thirst for profits and the lives of millions of human beings, with women once again in the crosshairs.

If *Bread and Roses: Gender and Class Under Capitalism* can inspire young women workers and students of the new generation in the heart of US imperialism and other parts of the world to take this task into their hands—the construction of a force fighting for a society without exploitation, in which no human being is oppressed by another because of their gender, their skin color, their nationality, or any other reason—then I will feel proud that this book, published by Pluto Press in English, has served its purpose.

Andrea D'Atri
Buenos Aires, September 2020

Acknowledgments

There are no individual elaborations. Books are the product of exchange and dialogue with many other people, and are influenced by them. Even more so in this case, as *Bread and Roses: Gender and Class under Capitalism* is nothing but a summary of a collective reflection and a militant practice of which I am a part. For this reason, this new corrected and expanded edition could not have been published without the collaboration—at times unintentional—of fellow comrades from the women's group *Pan y Rosas* (Bread and Roses) and the *Partido de Trabajadores Socialistas* (Party of Socialist Workers, PTS), as well as women from different latitudes, who over the last 15 years have attended numerous conferences, workshops, debates, forums, and seminars that we held in various cities in Argentina and that brought us to Chile, Brazil, Mexico, Venezuela, Peru, Costa Rica, El Salvador, Honduras, the Spanish State, Thailand, Italy, France, Germany, and the United Kingdom. Hundreds of women in different parts of the world offered suggestions, questions, and criticisms, which have enriched our own readings and elaborations. To all of them, my thanks.

I would also like to thank Celeste Murillo for her invaluable collaboration in revising the manuscript. She knows this work since its inception ten years ago, as she was present in the "kitchen," where it developed and transformed until finally reaching our readers in this new corrected and expanded edition.

I would like to express my special recognition for the sharp and critical review that Laura Lif provided of the first edition of *Bread and Roses: Gender and Class under Capitalism*, published in in 2004. It was this review that led to her proposal to revise and expand the book, ten years after its first publication. Her review identified gaps, controversies, and important connections that needed to be explored, contributing ideas and suggesting ways to develop them.

Biography

Andrea D'Atri was born in Buenos Aires in 1967. She graduated from the University of Buenos Aires with a degree in psychology, specializing in Women's Studies with a focus on teaching, research, and communication.

With a prominent role in the women's movement, she founded the women's group *Pan y Rosas* (Bread and Roses) in Argentina in 2003, which also has a presence in Chile, Brazil, Bolivia, Peru, Uruguay, Venezuela, Costa Rica, Mexico, Germany, France, Italy, and the Spanish State.

She is the author of *Bread and Roses: Gender and Class Under Capitalism*, which has been published in Buenos Aires, São Paulo, Caracas, Mexico, Rome, Berlin, Paris, and Barcelona. She is the co-author of *Luchadores: Historias de mujeres que hicieron historia* (*Women Fighters: Stories of Women who Made History*), which was published in Buenos Aires, São Paulo, Caracas, and Madrid. She also wrote the prologue to the first Spanish edition of Wendy Goldman's *Women, the State and Revolution: Soviet Family Policy and Social Life, 1917–1936*, which she presented at the 37th International Book Fair in Buenos Aires.

She contributed to the compilations *Femministe a parole: Grovigli da districare* by S. Marchetti, J. Mascat, and V. Perilli, Rome; *Emancipaciones feministas en el siglo XXI* by Gleidys Martínez Alonso and Yanet Martínez Toledo, Havana; *Building Feminist Movements: Global Perspectives* by Lydia Alpizar, Anahi Durán, and Anahi Russo Garrido, London; *Nosaltres les dones. Discursos i pràctiques feministes* by Aurora Mora, Barcelona; *Señoras, universitarias y mujeres (1910–2010): La Cuestión Femenina entre el Centenario y el Bicentenario de la Revolución de Mayo* by Héctor E. Recalde, Buenos Aires; and *Changing Their World: Concepts and Practices of Women's Movements* by Srilatha Batliwala, Toronto, among others.

She has given seminars and conferences in numerous countries. She is currently a member of the editorial board of the political and cultural magazine *Ideas de Izquierda* (*Left Ideas*).

She is a member of the national leadership of the *Partido de Trabajadores Socialistas* (Party of Socialist Workers, PTS), of which she has been a member since its foundation in 1988. She served as the PTS's candidate for the national congress in the city of Buenos Aires for the *Frente de Izquierda* (Left Front) in 2013. She was a speaker in favor of a bill for the legalization of abortion in Argentina's National Congress in 2018, and she currently works as an adviser for the Left Front in the parliament of the city of Buenos Aires.

Andrea D'Atri with the *Pan y Rosas* delegation, made up of 3,000 women, at the National Women's Meeting in Argentina in 2016 in the city of Rosario
Photo: © Enfoque Rojo

Introduction

While one part of feminism individually and comfortably reclines on the couch, asking itself, "who am I?" and another part searches anxiously for the reference needed for a footnote that certifies its work as trustworthy, [...] out there the world is bursting with poverty: millions of infants, born as women, look out upon a model of society that reserves a cradle of thorns for them.
—Victoria Sau Sánchez

GENDER AND CLASS ON INTERNATIONAL WOMEN'S DAY

Today, we still celebrate International Women's Day every year on March 8. However, among all the advertisements for flowers and chocolates, the great majority of people do not know the origin of this holiday. It began with an action organized by women workers in the nineteenth century to demand their rights: on March 8, 1857, the workers of a textile factory in New York went on strike against exhausting twelve-hour days and miserable wages. The demonstrators were attacked by the police.

Half a century later, in March 1909, 140 young workers were burned alive in a textile factory where they were trapped under inhumane conditions. And in that same year, 30,000 New York textile workers went on strike and were repressed by the police. In spite of the repression, however, these workers won the support of university students, suffragettes, socialists, and other sectors of society.

A few years later, at the beginning of 1912, the "Bread and Roses" strike broke out in the city of Lawrence, Massachusetts. The striking textile workers used this slogan to summarize their demands for increased wages and also for better living conditions. In this struggle, the strike committee sets up nurseries and communal kitchens for the children of the women workers in order to facilitate their participation in the conflict. The Industrial Workers of the World hold meetings for children in the union hall to discuss why their mothers and fathers are on strike. After several days of conflict, the children are sent to other cities. They are to be taken in by families in solidarity with the workers' struggle. On the first train, 120 children leave. As the second train is set to depart, the police unleash repression against the children and the women accompanying them. With this incident, the conflict reaches newspapers across the country and also the halls of congress, increasing solidarity with the strikers.

Two years earlier, during the Second International Socialist Women's Conference held in the city of Copenhagen, Clara Zetkin[1] from Germany had proposed to celebrate International Women's Day every year in March, to commemorate the women workers who had carried out the first organized actions against capitalist exploitation.

At this conference in August 1910, 100 socialist women from different European countries debated about voting rights for women and social welfare for working mothers, as well as measures to establish relations between socialist women around the world. They passed a motion to fight for the eight-hour working day, sixteen weeks of maternity leave, and other demands.

It was the German delegates who presented a motion that was passed unanimously and went down in history. The resolution presented by Clara Zetkin and Käte Duncker said:

> In agreement with the class-conscious political and trade organizations of the proletariat in their country the socialist women of all nationalities have to organize a special Women's Day, which primarily has to promote Women Suffrage propaganda. This demand must be discussed in connection with the whole women's question according to the socialist conception of social things. [Women's Day] must have an international character and be prepared carefully.[2]

In the following years, International Women's Day was celebrated in many countries—but on different days in March. It was not until 1914 that the German, Russian, and Swedish socialists agreed to hold it on March 8. This date became fixed in history as International Women's Day because on

---

1. Clara Zetkin (1857–1933) was a leader of the Social Democratic Party of Germany and organizer of its women's section. She founded the newspaper *Die Gleichheit* (*Equality*) and fought against the party leadership when it aligned itself with the national bourgeoisie and voted in favor of war bonds at the beginning of World War One.
2. International Socialist Conference, *Report of the Socialist Party Delegation and Proceedings of the International Socialist Congress at Copenhagen, 1910* (Chicago, IL: H.G. Adair, 1910). (This translation has been slightly corrected, based on the original German —trans.)

Introduction

March 8, 1917 (in February according to the Russian calendar at the time) the textile workers of Petrograd took to the streets demanding "bread, peace and freedom." This signaled the beginning of the greatest revolution of the twentieth century, which led to the seizure of power by the working class in October of that year.

As we can see, International Women's Day combines class and gender—a combination that, more than a century later, is still being debated both among Marxists and in the feminist movement.

OPPRESSION AND EXPLOITATION

For revolutionary Marxists, the question of women's oppression is written into the history of the class struggle. Therefore, our theoretical position is the same as that of our struggle: we stand beside all people exploited and oppressed by the capitalist system. We do this from the perspective of dialectical and historical materialism, which provides tools to understand this world—and to transform it.

Some specialists in Women's Studies have stated that it is "absolutely necessary to undertake a class analysis when dealing with the history of feminism," and add that:

> bourgeois feminism is the expression of the consciousness of bourgeois women who seek their equality with men in the political, legal and economic fields, within the framework of bourgeois society. Proletarian feminism, on the other hand, proposes overcoming social subordination within the framework of a classless society, according to the political model to which it adheres, be it socialist, anarchist or communist.[3]

Other authors highlight class differences in the analysis of women's oppression, noting that: "even if all women are oppressed by the patriarchal system in place in almost all contemporary societies, they are not oppressed for identical reasons; moreover, there are oppressed women who oppress others, and it is important to point that out."[4]

---

3. Mary Nash, "Nuevas dimensiones en la historia de la mujer," in Mary Nash (Ed.), *Presencia y protagonismo: Aspectos de la historia de la mujer* (Barcelona: Serbal, 1984), our translation.
4. Andrée Michel, *El feminismo* (México: Fondo de Cultura Económica-GREA, 1983), our translation.

From a Marxist perspective, therefore, we define **exploitation** as the relationship between classes. This describes the appropriation of the surplus labor of the working masses by the class that owns the means of production. It is a category with roots in the economic structure of society. Oppression, on the other hand, can be defined as a relation of subjugation of one group by another for cultural, racial, or sexual reasons. The category of **oppression** refers to the use of inequalities in order to put a particular social group at a disadvantage—a difference transformed into a justification for the domination of one social sector over another.

We can say that women belong to different social classes that are in conflict with one another. Women do not constitute a separate class but rather an inter-class group. Within this group, exploitation and oppression are combined in different ways. The class to which a person belongs determines the contours of their oppression. For example, laws that restrict a woman's right to control her own body apply equally to all women. But in reality, some women have better access to illegal procedures and are therefore better equipped to deal with possible complications. Some have access to abortion under hygienic conditions due to their economic, social, and educational level. Others bleed to death or die from infections after the operation. They become victims of a patriarchal order with a merciless capitalist visage.

Although all women suffer from legal, educational, political, economic, and cultural discrimination—to different degrees and in different forms—the fact is that there are clear class differences between them. These differences shape not only the subjective experience of oppression but also, and fundamentally, the objective possibilities of confronting and at least partially overcoming these social conditions of discrimination.

GENDER UNITES US, CLASS DIVIDES US

As the twenty-first century opens, the fight for women's rights would appear to have become socially acceptable and even "politically correct," to the point that most governments in the world, at different institutional levels, have incorporated gender issues into state agencies, working groups, public policy agendas, and multilateral organizations.

However, there are facts that are undeniable. We cannot deny, for example, the reality of a phenomenon known as the "glass ceiling," which refers to the fact that women, both in academia and industry, are not promoted to

Introduction

leading roles at the same rate as men, even if they have the same qualifications and performance. It is also known that in the vast majority of countries in all continents, the total wages of women are equivalent to 60 percent or 70 percent of those of men.

We can observe that women's oppression manifests itself, in various ways, in all social classes. But the female half of society is not distributed equally among the different classes: women make up the majority of the exploited and poor of this world, and a tiny, almost non-existent, minority of the powerful owners of multinational corporations who condemn us to exploitation and poverty. It is a categorical fact that while women are slightly more than 50 percent of the world's population, we make up 70 percent of the 1.3 billion poor people of the planet. On the other hand, just 1 percent of the world's private property is in the hands of women.

When we point out the double and triple chains that restrain women workers—whether they are hourly workers, salaried employees, rural workers, or unemployed—we do not intend to conceal the oppression suffered by half of humanity, no matter what class they belong to. On the contrary, we present a class perspective because we believe that the oppression of all women gains its "legitimacy" from a system based on the exploitation of the enormous majority of humanity by a small minority of capitalist parasites. The perpetuation of hierarchies and inequalities is a fundamental part of the system's functioning. These different divisions and fragmentations allow it to sustain one of the most abject dichotomous hierarchies: the one that condemns millions of people to sell their labor power so that a few can satisfy their thirst for ever-more exorbitant profits.

If class did not condition gender oppression in different ways, how could we explain that while some women climb the Forbes billionaires' list and several women occupy the presidency and other important posts in different countries, 60 million girls still do not have access to education?

Starting in the twentieth century, we have seen women as presidents, prime ministers, cabinet secretaries, soldiers and officers, scientists, artists and athletes, businesspeople, and successful professionals. It was the era of the birth control pill, the miniskirt and jeans, unisex fashion, and household appliances; but let us not forget that it was also an epoch of 20 million clandestine abortions per year around the world, thousands of women raped and murdered by "ethnic cleansing," and millions of women unemployed and living below the poverty line.

Therefore, when a woman in her thirties, on an "equal" footing with men, can "exercise her right" to be an officer in a NATO joint task force bombing semi-colonial countries, or to die from AIDS, at the same age, in an African village, it is paradoxical, and even a bit cynical, to speak of advancement and progress for women in general. Shouldn't we be speaking about different kinds of women? Are the lives of businesswomen and women workers, women from imperialist countries and women from semi-colonies, white and Black women, immigrant and refugee women really all the same? To suppose that there is something that links the Queen of England with unemployed English women, or the President of Argentina with domestic servants, or international Latin pop stars and businesswomen with workers in Mexican maquilas, just because they are women, ultimately means succumbing to the biological reductionism of the dominant patriarchal ideology, which feminists have severely criticized. To speak of gender in this way, therefore, is to use an abstract category, devoid of meaning and powerless to affect the transformation we want to push forward.

CAPITALISM AND PATRIARCHY: A WELL-MATCHED MARRIAGE

Many feminists are posing these questions today. Some even point out that a class-based feminism would need to use different tools to evaluate the problems faced by women. Thus, they say, above and beyond the condemnation of the patriarchal system, there should also be a condemnation of the World Bank and the International Monetary Fund, which are responsible for growing poverty and cuts to public services. They add that the most important assistance that feminists can offer to women in the third world is to condemn, from an openly anti-imperialist position, all "humanitarian" interventions that only serve the interests of the great powers.[5]

For our part, we maintain that, although it emerged before capitalism, the oppression of women took on particular characteristics under this mode of production, transforming patriarchy into an indispensable ally of exploitation and the maintenance of the *status quo*.

Capitalism, based on the exploitation and oppression of millions of individuals across the planet, conquering not only entire peoples but also

---

5. Alizia Stürtze, "Feminismo de clase," *Lahaine*, available at: www.lahaine.org/sturtze/feminismo_clase.htm.

virgin lands and inhospitable territories for the expansion of its markets, has introduced the exploitation of women and children into its machinery of domination. Even though it has pushed millions of women into the labor market, destroying the obscurantist myths that condemned them to remain exclusively in the private sphere, it has done so in order to double their exploitation, with wages lower than those of men. In this way, it lowers the wages of all workers.

Capitalism, with the development of technology, created the conditions for industrialization and thus for the socialization of domestic labor. But this socialization does not take place, precisely because unpaid domestic labor forms part of the capitalists' profits, since it exempts the capitalists from the need to pay workers for the tasks that guarantee their reproduction as a labor force (food, clothing, recreation, etc.). Encouraging and sustaining patriarchal culture, which declares household chores to be the "natural" jobs of women, makes this "theft" by the capitalists invisible, while also making the domestic labor that fundamentally falls on the shoulders of women and girls invisible.

Although capitalism has created the scientific, medical, and sanitary conditions that would allow women to control our own bodies as never before, this right is still denied to us. The development of contraceptive methods like the pill, intrauterine devices, tubal ligation, and even the possibility of aseptic abortions without health complications are unavoidable facts. If we are not allowed to control our own bodies, to decide if and when we want children, as well as how many, it is because the Church, with the complicity of the capitalist state, continues forcing itself into our lives. Clandestine abortions have become a very profitable business for a sector of professionals, laboratories, police mafias, and so on. Additionally, the possibility of separating pleasure from reproduction implies a freedom that is dangerous for the interests of the ruling class. Questioning that motherhood is the only path to women's self-realization, questioning that reproduction is the only purpose of sexuality, questioning that sexuality is only understood as heterosexual intercourse—all this endangers the norms that the system relies on to regulate our bodies. The system of exploitation conceives these bodies only as labor power, as bodies subjected to beauty stereotypes, as splintered and alienated bodies transformed into yet another commodity in a world of commodities.

WOMEN'S STRUGGLE AND CLASS STRUGGLE

The emergence and development of capitalism did not only increase the exploitation and oppression of women, but also led to profound changes in women's resistance and struggles against these chains. At the end of the eighteenth century, with the bourgeois revolutions, feminism emerged as a social movement and a theoretical, ideological, and political current. This movement passed through the nineteenth and twentieth centuries, taking on different forms and reaching the present day in the form of different theoretical tendencies, diverse practices, and multiple experiences of organization.

Almost from the beginning of capitalism, with the appearance of a powerful working class, antagonistic to the ruling bourgeoisie, feminism (and the movement against it) has been marked by the debate that the capitalist system forces on women and is at the center of our interest: in the words of the US Marxist Evelyn Reed, "sex against sex—or class against class?"[6]

We revolutionary Marxists continue to maintain that the class struggle is the motor of history, and that the working class, leading the poor masses and all oppressed sectors, is the subject of the social revolution that will liberate us from wage slavery and all forms of oppression, striking capitalism in its heart, paralyzing its mechanisms of extortion and plunder, and destroying its machinery of war against the subaltern classes. Today, that class has millions of women in its ranks. Capital produces this contradiction alongside so many others. The bourgeoisie permanently creates and recreates its own gravedigger. It is our conviction that the women of the working class will play a fundamental role in these future battles for the complete toppling of the exploiting class.

---

6. Evelyn Reed (1905–1979) was a member of the Socialist Workers Party (SWP) of the United States for more than 40 years. Evelyn met the SWP at the end of the 1930s and settled in Mexico in 1939, where she frequented the home of the Russian revolutionary Leon Trotsky, who was in exile in that country. She was a member of the SWP's National Committee from 1959 until 1975. Her most outstanding contributions were undoubtedly her writings on women's liberation, in which she applied the method of historical materialism to analyze the origin of women's oppression in class society, showing the indissoluble relationship.

1
Grain Riots and Civil Rights

Women, wake up; the tocsin [alarm bell] of reason sounds throughout the universe; recognize your rights.

—Olympe de Gouges

BREAD, CANNONS, AND REVOLUTION

In the epoch of the struggles against feudal absolutism and of the consolidation of the bourgeoisie as a ruling class, a wave of peasant revolts passed through Europe. From the sixteenth century onwards, these revolts continued without interruption, and only ended with the formation of modern nation-states in the nineteenth century. Women were the protagonists of these rebellions that frequently led the masses to use violence. On numerous occasions, it was women who led them.

In 1709 and 1710, at the dawn of the eighteenth century in England, the housewives of Essex led riots against their living conditions, together with the miners of Kingswood and the fishermen of Tyneside. In 1727, the tin miners of Cornwall and the coal miners of Gloucestershire did the same. In 1766, the revolts spread across Great Britain. In 1725 in France, there were revolts in Caen, Normandy, and Paris. In 1739 and 1740, the riots spread to Bordeaux, Caen, Bayeaux, Angoulême, and Lille. In 1747, the masses rose up in Toulouse and Guyenne. In 1752, in Arles, Bordeaux, and Metz; in 1768, in Le Havre and Nantes. Finally, in 1774 and 1775, the so-called "Flour War" spread throughout northern France.

These riots imposed "popular taxation" (price controls) and also raised political demands. The burden of rents and taxes, the shortage of food, the loss of rights, and the abuses by the nobility were the central motives for the rebellions. It was also very common for revolts to be caused by an increase in the price of wheat and bread, by the competition of foreign workers who threatened the job opportunities of native workers, or by the speculation of merchants who monopolized scarce goods.

According to the historian E.P. Thompson, women were often the main instigators of riots.

> In dozens of cases it is the same—the women pelting an unpopular dealer with his own potatoes, or cunningly combining fury with the calculation that they had slightly greater immunity than the men from the retaliation of the authorities.[1]

In all cases, the means of action were similar:

> The small-scale, spontaneous action might develop from a kind of ritualised hooting or groaning outside retailers' shops; from the interception of a wagon of grain or flour passing through a populous centre; or from the mere gathering of a menacing crowd.[2]

Thompson recounts numerous anecdotes, for example, in 1693, when women went to the Northampton market with knives hidden in their corsets to force the sale of grain at a price they had set themselves. According to contemporary reports, the people of Stockton rose up in 1740 after being incited by a woman armed with a stick and a bugle. Among these stories is also one about a justice of the peace who once complained that it was women who incited the men to fight, and who, like "perfect furies," beat him on the back.

On October 5, 1789, in France, the women of Les Halles and Saint Antoine, two crowded neighborhoods in Paris, demanded bread in front of the city hall and marched toward Versailles, where the kings resided. This women's march became one of the motors of the revolutionary mobilizations that led to what has entered into history under the name of the "French Revolution."

As in other historical processes, the great French Revolution, which united all classes and social sectors in the struggle against absolutism, began with a revolt led by the women of the poor neighborhoods of Paris.

We will allow ourselves to quote extensively from a text by Alexandra Kollontai, in which she points to the role of women throughout the revolution:

---

1. E.P. Thompson, *Customs in Common* (London: Penguin Books, 1993).
2. Ibid.

The "women of the people" in the provinces of Dauphiné and Brittany were the first to challenge the monarchy. [...] They took part in the election of deputies for the Estates General and their votes were universally accepted. [...] The women of Angers drew up a revolutionary manifesto against the tyranny of the royal house, and the proletarian women of Paris took part in the storming of the Bastille, entering with weapons in hand. Rose Lacombe, Luison Chabry, and René Ardou organized the women's march on Versailles and brought Louis XVI to Paris under strict guard. [...] The women of the fish market sent a delegate to the Estates General to "encourage the deputies and remind them of the women's demands." "Do not forget the people!" called out this delegate to the 1,200 members of the Estates General, that is, the National Assembly of France. [...] Long after the collapse of the revolution, the memory of the horribly cruel and bloodthirsty "tricoteuse" [knitting women] continued to haunt the dreams of the bourgeoisie. But who were these "knitters," these furies, as the oh-so-peaceful counter-revolution liked to call them? They were artisans, peasants, laborers in the home or the workshop, who suffered from hunger and all sorts of torments, and hated the aristocracy and the *ancien* régime with all their hearts and strength. Confronted with the luxury and waste of the arrogant and idle nobility, they reacted with a healthy class instinct and supported the most militant vanguard for a new France, in which all men and women would have a right to work and children would not starve to death. In order to avoid wasting time unnecessarily, these honest patriots and diligent workers knit stockings not just at festivities and demonstrations, but also at the sessions of the National Assembly and at the foot of the guillotine. They did not knit these stockings for themselves, by the way, but for the soldiers of the National Guard—the defenders of the revolution.[3]

The newspapers of the time describe some of the heroic women of the demonstrations of 1789 that led to the revolution, such as

---

3. Alexandra Kollontai's 14 lectures for women workers and peasants at the Sverdlov University in 1921 have never been published in English. This passage has been translated from the German: Alexandra Kollontai, *Die Situation der Frau in der gesellschaftlichen Entwicklung: vierzehn Vorlesungen vor Arbeiterinnen und Bäuerinnen an der Sverdlov-Universität 1921* (Frankfurt: Neue Kritik, 1975).

that 18-year-old girl who was seen fighting, dressed as a man, next to her lover, and that coal seller who, after the siege, is searching for the body of her son and responds with haughtiness to those who comment about her serenity: "In what more glorious place could I go to look for him? If he gave his life for his fatherland, is he not blessed?"[4]

Marie-Louise Lenoël, later a member of the National Assembly, remarks on these episodes:

> The first assembly attended only by women took place at eight o'clock in the morning in front of the city hall, in order to find out why it was so difficult to get bread and at such a high price; other women demanded that the king and queen should come and settle in Paris.[5]

According to another account from the time, women:

> tie ropes to the chassis of the cannons, but since they are cannons from ships, this artillery is difficult to move. So the women requisition carriages, load their cannons onto them, and tie them down with cables, loading gunpowder and cannonballs as well. Some lead the horses and others, seated on the cannons, carry the fearsome fuse and other instruments of death in their hands. At the beginning of the march at the Champs Élysées, their number already exceeds 4,000, and they are escorted by 400 or 500 men, who had armed themselves with everything they could find.[6]

The women of the Grenoble region, for their part, sent an insolent letter to the king: "We are not willing to bear children destined to live in a country subjected to despotism."[7]

There were also women whose names transcended this historic episode, like Madame Roland or the journalist and author Louise Robert-Kévalio,

---

[4]. Paule-Marie Duhet, *Les femmes et la Révolution 1789–1794* (Paris: Julliard, 1971), our translation.
[5]. Marie-Louise Lenoël, Événement de Paris et de Versailles par une des dames qui a eu l'honneur d'être de la Députation à l'*Assamblée Nationale*, quoted in Duhet, *Les femmes et la Révolution 1789–1794*, our translation.
[6]. *Les Révolutions de Paris*, #13, quoted in Duhet, *Les femmes et la Révolution 1789–1794*, our translation.
[7]. Quoted in Duhet, *Les femmes et la Révolution 1789–1794*, our translation.

who sympathized with the moderate wing of the Girondins. Or Théroigne de Méricourt, who called on the people to take up arms, took part in the storming of the Bastille, and received a sword from the National Assembly as a reward for her courage. As legend has it, on October 5, 1789, she went ahead of the march on Versailles and entered the city on horseback, dressed in red, trying to win the women for the revolutionary cause.

FEMALE CITIZENS DEMAND EQUALITY

In 1789, when the National Assembly voted for the *Declaration of the Rights of Man and of the Citizen*, two documents about women appeared. On January 1, 1789, the anonymous pamphlet *Petition of Women of the Third Estate to the King* was published. The other, titled *Notebook of Women's Grievances and Demands*, signed by one Madame B.B., proclaims in one of its paragraphs:

> Gather, daughters of Caux, and you, female citizens of provinces governed by customs as unjust as they are ridiculous, go to the feet of the monarch, the best of kings, take an interest in everything that surrounds him, demand, solicit the abolition of a law that reduces you to poverty as soon as you are born.[8]

The best-known manifestos for women's rights are *On the Admission of Women to the Rights of Citizenship* by the Marquis de Condorcet,[9] and the *Declaration of the Rights of Woman and the Female Citizen* by the legendary Olympe de Gouges, from 1790 and 1791 respectively. Olympe de Gouges' real name was Marie Gouze. She was born in 1748 and in 1765 married an officer named Pierre Aubry with whom she likely had a son. She later embarked on a career as a writer, chiefly of plays. In 1791, when the king was arrested, she declared: "In order to kill a king it is not enough to cut off his head; he lives on long after his death; he is only truly dead once he has survived his fall." In a pamphlet, she proposed holding a referendum about

---

8. Madame B.B., *Cahier des doléances et réclamations des femmes*, quoted in Duhet, *Les femmes et la Révolution 1789-1794*, our translation.
9. It is interesting to note that the Marquis of Condorcet, one of the men who was most resolutely in favor of women's struggle to win equal civil rights, concluded his well-known essay demanding the right to vote only for women who owned property.

the following alternatives: a single and indivisible republican government, a federal government, or a monarchic government. For this reason, she was arrested and guillotined on November 3, 1793.

It was not only in France that demands for the rights of female citizens were raised. In England, Mary Wollstonecraft published her *Vindication of the Rights of Woman* in 1792, lamenting that women "are only considered as females, and not as a part of the human species."[10] Wollstonecraft did not limit herself to demands for political rights; she spoke up against society's hypocrisy and against inequality. She had been born in England in 1759 and received instruction from a Protestant pastor. Her first job was as a governess, an experience that led her to write *Thoughts on the Education of Daughters*. She defended the French Revolution and moved in Girondin circles in Paris. Other works she wrote include *A Vindication of the Rights of Men, in a Letter to the Right Honourable Edmund Burke; Occasioned by His Reflections on the Revolution in France*, as well as *Letters Written During a Short Residence in Sweden, Norway, and Denmark*, and a posthumously published novel titled *Mary: A Fiction*. She died very young from sepsis caused by an infection of the placenta during the birth of her daughter.[11]

John Wilkes (1727–1797), an English writer, lawmaker, and mayor of London, also was active during these years. This fighter for civil liberties led a movement for democratic reform and was expelled from parliament for publishing a pamphlet titled *Essay on Woman*. In France as well, there were men who joined the feminist struggle, such as Labenette, a member of the Cordeliers Club, who in 1791 founded the *Journal of the Rights of Man*, whose motto was: "every time you attack them, I will defend them." The newspaper included passages like this one: "Women, who are more intelligent and knowledgeable than their husbands, instead of being cloistered in their homes, should devote themselves to the business of the community, and husbands should remain at home caring for children."[12] And of course he had to publish at some point: "Some of my male readers yesterday

---

10. Mary Wollstonecraft, *Vindication of the Rights of Woman* (London: Penguin, 2004).
11. Her daughter, Mary Godwin, who later married the poet Shelley and became worldrenowned for her novel *Frankenstein*, once said: "Mary Wollstonecraft was one of those beings who appear once perhaps in a generation, to gild humanity with a ray which no difference of opinion nor chance of circumstance can cloud."
12. *Journal des Droits d l'Homme*, #14, quoted in Duhet, *Les femmes et la Révolution 1789–1794*, our translation.

threatened to stop reading my newspaper if I persevered in my intention to continue speaking out on behalf of women."[13]

LIBERTY, FRATERNITY, AND INEQUALITY OF CLASS AND GENDER

Women from the working-class districts of Paris were once again the protagonists of popular mobilizations in January 1792, rebelling against the scarcity and high price of sugar. A year later, in 1793, a revolt initiated by the laundresses again took up the demand for popular taxation, calling for measures against hoarders and speculators.

During all these years, although they were excluded from any kind of participation in armed struggle, the women of the bourgeoisie and the urban poor carried out their struggle against the counter-revolutionary forces in women's clubs. These women's clubs, like the fraternal societies of the men, vigorously attacked the clergy and the nobility. Some, like the association of young women of Nantes, even swore never to marry aristocrats. In the women's revolutionary clubs, figures like Rose Lacombe stood out. She was the founder, together with the laundress Pauline Léonie, of the Society of Revolutionary Republican Women. On one occasion, Lacombe occupied the seat of the National Assembly with a multitude of unemployed Parisian women asking what the government intended to do to alleviate the misery of women workers.

But ultimately, with the return of reaction, the civil rights which had been conquered were lost again. After the first attempts to organize women in patriotic and revolutionary clubs, Napoleon's empire limited the movement, banning all public demonstrations and closing the clubs. The Civil Code of 1804, which inspired all European legislation of the time, and which is still reflected in the civil codes of semi-colonial nations today, stipulated that women are the property of men and their main task is the production of children.

In the French Revolution, for the first time, the women's question became a political question. Feminism emerged as a powerful political movement demanding equal rights for women, echoing the bourgeois discourse of abstract equality of all citizens before the law: equal rights for men and also

---

13. Ibid.

for women in the framework of the egalitarian project of the Enlightenment. Feminism represents the radicalization of this project, highlighting the contradiction that exists between the proclaimed universal equality and the absence of real civil and political rights for half of civil society. Women, who in this struggle referred to themselves as "the third estate of the third estate," fought for their inclusion in the emerging citizenry. As the feminist Cristina Molina Petit points out: "The Enlightenment does not fulfill its promises: reason is not Universal Reason. Women are excluded from it, as the sector that the leading lights of the Enlightenment do not wish to illuminate."[14]

Led by the women of the bourgeoisie and the educated middle classes, and supported by broad sectors of women from the working masses who ardently defended the revolution, this movement was the expression of the flagrant contradiction to which the development of capitalism was leading: the education and cultural level of bourgeois women, on the one hand, and the increasing participation of working women in production, on the other, did not correspond with the social and legal discrimination to which they were both subjected. Together in revolutionary clubs, with petitions and mobilizations, they fought for bread, work, and civil rights. This is exactly what the different social classes had done in order "to settle radically with the lords of the past."[15] This gigantic effort had been necessary to establish the unity of a nation in revolt against feudal despotism. As Leon Trotsky points out in his comparative analysis of the great revolutions: "The Great French Revolution was indeed a national revolution. And what is more, within the national framework, the world struggle of the bourgeoisie for domination, for power, and for undivided triumph found its classical expression."[16] Dragging the masses of the people behind it, the bourgeoisie was able to get rid of the aristocracy in an unprecedented revolutionary act.

The "equality" of all citizens before the state that was conquered is just an expression of bourgeois rule, since it denies that society is made up of antagonistically structured social classes. At the time of the French Revolution, the Jacobin Chaumette declared: "The indigent have not won anything

---

14. Cristina Molina Petit, *Dialéctica feminista de la Ilustración* (Madrid: Anthropos, 1994), our translation.
15. Leon Trotsky, *The Permanent Revolution and Results and Prospects* (London: New Park Publications, 1962).
16. Ibid.

from the revolution except the right to complain about their poverty."[17] This is the reason that the unity among the classes under the leadership of the revolutionary bourgeoisie—which at that time made it possible to form an enormously progressive movement for the whole of society, putting an end to nobility and aristocracy—would transform into its opposite over the course of the class struggle. The same thing happened with the development of feminism from the nineteenth century to the present day. Class antagonism and the confrontations between different national bourgeoisies in the form of world wars would permanently divide the women's liberation movements from then on. Without a class perspective, it is impossible to struggle against patriarchal oppression.

At the end of the eighteenth century, when the working masses participated in the revolutionary movement against the nobility, led by the bourgeoisie, the women of the working-class districts mobilized for bread, while the educated women of the middle classes and the bourgeoisie legitimized their demands for freedom with pamphlets, proclamations, petitions, and organizations that articulated their vision about the need for equal rights.

Thus, as poor women were mobilizing against food shortages, feminism was emerging as a political and ideological phenomenon, demanding civil and political rights for women on an equal footing with men—independence from husbands' tutelage, access to education, the right to political participation, and so forth. And although the ideas advocated by the most liberal sectors of society were not shared by the majority of women workers, the patriarchal ideology of the ruling class had established a contradiction that has not been resolved to this day. Women from the working masses were considered primarily responsible for the daily nourishment of the family, pushing them to join—and often lead—protests for popular taxation and bread riots, mostly in France and England. The historically stereotyped role of nourishing mothers would create, without intending to, energetic opponents of the living conditions imposed by the capitalist system.

It was these first grain riots and the participation in revolutionary struggles that enabled women from the working masses to experience collective

---

17. Pierre Chaumette (1763–1794) was a French revolutionary. He was part of the insurrectionary commune that was constituted on August 9, 1792, and was one of the organizers of the insurrection against the Girondins. Attacked by Robespierre for his atheism and radical political positions, he was the fiercest enemy of the landowners and the wealthy.

social and political action, breaking out of the isolation of the home. This combined with the enlightened critique from one sector of educated women against male, bourgeois politics that denied civil rights even to the women of the ruling class. Together, these are experiences that did not occur in vain, as will be demonstrated in the course of the nineteenth century.

2
Bourgeois Women and Proletarian Women

If the French nation consisted only of women, what a terrible nation it would be.

—correspondent of *The Times* in Paris, 1871

STEAM ENGINES, LOOMS, AND WOMEN

From the middle of the eighteenth to the middle of the nineteenth century, artisanal production persisted in the most developed countries of Europe. The method of piecework, carried out by women workers in their own homes, also expanded. And the textile industry, especially the cotton industry, developed rapidly. Both married and single women found a place in the "cottage industry" and also in the first textile factories, as well as in domestic service and in agriculture.

However, beyond the powerful trend in this period toward the proletarianization of women, historians like Joan Scott warn that the:

> woman worker was a product of the Industrial Revolution, not so much because mechanization created jobs for her where none had existed before (although that surely was the case in some areas), but because she became a troubling and visible figure in the course of it.[1]

In other words, although there were already women working in the fields, in artisanal sectors, and in domestic service, it was the Industrial Revolution

---

1. Joan Wallach Scott, "The Woman Worker in the Nineteenth Century," in Georges Duby and Michelle Perrot (Eds.), *History of Women in the West*, Vol. 4: Geneviève Fraisse (Ed.), *Emerging Feminism from Revolution to World War* (Cambridge, MA: Belknap Press of Harvard University Press, 1993).

that established the category of "woman worker" as a subject for discussion in science, politics, religion, education, and so on.

The woman worker became a troubling figure, moreover, because her very existence questioned the image of femininity mandated by the dominant patriarchal ideology. She exposed a contradiction between the ideal of femininity and wage labor, marking an antagonism between the home and the factory, between maternity and productivity, between traditional values and capitalist modernity. The "woman worker" began to give rise to profound debates between those who defended her right to inclusion in social production and those who dismissed such participation. The latter employed both emancipatory and deeply sexist arguments.

Revolutionary socialists also reflected on these contradictions that capital was creating in relation to women and the family. Marx, for example, maintained in *Capital*:

> In so far as machinery dispenses with muscular power, it becomes a means of employing labourers of slight muscular strength, and those whose bodily development is incomplete, but whose limbs are all the more supple. The labour of women and children was, therefore, the first thing sought for by capitalists who used machinery. That mighty substitute for labour and labourers was forthwith changed into a means for increasing the number of wage-labourers by enrolling, under the direct sway of capital, every member of the workman's family, without distinction of age or sex. Compulsory work for the capitalist usurped the place, not only of the children's play, but also of free labour at home within moderate limits for the support of the family.[2]

The numbers regarding this new phenomenon of the female workforce speak for themselves. To name one example, between 1851 and 1861, 25 percent of British women worked. Of this number, the majority belonged to the working class and the peasantry. A census from 1851 shows that of women above the age of 20 in London, over 140,000 worked as domestic servants, 125,000 in dress and shoe manufacturing, 11,000 as teachers, and 9,000 in the silk industry.

In his magnificent analysis of the capitalist system, Marx points out:

---

2. Karl Marx, *Capital Volume One* (London: Penguin, 1990).

In contrast with the manufacturing period, the division of labour is thenceforth based, wherever possible, on the employment of women, of children of all ages, and of unskilled labourers, in one word, on cheap labour, as it is characteristically called in England. This is the case not only with all production on a large scale, whether employing machinery or not, but also with the so-called domestic industry, whether carried on in the houses of the workpeople or in small workshops. This modern so-called domestic industry has nothing, except the name, in common with the old-fashioned domestic industry, the existence of which pre-supposes independent urban handicrafts, independent peasant farming, and above all, a dwelling-house for the labourer and his family. That old-fashioned industry has now been converted into an outside department of the factory, the manufactory, or the warehouse. Besides the factory operatives, the manufacturing workmen and the handicraftsman, whom it concentrates in large masses at one spot, and directly commands, capital also sets in motion, by means, of invisible threads, another army; that of the workers in the domestic industries, who dwell in the large towns and are also scattered over the face of the country.[3]

Starting in 1802, the Factory Acts passed by the UK Parliament regulated working conditions, especially for women and children. In the middle of the nineteenth century, similar laws followed throughout Europe, limiting the workday to twelve and, in some cases, ten hours, as well as prohibiting work at night, on Saturday afternoons, and in particularly dangerous places. Health and safety standards were also established. But it was not until the 1890s that women could become factory inspectors, and thus were able to ensure compliance with these regulations, which were supposed to protect them.

WOMEN WORKERS ORGANIZE TO FIGHT

One example of the early organization of women workers was in 1788, as the hand-spinners in Leicester, England, formed a clandestine sisterhood, which destroyed spinning machines as a form of protest. These women later affiliated to the Manchester Spinners Union, composed mostly of men. They

---

3. Ibid.

joined together in a strike in 1818. The women were later expelled from the union because, according to documents from the time, some of them "refused to abide by the rules."

It was not until 1874 that the Women's Trade Union League was founded, which contributed to the creation of more than 30 women's unions. If women organized independently of men, this was not so much a result of feminist conviction, but rather because the majority of the unions tried to protect the jobs and the wages of male workers, excluding women from their organizations and even fighting against their incorporation into the labor market. To understand the attitudes of union leaders toward the incorporation of women into production, it is enough to note the words of Henry Broadhurst. At the British Trade Unions Congress in 1877, Broadhurst argued about male workers that:

> it was their duty as men and husbands to use their utmost efforts to bring about a condition of things where their wives should be in their proper sphere at home, seeing after their house and family, instead of being dragged into the competition for livelihood against the great and strong men of the world.[4]

Women, due to the low wages imposed on them, appeared more like a threat to male workers than a potential ally. Historically, this was the role that the bosses had assigned to women workers: turning them into an army that would objectively press against the interests of male workers. Women, with their lower salaries, were competing for the same jobs, thus tending to lower the wages of the entire class, or even directly threatening to make male workers unemployed.

However, despite being exploited by the bosses, socially oppressed, and abandoned by the most important unions, women workers were the protagonists of important events of the class struggle in the nineteenth century. Among the exemplary struggles, we can mention: the Nottingham riots of 1812, calling for a limit to the price for flour; the strike of the ovalists (silk workers) in Lyon, led by Philomène Rosalie Rozan; the matchgirls' strike of 1888 in London, organized independently of the male unions, with which

---

4. Quoted in Jane Lewis, *Women in England 1870–1950: Sexual Divisions and Social Change* (London: Wheatsheaf, 1984).

the strikers won their demands; the strike of the Edinburgh women compositors (typesetters), who in a pamphlet titled "We, the Women" demanded their right to print in the name of the equality of the sexes; and the aforementioned strike of New York textile workers on March 8, 1857, which was attacked by police and led, decades later, to the creation of International Women's Day, as we indicated in the Introduction.

By the beginning of the twentieth century, there had still been no major improvements in the miserable working and living conditions of women workers. The most prominent women-led proletarian struggles on the American continent took place in the early years of the century. To name one example, we will recount the experience of the strike of the New York textile workers in 1909, which we also cited in the Introduction. In that year, inhumane working conditions drove 30,000 textile workers to strike. Many of these workers were just teenagers, leading to talk of a "girls' strike." One of their leaders, Clara Lemlich, was only 23 when she launched the slogan, "If not now, when?" She received applause and shouts of approval in a meeting of her union on November 23, where she harangued her colleagues with the words: "I have no further patience for talk. I am a working girl, one of those striking against intolerable conditions. [...] I make a motion that we go out in a general strike." The strike quickly spread to 40,000 workers, even though just 1,000 were members of the union. In the following five days, 19,000 new members signed up. The workers even demanded payment for the strike days.

The police brutally repressed the workers from the first day of the strike. As the strike progressed, public opinion forced the police to partially withdraw from the picket lines. One of the most important moments of the textile workers' struggle was the march to City Hall on December 3, demanding the withdrawal of the police from the streets. The police repressed that march as well and its leaders were injured. Finally, after these events, the police had to hold back. The strike aroused enormous solidarity from university students and the entire community. The newspapers, for their part, reported on the events day by day. According to newspaper accounts, strikers spent most of their time on the picket lines with revolutionary songs and rallying cries, mostly in Yiddish, since a large number of the workers were immigrants from Eastern Europe.

It would be impossible to understand the magnitude of this strike without knowing that, according to a census from 1905, there were more than 70,000 women workers manufacturing women's clothing, 40,000 of whom were in New York City. Of these, 31 percent earned less than $6 a week. The difference in wages between men and women was abysmal: while 45 percent of women in the industry earned an average of $6 or $7 a week, the average among men was $16 to $18.

These and other heroic struggles have engraved the names of many women into the history books: Mother Jones,[5] an organizer of miners across the USA for almost 40 years; Aunt Molly Jackson,[6] also a prominent union activist; Annie Besant,[7] a leader of the matchgirls' strike; Jean Deroin and Pauline Roland,[8] who built a Union of Workers' Associations that more than

---

5. Mother Jones was born in 1830 as Mary Harris in a home of Irish militants. In 1861, she married George Jones, a foundry worker with whom she had four children and who introduced her to the workers' cause. After her husband and children died in a yellow fever epidemic, she dedicated herself to activism. She joined the semi-clandestine organization *The Knights of Labor*, which brought together the most exploited sectors of the workers' movement, including women, Black workers, and immigrants. In 1890, she participated in the founding of the *United Mine Workers*. In 1904, she joined the *Socialist Party*, and in the following year, she was the only woman among the 27 signatories of the founding manifesto of the *Industrial Workers of the World*, which called for the organization of all industrial workers.
6. Aunt Molly Jackson, born in 1880, was a trade unionist who took part in miners' strikes and struggles. Her father and brothers, as well as her husband, were miners, and she experienced the harsh working conditions in the flesh. As a member of the miners' union, she became a nationally known activist thanks to her songs denouncing the living conditions of the workers and their families.
7. Annie Besant, born in 1847, was a socialist, and a women's rights and trade union activist. She played a leading role in the matchgirls' strike in 1888 in London, in order to form a union and fight for better working conditions and higher wages. She also became known for her role in the struggle for freedom and self-determination for Ireland and India.
8. Jean Deroin (1805–1894) was first associated with Saint-Simonianism, and then with Fourier and Cabet (utopian socialists). She contributed to the newspaper *The Women's Voice*, created the Club for the Emancipation of Women, and fought for equal rights. In 1849, she presented her candidacy for the Legislative Assembly, illegally, winning sympathy from the workers and mockery from the bourgeoisie. Together with Pauline Roland, she founded the Association of Socialist Teachers, and attempted to bring together all the workers' organizations in a Union of Workers' Associations that would fight against capitalism and achieve a socialist society peacefully. For this attempt, both women were sentenced to six months in prison. Finally, Deroin had to go into exile in London, where she died. Pauline Roland (1805–1852) was also a disciple of the Saint-Simonians. She rejected marriage and considered that the liberation of women could not be separated from the struggle of the proletariat for its emancipation. Under Emperor Napoleon III, she was accused of participating in resistance to his *coup d'état* and was deported to Algeria. Through the intercession of George Sand and de Béranger, she was pardoned a few months later. But on her return to France, she died in Lyon from illness and deprivation.

100 unions joined; the enslaved woman Sojourner Truth;[9] Elizabeth Gurley Flynn;[10] Clara Lemlich; and Louise Michel, one of the most incendiary heroes of the Paris Commune.

A GOVERNMENT OF THE WORKING PEOPLE OF PARIS

When the enemy forces of the Prussian army surrounded Paris, hunger forced the city to surrender, after a long siege, on January 28, 1871. Two weeks later, the French National Assembly voted for peace. The people of Paris denounced the reactionary Assembly for concluding a peace that humiliated the French nation, and the National Guard in Paris refused to hand over its weapons. The Assembly, faced with a rebellion of its own army and the Parisian people, moved to Versailles with the goal of subduing the insurrectionary capital from there.

The rebellion by the people of Paris installed a revolutionary city government on March 18, 1871. It called on the other municipalities of France to follow suit and unite in a federation. Raising a red flag on the mast of the city hall, this first workers' and people's government in history soon decreed the separation of church and state, the right to recall all government officials, the rule that parliamentarians could earn no more than a workers' wage, and equal rights for women.

Meanwhile, Adolphe Thièrs, the head of the Versailles government, intensified the attacks against the rebels, under the approving eye of the

---

9. On one occasion, Sojourner Truth responded to a preacher who had ridiculed women, claiming that because they were weak and defenseless, they did not deserve the right to vote. Truth ascended the stage and proclaimed:

> That man over there says that women need to be helped into carriages, and lifted over ditches, and to have the best place everywhere. Nobody ever helps me into carriages, or over mud-puddles, or gives me any best place! And ain't I a woman? Look at me! Look at my arm! I have ploughed and planted, and gathered into barns, and no man could head me! And ain't I a woman? I could work as much and eat as much as a man—when I could get it—and bear the lash as well! And ain't I a woman?

10. Elizabeth Gurley Flynn was only 22 years old when she was sent by the Industrial Workers of the World to replace activists who had been arrested during the Bread and Roses strike by the textile workers in Massachusetts. At 16, she gave her first speech, "What Socialism Will Do for Women." She was known for her defense of the working class, her activism on behalf of political prisoners, and her struggle for women's rights, including equal pay, the right to vote, and birth control.

Prussians. The resistance of the glorious Paris Commune could only be broken after weeks of bloody combat that ended with atrocious reprisals that cost between 10,000 and 20,000 lives, constituting one of the cruelest cases of repression in history.

Brave women participated in the Commune with a passion, taking up arms and resisting the troops of Thièrs and also those of the Prussians, until the defeat meant death in combat, deportation, or execution by firing squad. Newspapers of the time describe the women of the Commune with words like these: "I saw a young girl dressed as a national guard walking with her head held high among prisoners with downcast eyes. This woman, tall, her long blond hair floating on her shoulders, challenged everyone with her eyes."[11] These women were workers, housewives from poor neighborhoods, small merchants, teachers, prostitutes, and slum dwellers. They organized themselves in revolutionary clubs such as the Women's Vigilance Committee or the Women's Union for the Defense of Paris, just as women had done in the French Revolution of 1789. In contrast to the women who participated in the Great Revolution, this time women who wanted to fight were allowed to. The proletarians of Paris did not deny them weapons, as the bourgeois revolutionaries had done.

In an interesting study of the Paris Commune, Silvio Costa from Brazil highlights the names of numerous women who participated in different revolutionary organizations:

> Among the women of this period, the best known was the socialist activist Louise Michel, the founder of the Women's Union for the Defense of Paris and Care of the Wounded, and a member of the First International. Those who also stand out: Elisabeth Dmitrieff, socialist and feminist activist; André Léo, editor of the newspaper *La Sociale*; Beatrice Excoffon, Sophie Poirier, and Anna Jaclard, members of the Women's Vigilance Committee; Marie-Catherine Rigissart, who commanded a women's battalion; Adélaide Valentin, who rose to the rank of colonel, and Louise Neckebecker, a company captain; Nathalie Lemel, Aline Jacquier, Marcelle Tinayre, Otavine Tardif, and Blanche Lefebvre, founders of the Women's Union, the last of whom was executed by reactionary troops; and Jose-

---
11. *The Times*, May 29, 1871, quoted in French translation in *Le Site de la Commune de Paris* (1871), www.commune1871.org, our translation.

phine Courbois, who had fought on the streets of Lyon in 1848, where she was known as the queen of the barricades. One should also mention Jeanne Hachet, Victorine Louvert, Marguerite Lachaise, Josephine Marchais, Leontine Suétens, and Natalie Lemel.[12]

These are only a few names of the hundreds of women who, often anonymously, became martyrs of the world proletarian struggle, as victims of bourgeois repression. Many of the women who were captured after the defeat were accused of being "women incendiaries." In the words of one historian of the period:

> Some sources refer to women as incendiaries—*les pétroleuses*—setting fire to public buildings during the final *Semaine sanglante* ["Bloody Week"] of the Commune. Such stories appear to have been government-inspired anti-feminist scaremongering, and most foreign correspondents present did not believe them. Nonetheless, hundreds of women were summarily executed— even beaten to death—by government troops, who suspected them of being *pétroleuses*. Yet, despite the fact that many more women were later accused of being incendiaries, the councils of war did not find a single one guilty of that offence. However, there is evidence to suggest that, during the final days, women held out longer behind the barricades than men.[13]

THE WOMEN INCENDIARIES AND THE LADIES WITH PARASOLS

Among these women of the working class, the name Louise Michel shines out. Her biography illustrates the lives of fighting women of that epoch. She was born in 1830 as the illegitimate daughter of a servant. She was educated and became a teacher. In 1869, she was the secretary of the Democratic Society for Moralization, which aimed to help workers. During the Paris Commune, she led the Club of the Revolution and its armed militias. When the Commune was defeated and thousands of combatants were killed, deported, or shot, Louise Michel was condemned to ten years of exile.

---

12. Silvio Costa, *Comuna de París: O Proletariado Toma o Céu de Assalto* (São Paulo, Anita Garibaldi, 1998), our translation.
13. Allan Todd, *Revolutions 1789–1917* (Cambridge: Cambridge University Press, 1998).

In the summary trial that was held to convict her, she declared:

> I belong completely to the Social Revolution [...] What I demand from you, who claim you are a court-martial, who pass yourselves off as my judges, you who don't hide the way the Board of Pardons behaves, you who are from the military and who judge me publicly—what I call for is the field of Satory, where our revolutionary brothers have already fallen. I must be cut off from society. You have been told that, and the prosecutor is right. Since it seems that any heart which beats for liberty has the right only to a small lump of lead, I demand my share. If you let me live, I will not stop crying for vengeance, and I will denounce the assassins of the Board of Pardons to the vengeance of my brothers.[14]

Finally, deported to the French colony of New Caledonia, she collaborated with those fighting for the political independence of the islands. Two years after her return to France, in 1881, she was prosecuted for leading a demonstration of the unemployed that ended with the expropriation of shops. On that occasion, it is said, Louise carried a black banner for the first time, a color that was later taken by the anarchists as a symbol for their struggle. For that demonstration, she was sentenced to six more years in prison. She finally died in 1905 at a conference for workers in Marseilles. Her life is an example of heroism and dedication to the struggle against exploitation.

It is easy to understand that there could be no unity with bourgeois women on the barricades. Two classes were in open struggle, and women joined one side or the other according to their class interests. In Paris, the workers resisted the savage and shameful attacks of the army commanded by the French bourgeoisie. The bourgeoisie was collaborating with the former Prussian enemy, which freed its prisoners of war so that they could enlist and fight against the French proletariat in arms. The men and women of the bourgeoisie fled Paris in the face of the new workers' power that threatened their class privileges, and collaborated as agents and informants of the repressive government. After the defeat of the heroic Communards, the women of the bourgeoisie returned to their homes and strolled down the streets of Paris, rejoicing in the return of "order" and dipping, as some

---

14. Louise Michel, *The Red Virgin: Memoirs of Louise Michel* (Tuscaloosa, AL: University of Alabama Press, 1981).

engravings from the time show, the tips of their parasols into the still fresh blood of the men and women who had tragically become martyrs.

In the nineteenth century, all the contradictions that had begun to germinate in the previous century now unfolded in their full dimensions. The proletariat entered the historical stage as a distinct class that rebelled against the savage exploitation by capital. As these struggles show, among hundreds of strikes, rallies, acts of sabotage, and revolts by the workers' movement of the nineteenth century, the history of that century is that of the disintegration of the "united front" between the bourgeoisie and the proletariat who had fought against the clergy and the aristocracy in order to create modern capitalist states.

In 1830, with the century's first economic crisis, misery and discontent spread. These formed the foundations for the social revolution that swept through the European continent and gave rise to a wave of revolutions that became known as the 1848 revolutions. The conflict of interests, the antagonism between classes, unfolded for the first time in history in all its magnitude. The proletariat, which had been an ally of the bourgeoisie against feudal absolutism, was openly transformed into a potential enemy.

The bourgeoisie, cowering in fear of the proletariat in arms, became powerless to carry out its historical mission:

> In 1848 the bourgeoisie was already unable to play a comparable role [to that of 1789]. It did not want and was not able to undertake the revolutionary liquidation of the social system that stood in its path to power. We know now *why* that was so. Its aim was—and of this it was perfectly conscious—to introduce into the old system the necessary guarantees, not for its political domination, but merely for a sharing of power with the forces of the past. It was meanly wise through the experience of the French bourgeoisie, corrupted by its treachery and frightened by its failures. It not only failed to lead the masses in storming the old order, but placed its back against this order so as to repulse the masses who were pressing it forward.[15]

---

15. Leon Trotsky, *The Permanent Revolution and Results and Prospects* (London: New Park Publications, 1962).

This rejection of the masses transformed, during the Paris Commune, into rivers of blood—and there was no turning back. As different authors point out, in the new historical period that was taking shape on the horizon, both in the struggles and in the new forms of social organization, working and oppressed women constituted an important vanguard among those sectors of the masses who "pressed forward" in a struggle that pitted them against other women who had once been their allies.

3
Between Philanthropy and Revolution

The law which enslaves woman and deprives her of education oppresses you, proletarian men. [...] Thus, workers, it is up to you, who are the victims of real inequality and injustice, to establish the rule of justice and absolute equality between man and woman on this earth. [...] Workers, in 1791, your fathers proclaimed the immortal declaration of the rights of man [...] In your turn, proclaim the rights of woman.

—Flora Tristán

VOTING RIGHTS OR CHARITY?

The accentuation of class antagonisms, which we discussed in Chapter 2, split the women's movement into two major camps. Women who belonged to the ruling classes rebelled against their lack of formal rights in comparison to the men of their class, but only rarely did they show solidarity with women of the subaltern classes. Women from the working masses took part in the struggles to obtain rights for their class, and in this framework, they demanded their rights as women.[1] The first tendency was expressed organically in liberal and democratic associations, and in philanthropic societies. The second was expressed in utopian socialist organizations and the social movements of the nineteenth century, which were fundamentally led by the growing working class.

However, despite the differences between the different groups and social sectors, with their respective positions and demands, we can see that the women's question had been put on the table, and was turning into a topic of

---

1. See League for a Revolutionary Communist International, *Theses on Women's Oppression*.

    In particular in the USA the demands for equal white women's suffrage was argued for by the leading feminists on the basis that black men had no right to a vote that the white daughters of the bourgeoisie did not have. Their racism, and the support many of their leaders had given to the continuation of slavery, made them clear enemies of the working class.

great significance in the social life of the period. As one expert in women's history put it:

> Between the French Revolution and the First World War, feminism in Europe and the United States manifested itself in a variety of women's movements, publications, and organizations, each with its own tactics and alliances. Their claims and the hostility they provoked demonstrate that the "woman question" had become an issue of broad public debate and figured in a variety of social and political struggles.[2]

The movement led by women from the ruling classes has been called "bourgeois feminism." These women, mostly identified with the struggle for civil rights—particularly the right to vote—or with reformist struggles for the welfare of unmarried mothers, girls' education, and so on, were the driving force behind a flourishing feminist press and countless associations that denounced inequalities in the family and marital sphere, such as the husband's right to decide on all matters of family life, patriarchal authority, the husband's right to administer his wife's property, and so on. They opposed the injustices to which unmarried mothers and their children were subjected, as well as the denial of access to higher education, to suffrage, and to political office. Two of the most important demands were for equal pay for equal work, and for laws regulating prostitution, even though these were not specific demands of the social sector to which the women of this movement belonged.

Philanthropic movements such as the Young Women's Christian Association and the Woman's Christian Temperance Union focused primarily on the struggle for girls' education, professional training, housing for unmarried women, and other charitable works, often accompanying their actions with a strong evangelizing message. Their appeals and lobbying were factors that made it possible to establish compulsory primary education for both sexes throughout Europe.

One of the milestones of this period, and of this broad and widespread movement, was the Seneca Falls Convention, held in 1848, where the campaign for women's suffrage was launched. In the middle of the century,

---

2. Anne-Marie Käppeli, "Feminist Scenes," in Georges Duby and Michelle Perrot (Eds.), *History of Women in the West*, Vol. 4: Geneviève Fraisse (Ed.), *Emerging Feminism from Revolution to World War* (Cambridge, MA: Belknap Press of Harvard University Press, 1993).

women's associations were also created in England that supported the candidacy of the economist and politician John Stuart Mill, a fighter for women's rights. In 1884, the Frenchwoman Hubertine Auclert, founder of the newspaper *La Citoyenne* (*The Citizeness*), wrote to U.S. feminists asking for assistance with the struggle being waged by feminists in France. This link led to the foundation of the International Council of Women (ICW), which at its first meeting brought together 66 Americans and eight Europeans in Washington, DC, in 1888.[3] Only a year after its first meeting, the ICW convened a second international meeting in London with 5,000 women representing 600,000 feminists from the different affiliated sections. As early as 1882, Auclert had used the term "feminist" in her newspaper to describe herself and her supporters, a name that later spread to the entire movement.

These feminist associations often connected their activities to the struggle for world peace and the defense of oppressed peoples. In 1848, when the International Peace Congress was held in Brussels, many of the associations in attendance were made up entirely of women; at the same time, many feminist organizations identified with the banner of peace.

As we can see, different currents of feminism were emerging with different objectives. While some based their demands on the concept of equality, inspired by the revolutionary ideals of the bourgeois class—but expanding the scope of civil rights in relation to gender—others emphasized the specifics of gender, recovering the idea of femininity in its physical, psychological, and cultural dimensions, with a perspective of demanding reforms from the state for the welfare of women. In its origins, the first concept served as the basis for the suffragette movements. The second, emphasizing women's contributions to society, especially their maternal role, achieved important improvements in health care, education, and social welfare.

According to some authors, the two main currents of bourgeois feminism in the late nineteenth and early twentieth centuries can be classified as "individualist" and "relational." "Individualist" feminism, which is found primarily in Anglo-American culture, is based on women's struggle for an existence independent of the family, aspiring to emulate a model of the emancipated individual (which, according to critics of this current, was a

---

3. In a letter addressed to Susan B. Anthony, dated February 27, 1888, Aclert used the word "feminist" when responding to the invitation to participate in the women's congress that was finally held in Washington that same year.

male model). This type of feminism gave political priority to the struggle for equal rights. "Relational" feminism, on the other hand, is based on sexual dimorphism and the idea of specific and complementary responsibilities for men and women on the basis of this dimorphism. These assumptions were the basis for broad demands in relation to maternity protection.

This contradiction between equality as a universal concept (the equality of rights between individuals belonging to different genders, based on their equality as human beings, as members of the same species) and gender difference as a particularity of identity, which can be observed in embryonic form in nineteenth-century feminism, developed into an almost insuperable contradiction in the second wave of feminism in the 1970s, as we shall see in later chapters. This contradiction between equality and difference continues to permeate the theoretical elaborations and political practice of the feminist movement today.

REFORM OR REVOLUTION?

Within what has come to be called "proletarian feminism" or "socialist feminism," we can distinguish two sectors. On the one hand, there were utopian or reformist sectors, who believed that cooperation between capital and labor would improve the situation of the working class and, therefore, of all oppressed people, including women. On the other hand, there were revolutionary socialists who believed that only the end of capitalist exploitation and the construction of a different society could liberate the working class from wage slavery—and thus also liberate all groups who suffered from any form of oppression.

Among the former, we find utopian socialists like Saint-Simon, Fourier, Cabet, and Owen, who advocated a free union between the sexes, challenging traditional ideas regarding love and marriage. Charles Fourier proposed a society organized into what he called "phalansteries"—a neologism based on a combination of "phalanx" and "monastery," since these communities were to live in a communal building surrounded by land they worked together. However, the most striking element of his thought was his critique of the family and marriage in bourgeois society. Fourier assumed that women have innate virtues that make them superior to men, but that society degrades women, forcing them to prostitute themselves in exchange for money: either offering sexual favors to several men in order to survive, or selling themselves to a single man via bourgeois marriage. This is why Fourier believed that women's economic independence is essential to achieve their liberation; even though he argued, paradoxically, that women should not be incorporated into social production under the conditions of the capitalist system at the time, because this could worsen the general situation of the proletariat.

Fourier—who Engels believed to be the first to draw attention to the oppression of women—satirized the hypocrisy of bourgeois ideology:

> Adultery, seduction, are a credit to the seducer, are good tone [...] But, poor girl! Infanticide! What a crime! If she prizes her honour she must efface all traces of dishonour. But if she sacrifices her child to the prejudices of the world her ignominy is all the greater and she is a victim of the prejudices of the law [...] That is the vicious circle which every civilised mechanism describes. Is not the young daughter a ware held up for sale to the first bidder who wishes to obtain exclusive ownership of her? [...] Just as in grammar two negations are the equivalent of an affirmation, we can say that in the marriage trade two prostitutions are the equivalent of virtue [...] The change in a historical epoch can always be determined by women's progress towards freedom, because here, in the relation of woman to man, of the weak to the strong, the victory of human nature over brutality is most evident. The degree of emancipation of woman is the natural measure of general emancipation.[4]

In the second half of the nineteenth century, revolutionary socialism took shape. As we have already pointed out, this tendency believed that women's oppression is a result of the division of society into classes and the appearance of private property, a situation that is exacerbated by the capitalist mode of production.

Marx and Engels first analyzed the bourgeois family with a description in the *Communist Manifesto*, which is not without irony. This was followed by a scientific study of the origin and evolution of the family, which is based on men's domination over women via the institution of monogamy, in Engels' well-known pamphlet *The Origin of the Family, Private Property and the State*. A detailed description of the evils to which women workers are sub-

---

4. Quoted in Karl Marx and Friedrich Engels, *The Holy Family* (Moscow: Foreign Languages Publishing House, 1956).

jected under the whip of capitalist exploitation is provided in Engels' early work *The Condition of the Working Class in England*. Later, Marx's masterful work *Capital* offers a scientific analysis of the role of women workers in the extraction of surplus value as "cheap labour."

Although they considered the existence of the family inevitable, due to its role in the system of production, they also warned that industry, by driving children and women into the factories, destroys the family regime, radically disrupting the relations between parents and children and also between spouses. For Marx and Engels, the family cannot be destroyed by communist propaganda, nor substituted by other kinds of relations in a voluntary manner, until class society, which gave origin to the family, is destroyed. Nonetheless, the communists developed a profound ideological critique of the family and of the values that the bourgeoisie imposes on the exploited and oppressed classes through an institution based on the authority of the father over his children and also on monogamy, which subjects women without preventing adultery by the patriarchs.

In their *Communist Manifesto*, Marx and Engels responded to the accusations of the ruling class against the communists:

> Abolition of the family! Even the most radical flare up at this infamous proposal of the Communists. On what foundation is the present family, the bourgeois family, based? On capital, on private gain. In its completely developed form, this family exists only among the bourgeoisie. But this state of things finds its complement in the practical absence of the family among the proletarians, and in public prostitution.[5]

We will permit ourselves to quote at length from the section of this manifesto in which its authors clearly explain the position of the communists toward women and children:

> Do you charge us with wanting to stop the exploitation of children by their parents? To this crime we plead guilty. But, you say, we destroy the most hallowed of relations, when we replace home education by social. And your education! Is not that also social, and determined by the

---

5. Karl Marx and Friedrich Engels, *The Communist Manifesto*, in Karl Marx and Friedrich Engels, *Selected Works*, Vol. 1 (Moscow: Progress Publishers, 1969).

social conditions under which you educate, by the intervention direct or indirect, of society, by means of schools, etc.? The Communists have not invented the intervention of society in education; they do but seek to alter the character of that intervention, and to rescue education from the influence of the ruling class. The bourgeois clap-trap about the family and education, about the hallowed co-relation of parents and child, becomes all the more disgusting, the more, by the action of Modern Industry, all the family ties among the proletarians are torn asunder, and their children transformed into simple articles of commerce and instruments of labour. But you Communists would introduce community of women, screams the bourgeoisie in chorus. The bourgeois sees his wife a mere instrument of production. He hears that the instruments of production are to be exploited in common, and, naturally, can come to no other conclusion that the lot of being common to all will likewise fall to the women. He has not even a suspicion that the real point aimed at is to do away with the status of women as mere instruments of production. For the rest, nothing is more ridiculous than the virtuous indignation of our bourgeois at the community of women which, they pretend, is to be openly and officially established by the Communists. The Communists have no need to introduce community of women; it has existed almost from time immemorial. Our bourgeois, not content with having wives and daughters of their proletarians at their disposal, not to speak of common prostitutes, take the greatest pleasure in seducing each other's wives. Bourgeois marriage is, in reality, a system of wives in common and thus, at the most, what the Communists might possibly be reproached with is that they desire to introduce, in substitution for a hypocritically concealed, an openly legalised community of women. For the rest, it is self-evident that the abolition of the present system of production must bring with it the abolition of the community of women springing from that system, i.e., of prostitution both public and private.[6]

Marx and Engels also called for the organization of women workers together with their class brothers in order to break out of the isolation of the home. This would liberate them from backwardness, ignorance, and contempt for politics and the proletarian struggle. Engels pointed out that:

---

6. Ibid.

the peculiar character of the supremacy of the husband over the wife in the modern family, the necessity of creating real social equality between them, and the way to do it, will only be seen in the clear light of day when both possess legally complete equality of rights. Then it will be plain that the first condition for the liberation of the wife is to bring the whole female sex back into public industry, and that this in turn demands the abolition of the monogamous family as the economic unit of society.[7]

This was the opposite of the anarchist Proudhon, who declared:

I regard it as baneful and stupid all our dreams about the emancipation of women; I deny her any kind of right and political initiative; I believe that for women, liberty and well-being lie solely in marriage, motherhood, domestic concerns, fidelity as a spouse, chastity, and seclusion.[8]

In accordance with their teachings, Marx and Engels defended the political and economic rights of women in the trade unions and the International Workingmen's Association—more commonly known as the First International—even when this required an open confrontation with the reactionary positions of petty-bourgeois and reformist currents that had influence over sections of the proletariat. They encouraged the formation of the *Women's Union*, the women's section of the First International under the leadership of Elisabeth Dmitrieff, who was sent to the Paris Commune in 1871 as a representative of the International. There, as we saw, Dmitrieff was an active participant in the organization of women for the defense of the city. The English trade union organizer Henriette Law also played a prominent role in the International as a member of its General Council.

As is easy to imagine, Marxist ideas were not accepted quickly. The same anarchist Proudhon, quoted above, argued, for example, that a woman only had two possible destinies: as a housewife or a prostitute, which is why he opposed the incorporation of women into production. Marx and Engels also had to confront the reformist political program of Ferdinand Lassalle for

---

7. Friedrich Engels, *The Origin of the Family, Private Property and the State*, in Friedrich Engels, *Selected Works*, Vol. 3 (Moscow: Progress Publishers, 1970).
8. Pierre-Joseph Proudhon, *La pornocracia o la mujer en nuestros tiempos* (Madrid: Huerga y Fierro Editores, 1995). For the English translation of this quote, see Hal Draper, *Women and Class: Toward a Socialist Feminism* (Alameda, CA: Center for Socialist History, 2011).

the Socialist Workers' Party of Germany, which also rejected the inclusion of women into production. Marx opposed Lassalle's position in his famous *Critique of the Gotha Program*.[9]

In fact, in 1866, a document of the German section of the First International, fundamentally inspired by the ideas of Proudhon and Lassalle, noted:

> The rightful work of women and mothers is in the home and family, caring for, supervising, and providing the first education for the children, which, it is true, presupposes that the woman and children themselves receive an adequate training. Alongside the solemn duties of the man and father in public life and the family, the woman and mother should stand for the cosiness and poetry of domestic life, bring grace and beauty to social relations, and be an ennobling influence in the increase of humanity's enjoyment of life.[10]

It was not until 1891, at the end of the century, that the Social Democratic Party of Germany included the demand for equal rights for men and women in its program, as we will see later.

But we do not want to close this chapter without making special mention of a socialist woman who was a fundamental pioneer in thinking about women's emancipation in connection with the emancipation of the proletariat: Flora Tristán.

A WOMAN LIVING BETWEEN TWO ERAS

Growing up with the contradictory influence of romanticism, Flora Tristán enjoyed reading Bernardin de Saint-Pierre, Victor Hugo, and Lamartine, and lived a life that was worthy of a romantic heroine: sordid and dark episodes, extravagant adventures in exotic landscapes, beauty, love, sadness, melancholy, and loneliness. And although her ideas about women and socialism, feminism and the working class were truly innovative, it was her unique life

---

9. A congress held in Gotha on May 22–27, 1875 united the two workers' organizations that existed at the time in Germany: the Social Democratic Workers' Party of Germany (SDAP), led by Liebknecht and Bebel, and the General German Workers' Association (ADAV), led by Lassalle. They founded a single organization, the Socialist Workers' Party of Germany (SAPD), which later became the Social Democratic Party of Germany (SPD).

10. Quoted in Werner Thönessen, *The Emancipation of Women: The Rise and Decline of the Women's Movement in German Social Democracy, 1863–1933* (London: Pluto Press, 1976).

that has most captivated the attention of writers and historians. Her existence was marked by adversities and setbacks, and her own account of that life makes Flora Tristán a remarkable character: the pariah, the Woman-Messiah. And in spite of being "a woman alone against the world,"[11] she was venerated by the workers, to whom she dedicated her fervent final days. They offered the words on her gravestone: "To the memory of Flora Tristán, author of *The Workers' Union*, the grateful workers. Freedom, Equality, Fraternity, Solidarity."

Flore-Célestine-Thérèse-Henriette Tristán-Moscoco was born on April 7, 1803. Her father was a Creole colonel in the Spanish army in the Viceroyalty of Peru and her mother was a Frenchwoman who escaped the Revolution of 1789 and emigrated to Bilbao. There, her parents were married by a priest but the marriage was not recognized by the French authorities and laws, and this would have crucial consequences later in Tristán's life. In 1804, a new Civil Code replaced the laws of the Revolution: while preserving some aspects of the egalitarian spirit of 1789, it emphasized the right to property and the patriarchal authority of the man over his wife and children. The *pater familiae* of Roman law thus regained his power by the hand of Napoleon, who personally intervened in the drafting of these articles: divorce was restricted, illegitimate children were not recognized, and paternal authority recovered the strength it had had in the *ancien régime*.

When Tristán's family settled in the Rue de Vaugirard in Paris, their home was frequented by Simón Bolívar, the naturalist Aimé Bonpland, and the writer and philosopher Samuel Robinson, who was none other than Bolívar's mentor Simón Rodríguez.[12] These are the names that Flora, as an adult, provided to her uncle Pío de Tristán to prove that she was the daughter of his beloved brother Mariano—despite the illegality of her parents' marriage and therefore the illegitimacy of her own birth. The blood of Spanish saints, Italian popes, Creole soldiers, and Inca emperors ran through Flora Tristán's veins. Her short life did not prevent her from knowing both comfort in the Rue de Vaugirard and deprivation in Bordeaux, honor in Paris and contempt in Arequipa, slavery in Praia and modern wage slavery in London. Each of these experiences shaped her thinking, transforming this self-taught

---

11. This is the title of a biography of Flora Tristán by the Peruvian writer Luis Alberto Sánchez: *Una mujer sola contra el mundo: Flora Tristán* (Lima: UNMSM, 2004).
12. Simón Rodríguez (1769–1854), known during his exile as Samuel Robinson, was a Venezuelan educator who served as the mentor of Simón Bolívar. —translator

woman into "The Pariah," driving her to become a pagan prophet of socialism and women's emancipation.

Flora Tristán's life took place between two revolutions: she was born 14 years after the Great French Revolution of 1798 and she died just four years before the Springtime of the Peoples, the rebellion that swept through Europe in 1848—this uprising had France as its epicenter and the proletariat, to whom Tristán dedicated the final years of her life, as its protagonist. In a certain sense, her existence was defined by these events: a bourgeois revolution that had died and a proletarian revolution that could not yet be born. This also serves as a metaphor for the contradiction she was experiencing personally: on the one hand, a strenuous effort to regain her lost place in the aristocracy after the death of her father; on the other hand, an eagerness to conquer the collective emancipation of the proletariat, of all those pariahs to whom she also felt she belonged. And although the objective conditions for a workers' revolution were still unripe, her work was in all respects a product of this transition period between the "no more" of the bourgeois revolution and the "not yet" of the proletarian revolution. This is why we can say that Flora Tristán stands halfway between utopian socialism and scientific socialism: her articles and pamphlets cannot be classified, without some effort at conciliation, together with those of her teachers; nor can they be included among the works of scientific socialism, fundamentally due to her lack of knowledge of political economy and resulting insufficient class analysis. Her work nonetheless contains some of the fundamental ideas that Marx and Engels would make known to the world just a few years later in the *Communist Manifesto*.

Neither French nor Peruvian, neither bourgeois nor proletarian. Where does Flora Tristán belong? Her search for a place in the world leads her to the realization that she has no place. The rift in her life is only resolved through a journey to the distant and unknown American lands, which is in reality a journey into herself—she recognizes that she is a pariah but simultaneously transforms herself into a social fighter, an exquisite polemicist, and an innovative publicist. There, in Peru, she sees the possibility to transcend her miserable existence through literary work; she dedicates herself to rebellious writing that will denounce the oppression faced by women, the pariahs of the world who are violently subjected to the chains of matrimony, which she compares to those of slavery—something she also witnesses in the course of this journey, at a stop on the coast of Africa.

Who had Flora Tristán been before this voyage? Just a woman who, at 18 years of age, had aspired to become "a perfect woman," who intended to "be good to everyone, to be a philosopher, but in such a sweet and kind way that all men will desire a woman philosopher."[13] A girl who had seen her brother die at the same time as her father; who went from having a home frequented by famous writers, soldiers, and politicians, to living alone with her mother in a sordid Parisian neighborhood. A young woman who, at the age of 15, was rejected as a bastard by her suitor's father. A woman condemned for the illegality of her parents' marriage, stigmatized as an illegitimate daughter by French laws which reserved a miserable fate for her, and whose situation was resolved by an arranged marriage with the lithographer André Chazal. At the time, Tristán worked in the studio of the somewhat older artist, which she had entered as an apprentice. Women in this era had no options: the convent or prostitution were the only alternatives to a marriage of convenience. The Napoleonic Code stated that a wife "can only petition for divorce in the event that her husband brings a permanent mistress into the home." Tristán was therefore a woman for whom marriage only brought new misfortunes: faced with Chazal's violence, she quickly discovered that she did not even have the right to leave him, to divorce him, to break the supposed "mutual consent" in which the bond had been established. And yet, she dared to abandon him, with two small children in tow and a few months into a third pregnancy. During her flight, she discovered feminism by reading *Vindication of the Rights of Woman* by Mary Wollstonecraft.

Flora Tristán worked in a confectioner's shop, pretending to be a widow. She left her children in the care of other people but no longer returned to the marital home and instead accepted a job as a governess for an English family, with whom she traveled through Switzerland, Germany, Italy, and England in 1826–1828. During this time, she read not only the original ideas of Mary Wollstonecraft, but also Saint-Simon, Charles Fourier, and George Sand—that daring writer whose pseudonym hid a woman who was also longing for freedom. Tristán's memory accumulated the experiences of an ill-fated life, which would turn her into a writer who condemned the evils of a society based on profound inequalities. "Without a mother, without children, without a name, without a husband: an authentic pariah, on the

---

13. Letter to André Chazal from 1821, quoted in Stéphane Michaud (Ed.), *Lettres* (Paris: Du Seuil, 1980), our translation.

threshold of her own destiny."[14] For the moment, however, these experiences merely tormented her spirit—only later would she turn them into incendiary pamphlets and books that would provoke the most varied reactions among progressive circles of the time.

After working as a governess for a bourgeois family in London, Flora Tristán then returned to Paris and sued her husband in court. She demanded the separation of the property from the marriage, but the justice system that denied her the right to divorce also rejected this claim: according to the sentence, André Chazal lacked property or any means of subsistence. It was, thus, up to her to provide for her children on her own. Shortly after this, her first child died. However, as if providence did not want to abandon her completely, she then met an officer of the merchant marine who, during his trips to Peru, had established a relationship with Don Pío de Tristán, none other than her uncle. On his deathbed, Flora Tristán's father had told her, "My daughter, you still have Pío." Attempts to contact this uncle beyond the sea had been fruitless for years: dozens of letters that her mother sent to that esteemed Creole brother-in-law had received no reply. Now there was a unique opportunity: the niece who had been entrusted to him by her father on his deathbed could send him a letter via the sailor Zacarías Chabrié.

Flora Tristán had already come into contact with the disciples of Saint-Simon, who had formed an association based on fraternity and communal life. Their ideas about love and family, fidelity and women were enormously revolutionary—but they were quite at odds with the group's own practice. Engineers, doctors, and poets who spoke about progress and socialism had founded an association in which women could not participate, with the exception of Clara, the wife of Saint-Amand Bazard, who was one of the group's leaders alongside Prosper Enfantin. These "Supreme Fathers"—as they were referred to in the sect—did not agree on everything. Bazard advocated political reforms, while Enfantin leaned toward preaching and moral change, especially criticizing the "tyranny of marriage" and calling for free love. Eventually, he led his followers toward mysticism, searching for a Woman-Messiah he hoped to find in the East. These "fathers," who were persecuted by the French authorities, were divided by different conceptions of women: they would either have no role in the construction of socialism in

---

14. Luis A. Sánchez, *Una mujer sola contra el mundo: Flora Tristán* (Lima: UNMSM, 2004), our translation.

the future, or they would reveal the new moral order. Tristán did not share the opinions of either tendency, even though the messianic idea of a woman predestined to become the prophet of the new world enticed her enormously. As various biographers of Flora Tristán point out, mysticism is the form of her own process of individuation—she assumes the task entrusted to her in an almost prophetic way.

In 1832, two socialist women workers—who had not been allowed to join the association created by Saint-Simon's disciples—launched the newspaper *La Femme Libre* (*The Free Woman*), which would later be called *La Femme Nouvelle* (*The New Woman*) and *La Tribune des Femmes* (*The Women's Tribune*). From these pages, Suzanne Voilquin would petition for the right to divorce, after becoming romantically involved with another Saint-Simonian. In the following year, Eugénie Niboyet founded *Conseiller des Femmes* (*The Women's Advisor*) in Lyon—the first feminist periodical published outside of Paris. Niboyet, who had joined the ranks of the Saint-Simonians, broke with that organization and joined the Fourierists. Unlike the disciples of Saint-Simon, who debated about sexual freedom versus the defense of fidelity, and who derived a certain religious mysticism from the socialist principles of their teacher, the Fourierists concentrated on economic changes for the development of their "phalansteries," where work—including domestic labor—would be carried out by all members of the community on the basis of equality. Charles Fourier had argued that the situation of women was the measure of social progress, and this idea impressed Tristán, who by now had moved away from the Saint-Simonians and was more inclined to the ideas of Victor Considerant, a disciple of Fourier who was committed to constructing the "phalansteries" that his teacher had envisioned. These communities would organize cooperatively in order to peacefully reform the socio-economic system that was the source of all injustice. "It can be observed that the level of civilization attained by different human societies is in proportion to the independence that women enjoy," Tristán would write, paraphrasing Fourier, in the opening pages of *Peregrinations of a Pariah*.[15]

Meanwhile, Tristán received an answer from her Peruvian uncle: a parsimonious and distant response that crushed her hopes that her Creole family would offer assistance. Her hopes were rekindled, however, by a people's

---

15. Flora Tristán, *Peregrinaciones de una Paria* (Lima: UNMSM, 2003), our translation (the introduction is not included in the English edition).

revolt. Tristán was an active participant in the Three Glorious Days,[16] after Charles X, the Bourbon king of France, suspended the freedom of the press and dissolved the recently elected Chamber of Deputies. The people of Paris—who had just endured the consequences of a major economic crisis and an increase in food prices—took to the streets, defeating the army and reopening the liberal newspapers that had been closed down by royal decree. Workers and craftsmen, who gathered in front of the Royal Palace, formed the initial nucleus of the insurrection; barricades were erected in front of the City Hall as well as in the suburbs; the verses of La Marseillaise resounded in the streets of Paris, interrupted only by the cry, "Down with the Bourbons!" The mobilization included students and the middle classes; shopkeepers and bosses gave their employees leave to participate in the revolt. Finally, on July 30, 1830, the king abdicated and the Chamber of Deputies elevated Louis-Philippe d'Orléans, referred to as "the king of the barricades," to the throne. Though deeply moved by the people's mobilizations, Flora Tristán saw her hopes crumble yet again. The law on divorce was discussed in the Chamber, but it would not be passed until 1884. The bond that kept her enslaved to the hated André Chazal still could not be dissolved. The working class had pushed the revolutionary movement forward, achieving a triumph for the people, but the big bourgeoisie was again going to take the spoils of victory. Meanwhile, her husband was seeking custody of her son Ernesto, while Tristán demanded, in return, the signing of a separation agreement, which she trusted would be transformed into a divorce as soon as the law permitted it. Finally, having exhausted all her resources to survive in the face of so many misfortunes, she turned to Mariano de Goyeneche, her father's cousin from Arequipa, who lived in Bordeaux, and he assisted her in preparing for her trip to Peru.

On April 7, 1833, Tristán set off on her pilgrimage to Peru on board the ship *El Mexicano*, captained by the very Zacarías Chabrié whom she had met a few years prior. It would be a voyage of four-and-a-half months on a ship with 20 men and one woman: her. In the months that followed, the French working class experienced the highest levels of exploitation since the Restoration. As Tristán sailed toward her destination, the silk workers of Lyon rose up against their miserable wages and exhausting 18-hour workdays. Under

---

16. The *Trois Glorieuses* (Three Glorious Days) were July 27–29, 1830, also known as the July Revolution. —translator

the slogan "live working or die fighting," the workers threw themselves into the struggle, enduring fierce repression by government troops. Their defeat, however, was not in vain. Strengthened in their class-consciousness, the workers advanced in the construction of their organizations. Tristán was far away from these events, in mysterious Peru, the land of her father, which had recently been liberated from the Spanish yoke and was engulfed in a struggle between military strongmen for the presidency of the new republic. In 1834, the city of Arequipa—where her father's family originated—was shaken by the overthrow of the constitutional president, General Luis José de Orbegoso, by two other generals from the independence war, Agustín Gamarra and Pedro Pablo Bermúdez. The Arequipa army was defeated and the city fell into the hands of the usurpers, although a people's uprising was later able to end the occupation. Flora Tristán witnessed these revolts on American soil with a totally new perspective: in France, she had become a wage laborer, condemned to live in illegality by Napoleon's ban on divorce; but in Peru, she belonged to one of the wealthiest families of Arequipa, a representative of the reactionary oligarchy.

It was not until January 1834 that she first met her uncle Pío de Tristán. She achieved nothing that she had set out to resolve with this long journey across the ocean. Her family granted her a meager pension, but did not recognize her right to the inheritance that Tristán longed for; although she was accepted as one of them, her parents' illegal marriage still condemned her to a life as a bastard daughter without rights. Her journey, however, did transform her into the Flora Tristán who shines in the history of socialist and feminist ideas; it transformed her into the woman who expressed her recollections of that voyage in the famous pages of *Peregrinations of a Pariah*, which she closed with the words: "I remained alone, completely alone, between two immensities: the sea and the sky."[17]

ON THE NEED TO WELCOME FOREIGN WOMEN

We will not dwell on this voyage of initiation, recounted in *Peregrinations of a Pariah*, which was written in 1835 after Tristán had returned to Paris. On her journey back to Europe, she began to write her first essay, *On the Need to*

---

17. Flora Tristán, *Peregrinations of a Pariah* (London: Virago Press, 1985).

Welcome Foreign Women. At the beginning of this text, Flora Tristán argues that the masses need to unite in order to fight against the old institutions:

> From all sides one hears a unanimous call for new institutions adapted to new needs, a demand for associations working by common consent to bring relief to the many who suffer and languish without being able to help themselves; for, divided, they are weak, unable even to struggle against the last efforts of a decrepit, dying civilization.[18]

She compares the struggle for women's rights with the great revolution that pitched the people against the antiquated medieval institutions, with all of society forming a tremendous alliance against the throne. She appeals to women, but also to men, those who "see the need to ameliorate the lot of women"; she argues that those whose mission is to "bring peace and love to mankind" cannot continue to live in pain.

On the Need to Welcome Foreign Women shows the differences that separate her from the utopian socialists: Tristán questions the Fourierists' division between theory and practice; she points out that the "phalansteries" and other forms of communal living imagined by the utopians are mere dreams that fail to solve the problems of the masses condemned to misery. "Our objective here is not to create another brilliant utopia by describing the world as it should be, without indicating how to realize the beautiful dream of a universal Eden."[19]

For Tristán, utopia is an abstraction. The theories of the great thinkers of socialism of the time are merely discursive and not intended to sketch the practical steps for achieving human progress. She does not want to be confused "with those metaphysicists who dream more than they should."[20] Nor does she want to "save" a chosen few, predestined to live a communal life within a sea of hardships: "The limits of our love should not be the brambles that surround our garden, the walls that encircle our city, the mountains or the seas that border our country. From now on, our homeland must be

---

18. Flora Tristán, "De la necesidad de dar buena acogida a las mujeres extranjeras." Parts of this essay have been published in English, see Flora Tristán, *Utopian Feminist: Her Travel Diaries and Personal Crusade* (Bloomington, IN: Indiana University Press, 1993). The rest is our translation.
19. Ibid.
20. Ibid.

the universe."[21] Here, Flora Tristán foreshadows the idea of internationalism, which places her closer to scientific socialism than to the socialism of her teachers. In fact, her travels have shown her that pariahs everywhere live under the yoke of the same oppression. Later, these same conclusions will help her forge her central idea, the *Workers' Union*, a sketch of a proletarian international conceived more than 20 years before the foundation of the International Workingmen's Association, better known as the First International.

In *On the Need to Welcome Foreign Women*, Flora Tristán searches for a language to speak to the masses, and for arguments to convince them that her proposals regarding women will have advantages for all of society. In this initial text, Tristán starts becoming a publicist of socialist feminism. She does not only address women but all of society; she does not propose a utopia, nor does she merely want to describe the miserable conditions of the most unfortunate: she tries to develop convincing arguments that will lead her readers to undertake the practical task that she is proposing.

Why should travel not be considered, in itself, a source of progress and union among peoples, "hastening the moment when so many rival nations will become one family"? For this, it is necessary to implement reforms of the existing laws and institutions that govern the destiny of pariahs, in order to obtain "incremental improvements." This is why the pamphlet contains not only a detailed description of the woes afflicting immigrant women but also a proposal to create a *Society for Foreign Women*, showing the importance that the practical political dimension has for Tristán. Toward the end of the text, she proposes a statute for such a society, whose motto would be "Virtue—Prudence—Publicity."

Her attempt to connect class and gender in this work is impressive. She describes three different sectors of women to explain how oppression manifests itself in such diverse ways. Flora Tristán distinguishes between women "who undertake voyages for education or pleasure," which includes the "most distinguished and interesting" women; then there are those who are drawn to the city "by commercial transactions, lawsuits, or other business"; and finally the third and largest group, women on whom "all griefs seem to be concentrated" and who are worthy "of the deepest compassion." The first group experiences difficulties in walking around Paris alone under the

---

21. Ibid.

prejudiced gaze of men; the second group runs the risk of being deceived in the pursuit of their goals; and the third group enters the big city seeking to lose themselves in anonymity, victims of the dishonor, the inequality, and the injustice of the laws that bind them to a matrimonial destiny that they deplore. The latter are poor women, since "very few rich women feel the cruel necessity of separating from their husbands," according to the author. And it is society's rejection that condemns them to a "path of vice, cloaked in the most brilliant colors." Tristán invokes the Christian principle of doing unto others as we would have them do unto us. They are not only foreigners because of their homeland—they are foreigners because of the rules imposed by an unjust society that mandates brutal inequality for women.

Will not progress bring salvation to the plagues that afflict humanity? Contradictorily, the text begins with a call to struggle against the backwardness of antiquated institutions, but it points out that the progress imposed by "civilization" adds new hardships, now in a capitalist form: "the barbarism of modern civilizations."

Her *Society for Foreign Women*, which could be presided over by a man or a woman, native-born or immigrant, would aim:

> to welcome foreign women, listen to their demands, satisfy them, if possible, present them to society, and even introduce them to the world; to provide those who come to carry out scholarly research with all the information they may need; to put those who are artists in contact with artists; to put those who are foreigners in France in contact with their compatriots, if they so desire; to try to get those who come seeking an occupation one that is suitable to their position; and also to help those who come for business, court, illness, etc. etc. with everything.[22]

The language of *On the Need to Welcome Foreign Women* is still infused with the mysticism that the utopian socialists let flourish in their articles and speeches; for Tristán, her goal is holy and she trusts God to inspire her with words that will find an echo in sensitive hearts ready to hear her message.

PETITION TO REINSTATE DIVORCE

Three tumultuous years follow the publication of Tristán's first essay. There are endless fights with André Chazal over the custody of their daughter

---

22. Ibid.

Aline—who would later become the mother of the painter Paul Gauguin. The little girl is abducted by her father and recovered by her mother in an episode that culminates in a police chase and an arrest. Again, Tristán has to appear in court, and is ordered to place Aline in a boarding house so that both parents can visit her. But Chazal does not stop: as revenge for the fact that Tristán abandoned him, he abducts Aline once more to keep her out of contact with her mother. But this time, the girl escapes from her father's home and seeks refuge at Tristán's. The joy is short-lived, as Chazal immediately sends the police to get her back. A short time later, a letter from Aline shocks her mother: the little girl writes about her fear of her father, and hints that he has tried to abuse her. It is not necessary to recover her by force, since Aline escapes from André Chazal's home once again, and Tristán reports him to the police for the attempted rape of a minor. This time, the court comes to the aid of the desperate mother, sentencing the accused to 60 days in prison; in response, he alleges that Flora Tristán is an adulteress and a schemer. Despite all this, she has to wait until February 1838 for the court to rule on the dissolution of the marriage.

In the meantime, Charles Fourier, the great teacher to whom Tristán had presented a copy of her essay, *On the Need to Welcome Foreign Women*, has died. And the third pillar of utopian socialism, the Welshman Robert Owen, visits Paris, where Tristán speaks with him. Trapped in this atmosphere of domestic violence yet entering the circles of the most progressive thinkers of the time, Tristán sends a petition to several liberal deputies: her *Petition for the Reinstatement of Divorce*. In it, Tristán offers a tirade against marriage, which she calls an "institution against nature." This is because it is a union of two beings who do not enjoy the same rights nor social equality. For this reason, she asserts that:

> it is superfluous to show that concord between spouses, as in any kind of association, can only result from relations of equality; that the repugnant union of despotism and servitude perverts the master and the slave; and that such is our nature, that there can be no affection that is not destroyed by dependence.[23]

---

23. Flora Tristán, "Petición para el restablecimiento del divorcio," our translation.

There can be no such thing as marriage based on love as long as women continue to be oppressed under the male yoke. Later, in her book *The Workers' Union*, she would write: "Between master and slave there can only be the weariness of the chain's weight tying them together. When the lack of freedom is felt, happiness cannot exist."[24]

She also criticizes the Napoleonic Code, condemning the fact that the legislation inherited from the Revolution of 1789 prohibited divorce, "the only remedy for extreme misfortunes." If marriage between people with unequal rights brings misfortune, this is further reinforced by its indissolubility. Tristán explains that she has experienced this herself, although she tries to make clear that:

> personal interest is not the motive for the petition I am addressing to you: I have been guided by love for my peers, convinced by my own experience that happiness cannot exist in families unless there are conditions of freedom.[25]

In contrast to Saint-Simonianism, Tristán strives to criticize the institution of marriage, hoping that legal reforms will provide relief to the bitterness caused by the impossibility of living together under the yoke of oppression. She does not advocate free love, although she is conscious of the dominance that the husband exercises over the wife. Instead, she calls for divorce and the right of women to choose their spouses freely, without intervention by their parents. But what does she think about love? According to her biographer Yolanda Marco, love and marriage are antagonistic for Flora Tristán, who does not believe that love can be assimilated into the contracts imposed by the institution of marriage, which subjugate women as the property of their husbands. She also declares that in her own life, her passions were sublimated into a general love of humanity, as a social passion that encompasses women and the proletariat, the most oppressed of society. Her experience with matrimony, and that of her parents, prompts her to reflect on the institution of marriage and to "request that the Chamber reinstate divorce and base it on the principle of reciprocity and the will of one of the spouses, as

---

24. Flora Tristán, *The Workers' Union* (Urbana, IL: University of Illinois Press, 1983).
25. Tristán, "Petición para el restablecimiento del divorcio," our translation.

the laws had done prior to the Napoleonic Code."²⁶ This made her one of the most ardent defenders of women's rights of the time.

In the meanwhile, she publishes *Peregrinations of a Pariah* and survives an attempt on her life: André Chazal shoots her in the back in the middle of the street. He is arrested, while Tristán is taken to hospital with a serious injury. However, displaying an unparalleled altruism, as soon as she recovers, she submits another petition to the Chamber of Deputies for the abolition of the death penalty. This document is followed by other articles published in the most important socialist magazines of the time, including a profile of Simón Bolívar based on the correspondence that *El Libertador* maintained with her parents, adding her own childhood memories. Before long, *Peregrinations of a Pariah* is reprinted and some of its passages are read out during the trial against Chazal. Her "philosophical and social novel," *Méphis, or the Proletarian*, appears. Visiting London for the fourth time, she visits the House of Commons disguised as a man and attends meetings of the English workers' Chartist movement. Her impressions of the cradle of the Industrial Revolution are published in her *London Journal*, which is very well received by critics. Not only are fragments published in the press but it is also reprinted twice.

THE WORKERS' UNION

Flora Tristán then begins composing *The Workers' Union*. The Fourierist Victor Considérant publishes extracts in his newspaper *La Falange*, and the book appears in June 1843.²⁷ Deeply moved by her experiences in London,

---

26. Ibid.
27. In September of that year, a young German Jew, just 25 years old, wrote to a friend, "I shall be in Paris by the end of this month, since the atmosphere here makes one a serf, and in Germany I see no scope at all for free activity." It was Karl Marx, the editor of the *Rheinische Zeitung*, a publication that was targeted by the censors and whose editor soon had to go into exile. His friend in Paris was Arnold Ruge, with whom he founded the journal *Deutsch-Französische Jahrbücher* (German-French Annals), and who, in turn, introduced him to Flora Tristán. With the beginning of the friendship between Marx and Friedrich Engels, who was also in Paris, scientific socialism began to take shape. Soon, they would join forces to resolve their philosophical doubts in writing, in an incisive and poignant polemic with the journal published by the brothers Bruno, Edgar, and Egbert Bauer. This polemic dedicated a section of the third chapter to Flora Tristán's *Workers' Union*. Mocking Edgar Bauer and defending Tristán, they write,

> Criticism's own proposition, if taken in the only reasonable sense it can possibly have, demands the organization of labour. Flora Tristán, in an assessment of whose work this

Tristán intends to collaborate in the organization of the French workers' movement. In the city of misery and overcrowding, of the steam engine and the fog on the Thames, Tristán had also discovered an organized workers' movement, which held public rallies and clandestine meetings, fighting not only for social but also for political reforms. In 1838, the vigorous British proletariat had put forward its demands in a *People's Charter*, calling for universal male suffrage for adults, equal constituencies with the same number of voters, secret ballots, no property qualifications to obtain a seat in parliament, a stipend for members of parliament, and annual parliamentary elections. From this, Tristán concludes that in order to combine efforts and share experiences in the struggle for the emancipation of the proletariat, it is necessary to unite internationally; but also that it is necessary to have a representative in parliament, as the English Chartists had won, a Defender of the People, who would fight from the rostrum for measures to benefit the working class: the right to a job and a wage, as well as the right to organize. In order to transform society, the proletariat would need an instrument: an international union of workers, which would fight inequality and misery with peaceful means, persuasion, and political pressure on the institutions of the regime. This is what Flora Tristán envisaged, and in six weeks, she drafted *The Workers' Union*. She planned a tour of France to bring the good news to the Gallic workers.

> I realized that, with my book published, I had another task to accomplish, which is to go from town to town and from one end of France to the other with my union plan in hand to speak to those workers who do not know how to read or have no time to read. I told myself that the time had come to act.[28]

---

  great proposition appears, puts forward the same demand and is treated *en canaille* for her insolence in anticipating Critical Criticism.

This first quote is from Letter from Marx to Arnold Ruge from September 1843, published in *Deutsch–Französische Jahrbücher* (Paris, 1844), in Karl Marx and Friedrich Engels, *Collected Works, Vol. 3* (London: Lawrence & Wishart, 1975); the second quote is from Karl Marx and Friedrich Engels, *The Holy Family, or Critique of Critical Criticism* (Moscow: Foreign Language Publishing House, 1956).

28. Flora Tristán, *The Workers' Union* (Urbana, IL: University of Illinois Press, 1983).

In contrast to the French trade unions, which stand in the tradition of the craft guilds and the journeyman system, Flora Tristán's *Workers' Union* aims to unite the entire working class without distinction. Saint-Simon considered this class to be the most numerous and the poorest in society, but Tristán gives it a new definition: paraphrasing her teacher, she calls it the most numerous and useful class. Its unity would make it strong, and this social power would enable its parliamentary representatives to impose the demands of the proletariat on the bourgeoisie. The guilds help workers in times of illness or unemployment, but she warns: "alleviating misery does not *destroy* it; mitigating the evil is not the same as *eradicating* it."[29] And the only way to get to the root of the problem is to overcome the existing trade associations with a universal union that encompasses the entire class. Had not the dissolution of narrow borders dividing countries into small fiefdoms allowed for the formation of great empires? Tristán explains to the workers how the bourgeoisie constituted itself as a class and conquered power:

> Workers, for more than two hundred years the bourgeois have fought courageously and ardently against the privileges of the nobility and for the victory of their rights. But when the day of victory came, and though they recognized *de facto* equal rights for all, they seized all the gains and advantages of the conquest for themselves alone. The bourgeois class has been established since 1789. Note what strength a body united in the same interest can have.[30]

Her thesis is convincing: at the bottom of the page she clarifies that the bourgeoisie had represented the "head" of the revolution, and had used the people as "arms"; but the working class has no one to come to its aid, to be its "arms." So it "must be the head as well as arms." Later, Marx and Engels would say that the proletariat has nothing to lose but its chains. The proletariat was emerging in history as the class called upon to be the gravedigger, not only of the bourgeoisie, but also of all existing class societies.

Tristán's concern, like that of the founders of scientific socialism, is not economistic. She is determined to contribute to the constitution of the working class as a political subject, and for this, she believes that it is nec-

---

29. Ibid.
30. Ibid.

essary to start by fighting for the widest possible unity. That is why her book *The Workers' Union* begins with a phrase from the typesetter Adolphe Boyer: "Today, the worker creates everything, does everything, produces everything, and yet he has no rights, possesses nothing, absolutely nothing." This is accompanied by a proverb from Tristán's pen: "Workers, unite—unity gives you strength."[31] The proletarian internationalism proposed by Flora Tristán is deeply political and traces the outlines of a new praxis. For this reason, Tristán begins by distancing herself from the utopian socialists: they have already said everything about the workers' cause and unfortunate situation; now it is imperative to act. "Only one thing remains to be done: *to act by virtue of the rights inscribed in the Charter*,"[32] Tristán writes, in reference to the *People's Charter* of the British workers. In opposition to utopian projects at the fringes of society, and to all narrow trade associations, Tristán is calling for a union of the proletariat to peacefully intervene in the political sphere. Others have spoken about workers, "but no one has yet tried to speak *to* them."[33]

Another striking element of Tristán's thought is expressed in *The Workers' Union*: in addition to internationalism and the foreshadowing of the proletarian party, Tristán points out that the emancipation of the workers must be conquered by the workers themselves, but for this they would need to establish a sort of alliance with other socially oppressed classes and strata. Oppression results from the existence of "the privileges of property" that weigh on all the dispossessed and the expropriated: "artists, teachers, employees, small businessmen, and many others, even small investors who own no property such as land, houses, or capital, are fatally subjected to the laws passed by the landowners sitting in the legislature."[34] Thus, she lists, in a footnote, the allies of the proletariat in its struggle for emancipation. Her conception is very different from that of Saint-Simon, who believed the "producing classes"—those called upon to determine the destiny of humanity—included both workers and industrialists. In fact, Tristán's conception is closer to the revolutionary Marxism of the twentieth century, which calls on the working class, in its fierce struggle against blood-drenched capital, to lead all the oppressed sectors of the nation, to

---

31. Ibid.
32. Ibid.
33. Ibid.
34. Ibid.

gain hegemony over all the exploited, and to form an alliance with the peasantry and the urban poor.

The Workers' Union reveals a connection that still echoes in the reflections of contemporary socialist feminists: Tristán argues that woman is the proletarian of the proletariat, and that women will only win their emancipation hand in hand with the working class. But male workers cannot aspire to liberate themselves from the yoke of wage slavery unless they summon women to fight alongside them under the banner of their own freedom and the struggle for their rights. Flora Tristán's feminism, which was already outlined in her first essay, *On the Need to Welcome Foreign Women*, evolves from utopian to scientific socialism in the few short years of literary and political production between her trip to Peru and her early death. This analysis, which combines the categories of class and gender in a single strategy for liberation, makes her the most illustrious pioneer of socialist feminism in history.

In the third chapter of *The Workers' Union*, titled "Why I Mention Women," Tristán sketches a brilliant analysis of the union between feminism and socialism, between women and proletarians. With a particular crudeness that no one had ever employed before, she describes the unequal relations in the home between the worker and his wife. The exclusion of women from progress and social wealth has condemned them to be treated as pariahs by "the priest, the lawmaker, and the philosopher."[35] Some of them condemned women to represent the sins of the flesh; others condemned them to be the property of their fathers or husbands, denying them access to the rights granted by civilization; finally, the sciences always claimed that women were inferior beings, lacking intelligence, logic, and reasoning. "Their 1789" had not arrived yet, Tristán writes, returning to the analogy with the French Revolution which is so dear to her. The author deduces that if these prejudices are defended as valid principles, then the result is reinforced from all sides as a tautology: If it is claimed that women are ignorant and incapable of accessing the highest levels of education and culture, then they are denied this right—a situation which undoubtedly makes them ignorant beings. But this condemnation, which for centuries has weighed down on the perception of women, can come to an end. There is nothing "natural" about it. Was not the proletarian considered a beast of burden, while the princes and nobles pre-

---

35. Ibid.

sented themselves as superior beings anointed by God? And yet "89" came, showing "that the lower orders are to be called the *people*, and that the serfs and peasants are to be called *citizens*."[36] What will happen when women get "their 1789"?

For this reason, the right to education is vital for Tristán. She recognizes that the refusal to send women to school has the "advantage" of making them work for free in the home. She also warns, again in a footnote, that the status of women as a subordinate social group is advantageous for the capitalists, who can pay them half the wage of a male worker for the same workday. And yet, the central role of women in the constitution of proletarian families makes them a fundamental factor in the education of the workers and the new generations. This is an insurmountable contradiction that Tristán hopes to resolve by persuading the workers she is addressing. If women are educated, they can act as "moralizing agents" for the men over whom they have influence: their sons and husbands.

> Are you beginning to understand, you men, who cry scandal before being willing to examine the issue, why I demand rights for women? Why I would like women placed in society on a footing of *absolute equality* with men to enjoy the legal birthright all beings have?[37]

All misfortunes originate with this fundamental neglect of women's rights. All hopes for a different future are based on the conviction that women have never accepted this fate without permanently rebelling against it. This rebellion has, since the *Declaration of the Rights of Man and the Citizen*, only led to exasperation. But the workers should be conscious of the situation of women, in order to fight for changes that will transform women into their companions, lovers, and friends. She insists: "try to understand: the law which enslaves woman and deprives her of education oppresses you, proletarian men."[38] As long as women remain in such a state of brutalization, they will fall prey to conservatism and oppose all progress, subject to the most basic and mundane needs and unable to have greater aspirations than those imposed by the routines of daily life. In this situation, women often oppose their husbands when the latter want to organize, to embrace the cause of

---

36. Ibid.
37. Ibid.
38. Ibid.

proletarian emancipation, and to fight selflessly for the ideals of their class. Flora Tristán goes so far as to mention that she has been attacked by these brutalized women, who insulted and beat her on one occasion "because I commit the big crime, they say, of putting ideas in their men's heads which move them to read, write and speak among themselves, all useless things that are a waste of time."[39]

Far from romanticizing the working-class family, Tristán precisely describes the human miseries caused by inequality within the home, as well as the discontent that is generated when male workers advance in their consciousness but they are not understood and accompanied by women. Without scruples, Flora Tristán paints a picture that penetrates to the heart of the class, laying bare the dire consequences for all members of the family if woman is "the proletarian of the proletariat." She does not idealize the proletariat; she knows that her ideas are strange and incomprehensible to them; on more than one occasion, she would lament that the workers do not understand two fundamental words of her apostolic message: "act" and "union." Later, in her account of the labors that culminated in the book and the tour of France, she recalls being confronted by workers who did not want her to publish the chapter "Why I Mention Women"; they argued that the miseries of proletarian life described there did not need to be exposed before the attentive eyes of the bourgeoisie. Tristán, overcome by a feeling of mystical and spiritual transcendence, did not consent to lie about the reality that she wished to transform.

In this way, she established a double alliance: on the one hand, there would be no emancipation of the workers from the capitalist yoke if they did not ensure that the women of the working class joined in this struggle. For that, first of all, it was necessary for them to have access to education. On the other hand, there would be no emancipation of women if they did not embrace the cause of the workers' union, because the bourgeoisie makes laws to serve its own interests, and society must be transformed in order for all pariahs, men and women, to achieve happiness and fulfillment. This task fell on the shoulders of the most numerous and the only useful class. "You are oppressed by law and prejudice. Unite with the oppressed, and this legitimate, sacred alliance will enable us to struggle legally, and loyally against oppressive laws and prejudices."[40] In Tristán's thinking, the bourgeoisie and

---

39. Ibid.
40. Ibid.

the proletariat are two distinct social classes, but she is keen to emphasize that while proletarian women are exploited, both they and the women of the bourgeoisie are united in a common suffering, which is that of being enslaved by laws that make them the property of their fathers and husbands. More than a century ahead of contemporary feminist elaborations on gender theory, Tristán would appear to have been warning us from the distant past: gender unites us, class divides us.

Flora Tristán could not delve much deeper in her understanding of this complex society that was developing before her eyes. Her lack of knowledge of political economy prevented her from arriving at the definitions that Marx would later elaborate. For Tristán, the working class or the proletariat did not mean the same thing as for the author of *Capital*: her concept included all the poor, the miserable, and the marginalized—all those impoverished by the creation of wealth. Even though her vision included only those who did not own property (a notable difference from utopian socialism), it failed to unravel the knot of wage slavery, the exploitation of labor, and the expropriation of surplus value. She could not discern the link between the two parts of an equation that plunges the masses into ever-greater misery. Her gaze remained focused on "civil society" and, in a Manichean way, she separated the production of wealth from its distribution, confusing cause and effect in her diatribes against injustice. In an appeal to the factory owners in *The Workers' Union*, she declares, "You amass more or less huge fortunes. In working for you, we can scarcely survive and feed our poor families. This is a legal issue."[41] She even concludes with an appeal to the understanding bosses to make donations to the Union.

Flora Tristán, imbued with a profound pacifism, was committed to the path of legal reforms precisely to avoid the revolutions that had brought only blood and death to the proletarians of Lyon.

> My mission is sublime; it is to put men on the path of legality, of the law. I must make them understand that brute force cannot organize anything, that it can only destroy, and that we have reached an epoch in which we must dream of building.[42]

---

41. Ibid.
42. Flora Tristán, *El tour de Francia* (Lima: UNMSM, 2007), our translation.

Nonetheless, she has the merit of having conceived the idea that the proletariat is a universal class and as such must organize itself internationally; and that its existence and its strength are defined by its lack of property, by its majority in society, and by its nature as the only truly productive class. It cannot achieve its emancipation, however, unless it establishes an alliance based on its ideals including all social strata that are also oppressed by capital. The proletariat must especially rally the women of all classes to its side, in order to free them from the yoke of slavery imposed by marriage and the prejudices that keep them under patriarchal authority from their earliest infancy. For this reason alone, Flora Tristán deserves a place among the great leaders and thinkers of socialism and feminism. As Karl Marx would point out, Flora Tristán was a "precursor to the highest noble ideals."

The Workers' Union, whose first two editions of 1843 and 1844 were paid for by friends and relatives of the author, was republished in Lyon in 1845, with the advance provided by groups of workers via anonymous and collective subscriptions. This is perhaps a testimony to the support her ideas were gaining in her beloved proletariat.

THE *TOUR DE FRANCE*

Flora Tristán's final work is a diary that she wrote as she toured through different French cities to promote *The Workers' Union*, with the goal of organizing the workers as a class. In the initiation practice of the *compagnonnage*, young craftsmen learn their trade while traveling through France. Reminiscent of this *tour de France*, Tristán began her journey in Auxerre in mid-April 1844, from where she traveled to Lyon, then from there to Marseilles, and from there to Bordeaux, where she died. But the diary begins in Paris and records a previous trip to Bordeaux from September 1843. She could not have known it, but the diary would become a valuable testimony of the last days of Flora Tristán's life, before her death on November 14, 1844, from typhoid fever.

Since the Middle Ages, French artisans and workers have kept up the tradition of these tours, in which they learn a craft, following a route through different cities in a clockwise direction. Tristán was herself completing a work as majestic and imposing as the cathedrals that the workers and artisans had raised to the heavens: she was building *The Workers' Union*. These were months of strenuous activity, endless meetings, appointments,

Between Philanthropy and Revolution

heated discussions, conferences, energetic speeches ... After her tour of France, Tristán intended to continue with trips to other European countries.

Attacked by typhoid fever and the police, she was ultimately unable to complete her mission. Her tour was nonetheless intense—like her entire life. It allowed her to meet workers from all professions and trades, workers from the most diverse cities in France, workers with all different ideologies or without any. Shortly before her death, she wrote a premonition in her diary:

> Oh! how unfortunate is the person who is born, lives and dies in the same place and circumstances. In this respect I am very privileged.—What life was ever more varied than mine! In these 40 years, I have lived through so many centuries![43]

That is how rewarding the tour must have been for Flora Tristán, although it demanded of her enormous sacrifices, crises, fears, and even police persecution. Despite fever and pain, she did not want to abandon it.

The *Tour de France* is a remarkable work that combines the intimate confessions of a personal diary, the vivid impressions of a travel journal, the detailed descriptions and analysis of a sociological study, and the novelized transcriptions of the most extraordinary experiences. In addition, some ideas are always present in Tristán's thoughts, and these are presented masterfully among the most picturesque pages: ideas about the church, property, and love are among the themes developed here.

Flora Tristán accuses the church and the priests of keeping the people in ignorance for the benefit of the ruling classes. "There is an unholy alliance between the priests and the bourgeoisie!"[44] she exclaims. She reserves some invectives for the state, the bourgeoisie's organ of rule, but she finds the clergy even more despicable: "As long as there are priests who have some power over the people, it is impossible to envisage the liberation of the proletarians."[45] And the cult of property, is it not every bit as despicable? After a strange episode in which she finds a small gold watch in her hotel room that she hesitates to keep, she reflects on private property. She repeats the words that Proudhon wrote four years earlier: property is theft. "The slogan of the first

---

43. Quoted in Susan Grogan, *Flora Tristán: Life Stories* (London: Routledge, 2002).
44. Quoted in Ibid.
45. Quoted in Ibid.

revolution must be: 'No more property of any kind.'"[46] Tristán realizes that after this tour, in which she lived with the most exploited and oppressed beings in France, she would no longer be able to endure standing in front of a bourgeois, those beings of a "nauseating race."

More than 200 years have passed since her birth, yet Flora Tristán's work has not lost its relevance: it continues to inspire young generations of women who carry on the struggle for liberation from all forms of oppression. Tristán initiates fundamental debates about feminism and socialism, which today, two centuries later, are still full of vigor and controversy: the relation between bourgeois matrimony and women's oppression, later studied in depth by Friedrich Engels; the inequality of men and women before the law; the additional difficulties a woman must face if she is far from her homeland; and the necessary relationship between the emancipation of women and the struggle for socialism in order to reach a society liberated from all forms of oppression and exploitation.

Her innovative thinking links the women's question to the proletarian cause, in an absolutely unprecedented and penetrating dialectic. For this reason, we could say that she had everyone against her: men, because she called for the emancipation of women; and the bourgeoisie, because she fought for the emancipation of the proletariat.

---

46. Tristán, *Utopian Feminist*.

4
Imperialism, War, and Gender

As long as the war lasts, the women of the enemy will also be our enemy.
—Jane Misme

DEBATES IN THE SECOND INTERNATIONAL

In 1879, the Marxist August Bebel, who would later become the leader of the Social Democratic Party of Germany, published *Woman and Socialism*, in which he demonstrates how the family has transformed in tandem with the development of the mode of production, and how the situation of women, trapped in inequality, is linked to the existence of private property:

> Regardless of the question whether woman is oppressed as a proletarian, we must recognize that in this world of private property she is oppressed as a sex being. On all sides she is hemmed in by restrictions and obstacles unknown to the man.[1]

From these precepts, he deduces that "in the new society woman will be entirely independent, both socially and economically. She will not be subjected to even a trace of domination and exploitation, but will be free and man's equal, and mistress of her own lot."[2] He also emphasizes the progressive character of women's incorporation into industrial production, even though this runs counter to the prevailing ideas of the time:

> There are Socialists who are not less opposed to the emancipation of women than the capitalist to Socialism. Every Socialist recognizes the dependence of the workman on the capitalist, and cannot understand that others, and especially the capitalists themselves, should fail to recognize

---
1. August Bebel, *Woman and Socialism* (New York: Socialist Literature Co., 1910).
2. Ibid.

it also; but the same Socialist often does not recognize the dependence of women on men because the question touches his own dear self more or less nearly.[3]

His concern was not exaggerated: everywhere there were socialists arguing against women's incorporation into production and against their democratic rights, such as the right to vote. Nonetheless, the socialist parties were the first to include the demand for women's suffrage in their political programs, after extensive debates.

As early as 1875, when two tendencies of the German workers' movement—the Social Democratic Workers' Party (SDAP), led by Bebel and Liebknecht, and the General German Workers' Association (ADAV), led by Lassalle—unified at the Gotha Congress, the leaders of the former tendency proposed the inclusion of the following amendment in the new party's program: "the right to vote for citizens of both sexes." Their proposal was rejected, however, and it is only in 1891 that the party adopted the demand for universal suffrage for all citizens "without distinction of sex." After arduous battles within the social democracy, the parties of the Second International eventually passed motions to include the struggle for women's suffrage as part of their programmatic platforms. The sixth congress of the Socialist International, held in Amsterdam in 1904, affirmed:

> In the proletariat's struggles for the conquest of universal, equal, secret, and direct suffrage in state and municipal elections, the socialist parties must propose women's suffrage in the legislative bodies, adhere to it in their agitation as a matter of principle, and argue for it vigorously.[4]

Seven years after the German section inscribed this right in its statutes, misogynist arguments could still be heard at party congresses, such as when Ignaz Auer interjected after a speech by Clara Zetkin:

> Where is it supposed to lead when we hear speeches from representatives of the supposedly oppressed sex? I am no great enthusiast of this line, as is

---

3. August Bebel, *Woman in the Past, Present and Future* (San Francisco, CA: G.B. Benham, 1897).
4. "Resolution über das Frauen-Stimmrecht," in *Internationaler Sozialisten-Kongreß zu Amsterdam 1904* (Berlin: Expedition der Buchhandlung Vorwärts, 1904), our translation.

known, but when I heard comrade Zetkin rattling off her attacks yesterday, I said to myself: That is the oppressed sex! What on earth will happen when they are free and equal?[5]

On more than one occasion, Clara Zetkin had to argue that the right to vote would not guarantee women's liberation, but was merely a formal democratic right; the right wing of social democracy believed that women's suffrage would end women's oppression. In 1901, she replied to critics in the party, who claimed that the articles in the newspaper she founded and edited, *Die Gleichheit* (*Equality*), had an elitist character:

> Only in such a [socialist] society, with the disappearance of the currently dominant economic and property relations, will the social contradictions disappear between the haves and the have-nots, between man and woman, between intellectual and physical work. The abolition of such contradictions, however, can only come through class struggle: the liberation of the proletariat can only be the work of the proletariat itself. If the proletarian woman wants to be free, she must join forces with the general socialist movement.[6]

In the same party, Edmund Fischer argued that socialists should aim for a society in which each male worker could support a wife with his salary: "It is not the emancipation of women from men that will then be achieved, but rather something else: women will be returned to the family. And this goal can and should be the goal of socialists."[7] Paradoxically, this aphoristic statement by the socialist Fischer was not very different from a speech by the Prussian emperor, who affirmed that:

> the main task of women is not to participate in meetings nor to conquer rights that make them equal to men, but rather to carry out their duties in

---

5. *Protokoll über die Verhandlungen des Parteitags der Sozialdemokratischen Partei Deutschlands. Abgehalten zu Stuttgart vom 3. bis 8. Oktober 1898* (Berlin: Expedition der Buchhandlung Vorwärts, 1898), our translation.
6. Quoted in Werner Thönnessen, *The Emancipation of Women: The Rise and Decline of the Women's Movement in German Social Democracy 1868–1933* (London: Pluto Press, 1976), translation slightly revised, based on the original German.
7. Edmund Fischer, "Die Frauenfrage," in Wally Zepler (Ed.), *Sozialismus und Frauenfrage* (Berlin: Cassirer, 1919), our translation.

the home and the family in silence, to educate the new generation, and to teach them above all obedience and respect for their elders.[8]

Even in 1913, we find socialists like Ernest Belfort Bax, who published *The Fraud of Feminism* to demonstrate that women's oppression did not exist, and that, on the contrary, the real problem was female privilege. Even though women's suffrage had already been incorporated into the socialist party program, Bax maintained that:

> given an average intellectual, and in certain aspects, moral inferiority of woman as against man, and there is obvious reason for refusing to concede to woman the right to exercise, let us say, administrative and legislative functions such as hitherto accrued to men.[9]

The debate about women's inclusion in production and social organizations was not easy to resolve. Until 1889, Clara Zetkin herself opposed all legislation protecting motherhood, concerned that it could serve the ruling class as a pretext for refusing to incorporate women into production, or that it could be used as an argument in support of the reactionary idea that women were inferior beings. At the Paris congress of the Second International in 1889, she stated:

> Because we do not want to separate our cause from that of the working class in general, we will not formulate any special demands. We demand no other type of protection than that which labor demands in general from the capitalists.[10]

Then she added, "We will permit only one exception: that of a pregnant woman whose condition requires special protective measures."[11] Anna Kuliscioff, a socialist from Italy, had made the same argument. However,

---

8. Quoted in Gilbert Badia, *Clara Zetkin: féministe sans frontières* (Paris: Les Éditions Ouvrières, 1993), our translation.
9. E. Belfort Bax, "Socialism and the Feminist Movement," *The New Review* (New York, May 1914), 2(5).
10. Clara Zetkin, "For the Liberation of Women: Speech at the International Workers' Congress, Paris, July 19th, 1889," in Clara Zetkin, *Selected Writings* (Chicago, IL: Haymarket, 2015).
11. Ibid.

both of them would change their position when they came to realize that equal rights alone could not remedy a situation of initial inequality. This is how socialism began to include demands such as the prohibition of night work for women, paid maternity leave, the protection of women in certain branches of production that were thought to affect their health, etc.—at a time when women workers had up to 112-hour-weeks!

As the feminist movement for equal rights was emerging in Europe and the United States, centered on the struggle for suffrage, socialism presented a more profound concept of egalitarianism that was not limited to formal rights but also addressed the exploitation to which millions of women were subjected as the most exploited of the proletariat—a situation that feminists often failed to take into account. In 1894, for example, the *League of German Women's Associations* refused to admit women's organizations that defended the rights of women workers; in 1900, it opposed a motion to cooperate with the social democratic women's movement. The British feminists of the *Women's Social and Political Union*, led by the well-known suffragette Emmeline Pankhurst, decided—after carrying out some very militant street actions—to demand the right to vote only for women who owned property. Although the most progressive wing of bourgeois feminism tended to join the militant social democratic women in their daily activities, in the election campaigns, it ended up supporting the liberal parties—even though liberalism, in contrast to social democracy, did not uphold the principles that feminists were fighting for. This division was accentuated, as we will see later, during World War One.

Social democracy, in its attempt to defend women workers from overexploitation, had to confront not only bourgeois feminism, but also trade unionists who opposed women's incorporation into production, seeing them as competitors with the male workforce. We even find this rather frequently in the statutes of the workers' organizations of the period. "Aren't women already too busy taking care of the daily housework to be interested in union life?" one French trade unionist asked. The demands of social democracy were not detached from the real struggles that women were carrying out, despite the fact that union leaders forced them to organize their own separate unions, or on more than one occasion even initiated strikes to get women dismissed. Due to the union bureaucracy's narrow-mindedness, women tended to organize separately; this defensive policy by women workers went against the program of social democracy, but the party's more illustrious sectors accepted it with sympathy. Clara Zetkin argued that: "The unionization of women workers will make significant progress only when it is no longer merely aided by the few, but by every single union member making every effort to enlist their female colleagues from the factory and workshop."[12]

All these debates about the situation of women and the program that socialists should raise for their emancipation reflected a struggle taking place within social democracy between reformists and revolutionaries, in all areas of theory, program, and politics.

In 1899, Eduard Bernstein, a leader of the Social Democratic Party of Germany, had published *The Preconditions of Socialism*, in which he argued that Marxism was wrong because under capitalism, workers were beginning to live better lives as a result of favorable labor laws, social reforms, greater abundance, and so on. The most implacable fighter against the right wing of German social democracy, in its slide toward reformism, was a woman: Rosa Luxemburg. Her struggle for revolutionary principles led Bebel himself to refer to her with these words:

> It is an odd thing about women. If their partialities or passions or vanities come anywhere into question and are not given consideration, then even the most intelligent of them flies off the handle and becomes hostile to the point of absurdity.[13]

Rosa Luxemburg, who was a friend of Clara Zetkin and a Polish immigrant, was also concerned with increasing the influence of her revolutionary ideas in the party's women's section:

> with the political emancipation of women a strong fresh wind must also blow into [social democracy's] political and spiritual life, dispelling the suffocating atmosphere of the present philistine family life which so unmistakably rubs off on our party members too, the workers as well as the leaders.[14]

---

12. Clara Zetkin, "Women's Work and the Organization of Trade Unions," in Clara Zetkin, *Selected Writings* (Chicago, IL: Haymarket, 2015).
13. August Bebel, Letter to Karl Kautsky, quoted in Rosa Luxemburg, *The Rosa Luxemburg Reader* (New York: Monthly Review Press, 2004).
14. Quoted in Raya Dunayevskaya, *Rosa Luxemburg, Women's Liberation, and Marx's Philosophy of Revolution* (Champaign, IL: University of Illinois Press, 1991).

Imperialism, War, and Gender

Later, in the face of the Second International's outright betrayal—as its parliamentary representatives voted for the bonds that financed the massacre of World War One—Clara Zetkin and Rosa Luxemburg joined the efforts of Lenin, Trotsky, and other internationalist social democrats to defend the principles of revolutionary Marxism.

WOMEN AT WAR

At the outset of World War One, all the belligerent countries incorporated women into production. In Europe, women poured into factories, companies, and state offices. This is no minor detail, and it will help us to understand the role of women in the Russian Revolution, as we will see later. But although they entered the world of production as never before, women faced a truly unbearable situation. The exhausting workdays—including in heavy industry—continued in the home, harming women's health and increasing their mortality rates. Living conditions were made worse by inflation, scarcity, and misery. Nervous disorders and mental illnesses spread as a result of deprivation, exhaustion, and anguish for husbands, sons, and brothers at the front.

As a result, most of the belligerent countries experienced violent riots by women against inflation and the war. In 1915, women workers in Berlin organized a mass demonstration against the war that headed toward the parliament. In Paris, in 1916, women stormed warehouses and looted coal depots. In June 1916, there was a three-day insurrection in Austria after women began to demonstrate against inflation and the war. After the declaration of war and during the mobilization of the troops, women would lie down on railway tracks to delay the soldiers' departure. In Russia, in 1915, women were the instigators of disturbances that spread from St. Petersburg and Moscow to the entire country.

In order to understand this uprising by women workers in the central countries, and to draw lessons from these struggles for the resistance against the world war, Clara Zetkin launched an appeal to socialist women and convened an international conference that took place on March 26–28, 1915, in Berne, Switzerland.[15] Seventy delegates from Germany, France,

---

15. This International Socialist Women's Conference against the war took place six months before the better-known Zimmerwald Conference, where the revolutionary wing of the Second International spoke out against the imperialist war and against the betrayal by the International's

England, Holland, Russia, Italy, and Switzerland participated and discussed the betrayal by their parties, who had decided to support the war. The resolution adopted by the conference denounced the capitalist war with the slogan: "War against war!"

The Berne conference is the third one organized by socialist women. The previous two—in Stuttgart in 1907 and in Copenhagen in 1910, which we have already mentioned—had spoken out in favor of women's suffrage and the struggle for the preservation of peace, against hoarding food and the high cost of living, against tsarist repression in Finland, and for social security for women and children. One of the Copenhagen resolutions noted that they saw the causes of war "in the social antagonisms which are the consequence of the capitalist system of production" and that:

> peace can only be maintained by the energetic and conscious action of the working class and finally by the victory of socialism. It is the particular duty of Socialist women to share in the world of maintaining peace according to the views expressed by the International Socialist Congress at Stuttgart.[16]

But the Berne conference was to become the first international socialist conference whose central axis was opposition to the ongoing war.

---

most important section, the Social Democratic Party of Germany. That international socialist conference took place in Zimmerwald, Switzerland on September 5-8, 1915, and many considered it to be the first general meeting of internationalist socialists after the outbreak of the war. The position of the Bolsheviks (the Russian party of the Second International) was for the immediate creation of a new international. Lenin argued that socialists should break off collaboration with bourgeois governments, that mass mobilizations against social chauvinism were necessary, and that the war must be transformed into a civil war. Their position was rejected by 19 votes to 12. The conference sent greetings to Rosa Luxemburg and Clara Zetkin, who were imprisoned in Germany due to their opposition to the war. On April 24-29, 1916, the internationalists met again in Kienthal, near Berne. Lenin again proclaimed the treachery and irredeemable collapse of the Second International. Eventually, those who continued to defend the revolutionary principles of proletarian internationalism founded communist parties and the Third International. Inessa Armand (1875-1920), the daughter of an English father and a French mother who married a Russian in 1893, participated in both of these meetings. A Bolshevik since 1904, she emigrated in 1909 and became a personal friend of Lenin in exile. She represented the Bolsheviks in Brussels in 1914, as well as in Zimmerwald and Kienthal. On her return to Russia in 1917, she worked for the Third International but died of cholera in 1920.
16. Quoted in Friedrich Ebert Stiftung, "Sources on the Development of the Socialist International (1907–1919)," http://library.fes.de/si-online/index.html.

Later, imprisoned and suffering from heart problems, Clara Zetkin could no longer actively intervene in this struggle. After she was prohibited from speaking in public in 1916, she was expelled from the Social Democratic Party of Germany together with other members, and 20,000 of them formed a group in opposition to the majority line of the German social democracy.

The bankruptcy of the Second International, which had united the social democratic parties, was impossible to deny. Their collaboration with the national bourgeoisies of the belligerent states led to the massacre of millions of workers, facing each other in the trenches in defense of their bosses' interests, and caused enormous misery for women. Clara Zetkin said later, in 1919: "The old international gave its death rattle with dishonor and infamy on the imperialist battlefields. It cannot be resurrected." Finally, she became one of the delegates of the Third International, founded by Lenin with different internationalist organizations.

In 1891, Clara Zetkin had founded the social democratic newspaper *Die Gleichheit* (*Equality*), aimed at women workers. By 1913, it had nearly 140,000 readers whom Zetkin influenced with her ideas, which often went against those of the party leadership. These included support for the Russian Revolution of 1905 or opposition to the imperialist war. She expressed herself not only through this newspaper, but had also managed to organize the International Socialist Women's Conferences starting in 1907. This policy, which Clara Zetkin carried out with the support of her friend Rosa Luxemburg, explains, in part, why the majority of the women in the Social Democratic Party of Germany, in the face of the flagrant betrayal by the leadership, followed those who led the split with that party.

WOMEN AND NATIONS

At the beginning of the twentieth century, smashed windows and firebombs drew the world's attention to radicalized women's mobilizations demanding the right to vote. On July 5, 1914, suffragettes held a massive demonstration in Paris in honor of the Marquis de Condorcet, who, as we saw earlier, had proposed the inclusion of women in the rights of the citizen in 1790. This demonstration became a show of force to demand political rights for women. In this same year, 53,000 women marched in London for the right to vote.

This movement suffered a partial defeat, however, when war was declared. The world war blocked the emancipatory democratic movement that had been taking shape in the most important countries of Europe, threatening to become a massive feminist movement for equality. In addition to the limitations imposed by government repression and censorship in the belligerent countries, the majority of feminist organizations voluntarily decided to join the cause of their "fatherland" and suspended their demands, fulfilling the duties that patriotism demanded of them in order to prove their respectability to their respective national governments.

In the face of the imperialist war, we find the feminists of the Pankhurst family with a position diametrically opposed to that of Clara Zetkin and Rosa Luxemburg. Emmeline Pankhurst[17] and her daughters Sylvia and Christabel were the principal standard-bearers of the suffragette movement in England in the early years of the twentieth century, and they also fought to raise the workers' level of education. In 1904, they won the support of the Labour Party, which introduced a bill in parliament in favor of women's suffrage, but this was defeated. On June 21, 1908, they led a demonstration of 400,000 suffragettes through the streets of London and began to take direct action. They destroyed mailboxes, smashed windows, and set churches and shops on fire, before being imprisoned. One of their followers was trampled to death by a horse at the famous Derby races when she stood in front of the Prince of Wales demanding the right to vote.

Initially, the Pankhursts' struggle for women's suffrage was linked, at least partially, to the demands of women workers. But the world war that broke out in 1914 transformed Emmeline Pankhurst's struggle, as she put herself at the service of the British government. Faced with this political turn, her daughter Sylvia broke from her and joined the socialist workers' movement.

By the age of 24, the young Sylvia had already abandoned her studies at the Royal College and served time in prison. In 1911, at just 29, she published her first book, *The Suffragette: The History of the Women's Militant Suffrage Movement*. She was already beginning to differentiate herself from

---

17. Emmeline Pankhurst was born in Manchester in 1858 to a family of reform-minded industrialists and was educated in Paris. She married a lawyer who was a member of the suffragette society founded by John Stuart Mill, and she became a feminist. In 1903, together with her daughters Christabel and Sylvia, she founded the *Women's Social and Political Union*, and in 1905, she decided to use illegal and violent methods to attract attention from the public and politicians. Arrested on multiple occasions, Emmeline carried out hunger, thirst, and sleep strikes as a form of protest, and she defended herself in court.

the *Union* her mother had founded, which she believed was moving away from its socialist principles. With the outbreak of World War One, these differences deepened. Sylvia was a pacifist and did not agree with the *Union*'s strong support for the British government in the war. She wrote:

> When I read in the newspapers that Mrs Pankhurst and Christabel were returning to England for a recruiting campaign, I wept. To me this seemed a tragic betrayal of the great movement [...]. We worked continuously for peace, in face of the bitterest opposition from old enemies, and sometimes unhappily from old friends.

Her sentiment was justified: the *Women's Social and Political Union*, which published the newspaper *The Suffragette*, changed the name of its organ to *Britannia* and the motto to "For King, For Country, For Freedom." Sylvia, along with her friend Charlotte Despard, founded the *Women's Peace Army* and threw herself into activity in the ranks of the Labour Party, where she published a newspaper for women workers. Sylvia's activities centered on visiting working-class neighborhoods, organizing women workers, and fighting for their demands, all of which led her to profoundly question the line of the *Women's Social and Political Union* headed by her mother and her sister Christabel. Christabel aspired to total independence from political parties, which were made up of men, and pressured the sector headed by Sylvia to leave the *Union* for good, as she was annoyed by their permanent activism alongside women workers.

Obviously, this break was shaped by the social polarization running through the country. Between 1911 and 1914, as the bourgeoisie was preparing to wage an imperialist war, all the key sectors of the British proletariat went on strike at some point. In the midst of this situation, Sylvia's group continued to campaign for women's suffrage, to fight for equal wages, and to defend a pacifist position, as most of the workers' organizations did as well. These positions were in complete opposition to those of the *Union*, which argued that women's sectoral demands should be suspended in order to support the government's war effort. Sylvia also fervently supported the Russian Revolution of 1917 and later visited the Soviet Union, where she met Lenin—this trip cost her a five-month prison sentence upon her return to England, after she was charged with sedition for her "pro-communist" articles. The influence that the Russian Revolution had on her can be seen in the name of her newspaper, which was originally called *The Women's Dreadnought* and in July 1917 was changed to *The Workers' Dreadnought*. Sylvia even earned the nickname "Little Miss Russia." In 1918, when the right to vote was extended to some women over the age of 30, Sylvia denounced the fact that this right was limited to women who owned property, had attended university, and so on. And although she was a founding member of the Communist Party of Great Britain, Sylvia later abandoned the party, and was horrified by the purges the Stalinist regime carried out against all opposition. In the 1930s, she supported the Spanish Revolution, then helped Jews persecuted by the Nazi regime in Germany. She finally died in 1960 without having been able to witness the resurgence of the feminist movement in what has become known as the second wave.[18]

The feminists who stuck to their pacifist principles were unable to provide an organized perspective for the movement, due to the boycott by warmongering nationalists of both sexes. In 1915, the *International Women's Peace Conference* met in The Hague, with the participation of pacifist feminists from different countries. They formed an *International Committee of Women for Permanent Peace*, which sent delegates all around the world. But in France, their representative was expelled from the *National Council of French Women* on the charge of being a "feminist in the service of Wilhelm" (in reference to the German Kaiser). Meanwhile, the majority of the worldwide feminist movement dedicated itself to subscribing to national bonds, denouncing deserters, and supporting the campaign to raise funds for the war.[19]

Emmeline Pankhurst and her daughter Christabel, for example, dedicated themselves to recruiting women volunteers. "The situation is serious, women must help save it," read the banners at the impressive demonstration on July 17, 1915, called the Right to Serve March. The old demand for women's

---

18. Let us hold onto the following words from Sylvia:

> I wanted to rouse these women of the submerged mass to be, not merely the argument of more fortunate people, but to be fighters on their own account, despising mere platitudes and catch-cries, revolting against the hideous conditions about them, and demanding for themselves and their families a full share of the benefits of civilization and progress.

From E. Sylvia Pankhurst, *The Suffragette Movement: An Intimate Account of Persons and Ideals* (London: Virago Press, 1977 [1931]).

19. A British propaganda poster read: "Joan of Arc saved France. Women of Britain, save your country. Buy war savings certificates."

suffrage became a weapon in the service of the war: "Votes for Heroines as well as Heroes" was the new formulation of this demand. The march, organized by the Pankhursts with the help of the new Ministry of Munitions, was a symbol of the sharp divide in the women's movement: no longer was it bourgeois women pitted against proletarian women; it was bourgeois women of one country against bourgeois women of another, thus breaking with the movement's short-lived but progressive international tradition. Let us recall that until 1914, feminism still appeared to be an international movement that fought for the common demand of suffrage. The pacifism proclaimed by the various organizations of the feminist international disappeared at the very moment the world war broke out—a trial by fire for the movement. This was the moment when, in addition to suspending their demands, the feminists of the belligerent countries shattered their international alliances in favor of a national-feminism that called on women to serve the fatherland, thus imposing the discipline of the national bourgeoisies.

The tradition of international friendship that had prevailed between the different groups of the women's movement proved to be full of holes when faced with the test of the world war. Internationalism and the struggle against war were left exclusively in the hands of revolutionary socialism. Taking the lead in the struggle against the world war were revolutionary women like Clara Zetkin, Rosa Luxemburg, Inessa Armand, Nadezhda Krupskaya, and others.

FREEDOM DURING WARTIME, OPPRESSION DURING PEACETIME?

During the course of the war, and even after its end, the idea gained traction that women had made big steps toward their emancipation because the conflict had disrupted the relations between the sexes. While the war raged, peasant and merchant women took over tasks that men had been forced to abandon. At the same time, the new war industries, manufacturing munitions and modern weapons at an enormous scale, multiplied the jobs on offer. By force of necessity, the war temporarily eliminated the barriers that separated male and female labor.

Women's "achievements" were ephemeral, however. The patriarchal order of capitalism was only temporarily modified due to labor shortages, using women to run the machines that sustained capitalist profits in times of a "scarcity of men." When the soldiers returned from the front, they were given priority in the workplace. Emancipatory promises to women were replaced with bugle calls instructing women to return to the home. In England, for example, as long as the war lasted, agreements between companies and unions were common. Through mediation and social reform, women's work in factories was accepted under the regime known as substitution, which meant that women could take on "male" jobs but only if they promised to withdraw after the war.

Of course, while they were filling vacancies in factories and companies, these new women workers were the first to criticize the war, while the women of the bourgeoisie were subordinating the feminist movement, from head to toe, to the defense of the nation. The former provoked enormous disturbances with the theft of food from the shops or the countryside, illegal procurement on the black market, and other forms of sabotage. In some cases, they became the instigators of hunger riots, transforming their cities into scenes of a genuine civil war. In France, in 1917, women munitions workers and seamstresses made up the majority of the people on strike.

When the war ended, the demobilization of women from the front and from the factories was accompanied by a loud propaganda campaign against feminism and emancipated women, with official speeches praising mothers and housewives. It is no coincidence that Mother's Day, which is still celebrated around the world today, was established at this time. Liberal and reformist governments even began to introduce women's suffrage in Europe at the end of the war, as a concession to pre-empt the fledgling proletarian revolution and establish solid regimes of bourgeois democracy after the fighting. As Leon Trotsky points out:

> The defeat of the revolution of 1848 weakened the British workers; the Russian revolution of 1905 immediately strengthened them. As the result of the General Election of 1906 the Labour Party for the first time formed a large fraction with forty-two members. Without doubt the influence of the 1905 revolution is manifest in this. In 1918, before the end of the war, a new electoral reform was introduced in Great Britain which greatly enlarged the ranks of worker voters, and for the first time permitted women to participate in elections. Surely Mr. Baldwin will not trouble to deny that the Russian Revolution was an important motive for this

reform. The British bourgeoisie reckoned that by such means a revolution could be avoided.[20]

Between the two world wars, the working class underwent countless experiences of great historical significance. In this period, it went through the economic boom of the Roaring Twenties, with the development of large-scale production, the consolidation of the Soviet Union as a workers' state that emerged from the proletarian revolution of 1917, the crash of 1929 with the fall of the New York Stock Exchange and the Great Depression, mass unemployment, fascism, the popular fronts, the heroic Spanish Revolution, the emergence of mass unions in the USA, and so on. The situation of women developed in tandem with these events of the class struggle.

The revolutionary experience in Spain in the 1930s demonstrated once again that major democratic rights for women are obtained as a result of revolutionary uprisings against the entire existing order. In 1931, with the beginning of the revolutionary process in Spain, women won the right to vote in that country. But it was not until 1936, with the resurgence of revolutionary agitation among the masses, the electoral victory of the Popular Front, and the spread of a gigantic strike wave throughout Spain, accompanied by land occupations, that the right to abortion was legalized—in a situation where power had passed into the hands of workers' committees and militias. During their heroic insurrection of 1934, the workers of Asturias took control of the territory, but remained isolated and were defeated by Franco's troops after multiple battles. The wives and daughters of the Asturian miners took part in the struggle by joining the committees and taking up arms. During this period, communist and anarchist women's newspapers flourished. The formation of people's militias led to the inclusion of women on the front lines of battle. But starting in September 1936, the republican government of the Popular Front attempted to organize a regular army, with the aim of preventing the workers and peasants from organizing and arming themselves autonomously. The government prohibited the militias and persecuted revolutionaries, and as a result, the anarchists and the sympathizers of Trotskyism were crushed—and women were sent back to the rearguard.

A vivid description of these days, including the courageous actions of women workers, the attitudes of the different political organizations toward

---

20. Leon Trotsky, *Where Is Britain Going?* (Abingdon: Routledge, 2012).

women, and the perfidious role played by Stalinism in this heroic chapter of worldwide workers' history, can be found in the memoirs of Mika Etchebéhère, who served as a captain in the militia of the Workers' Party of Marxist Unification (POUM).[21] In her book, *Mi Guerra de España* (*My War in Spain*), the Argentinian woman recounts—in pages full of heroism, emotion, and profound reflections—how she crossed the border from France with her husband to participate in the Spanish revolution and joined a column of the POUM. Shortly after her arrival, her husband died in battle and she took command of the column, overcoming the prejudices of the militiamen and winning their respect in battle.

Another notable woman from this period is Carlota Durany Vives, secretary of the POUM's leader, Andreu Nin. Durany was a member of the leadership commission of the *Sindicato Mercantil* (commerce union) and worked intensely for the strikes in this sector. Those who knew her say that the anarchists in her union did everything they could to attract her to their ranks because of her great revolutionary activity and personality. The clandestine founding conference of the POUM was held in her home on September 29, 1935, making her the main target of the Stalinist secret police in Barcelona. At the height of the Spanish Civil War, Durany began writing short articles for the newspaper *Emancipación*, the organ of the POUM's Women's Secretariat, from which we quote these lines:

> On July 19, women rushed onto the streets with insurmountable enthusiasm to fight alongside their male comrades, to care for the wounded, to donate their blood. But one cannot live with such tension for months on end. Little by little, we are getting used to things that once inflamed our enthusiasm, and daily life, with its demands and worries, saps our revolutionary fervor. […] This is precisely the task of women! To constantly create the new, the revolutionary spirit! Women produce the spiritual atmosphere […]. And women have another task of utmost importance: to lay the revolutionary foundation in the future generation […]. From a

---

21. The POUM was a party led by Andreu Nin that was close to Trotskyism. It had emerged from the fusion of the old Left Opposition of the Communist Party of Spain and the Workers and Peasants Bloc of Catalonia (BOC), led by Joaquín Maurín. The POUM definitively broke off its relations with Trotskyism when—against Trotsky's advice regarding the necessity of the political independence of the working class—it joined the Popular Front and collaborated with the bourgeoisie.

very young age, children must learn that others do not live exclusively for them. This communal sentiment will later become class consciousness.[22]

The repression unleashed by the Stalinists is particularly focused on annihilating POUM militants. Durany, who had once been imprisoned for several weeks, was detained five days before the fascist troops under the command of general Franco entered Barcelona. When they arrested her, they left behind her three-year-old son, who was later recovered by neighbors. They loaded her into a car and drove her to a highway, while they interrogated and insulted her so she would tell them where her partner was. She replied, again and again, that she only knew that he was at the front, which further enraged her captors, who carried out a mock execution by firing squad. Durany was finally transferred to a prison of the Stalinist secret police along with other POUM women, and she was able to escape before the building fell into the hands of the fascists. She had just enough time to reunite with her son and leave for the French border in a truck organized by the party's Evacuation Committee. Only 35 years later did her ashes return to her native country, where they were scattered in the sea off the Costa Brava.

Fascism was not just a Spanish phenomenon: it was the political expression of big monopoly capital, which in certain situations substitutes the bourgeois-democratic regime with dictatorial forms in order to guarantee its profits. Fascism considered that women's emancipation was a perverse, unpatriotic, anti-regime ideology. For the Nazis in Germany, for example, motherhood was the central goal that women should have for their lives—but it was not desirable for all women. They claimed that 20 percent of the German population was unsuitable for motherhood or fatherhood because they were not "racially pure." Forced sterilization was applied to both men and women for reasons such as "imbecility," epilepsy, schizophrenia, manic-depressive syndrome, or being Black, Jewish, Romani, and so on. This demographic policy led young women to what were called "protest pregnancies" before they could be subject to sterilization. The data on women's employment in fascist Germany shows another side of the Nazi regime's cruelty:

> During World War II about 2.5 million foreign women were brought to work in German industry and agriculture, along with many more foreign

---

22. Carlota Durany Vives, "El doble papel de la mujer," *Emancipación*, May 29, 1937, our translation.

men; most of them were from Eastern Europe and were forced to work. The lower their "racial value"—the lowest was that of Russians, followed by that of Poles—the higher was the percentage of women workers among their national group, particularly in the heavy munitions industry.[23]

Women also enrolled in the resistance against fascism. In the Soviet Union, women actively participated in the defense of their territory against the invasion by the Nazi army. Shortly after the outbreak of World War Two, the *Soviet Women's Anti-Fascist Committee* was founded and received solidarity from women in England, the USA, India, Austria, and so on. In Yugoslavia, more than 100,000 women enrolled in the partisan units and Tito's army. In France, women were part of the *maquis*, the partisans of the resistance, creating networks in the businesses where they worked, acting as couriers and agents, organizing the struggle in the concentration camps, and taking part in combat. In Italy, there were about 35,000 women in the armed resistance, while 70,000 formed part of the women's volunteer defense groups, suffering torture, arrests, deportations, firing squads, or death in combat.

During World War Two, the same stereotypes about women that had emerged in 1914 were repeated: women either worked in the arms and munitions factories in the service of the fatherland, or they were protective mothers who looked after the home in the absence of the soldier. In England, private companies were prohibited from hiring women between 20 and 30—they were to remain under the control of the state and be sent into the arms factories if necessary. With the same goal, women's access to universities was limited—in order to have more labor power available. In 1944, industry and the auxiliary services of civil defense employed 2 million more women than before the war. In the USA, women were recruited with newspaper and radio campaigns, and the number of American women performing waged labor grew from 10 million in 1941 to 18 million in 1944.[24]

---

23. Gisela Bock, "Nazi Gender Policies and Women's History," in Georges Duby and Michelle Perrot (Eds.), *History of Women in the West*, Vol. 5: Françoise Thébaud (Ed.), *Toward a Cultural Identity in the Twentieth Century* (Cambridge, MA: Belknap Press of Harvard University Press, 1996).

24. An American poster shows a mother with a child and a baby in her arms. The caption reads: "I gave a man! Will you give at least 10% of your pay in War Bonds?" Another says: "Women, there's work to be done and a war to be won."

But as soon as the war ended, women were expected to return to the home. In England and the USA, for example, the nurseries that had been set up to make it easier for women to work disappeared. Women had the same experience as after World War One, but with greater resistance on the part of women workers and employees refusing to leave their jobs. A certain "discomfort" developed among women who did not want to see their role again reduced to that of mother, wife, and consumer, and this would find expression in the mass feminist movements that emerged years later, especially in the USA and the countries of Western Europe.

5
Women in the First Workers' State in History

In place of the old relationship between men and women, a new one is developing: a union of affection and comradeship, a union of two equal members of communist society, both of them free, both of them independent and both of them workers. [...] In place of the individual and egoistic family, a great universal family of workers will develop, in which all the workers, men and women, will above all be comrades.

—Alexandra Kollontai

THE SPARK THAT COULD LIGHT THE FLAME

With the workers' revolution of October 1917 in Russia, led by the Bolshevik Party, women achieved some inalienable rights, earlier than in the most developed capitalist countries of the world. Far-reaching reforms that had only been promised in the advanced democracies in the West became a reality in the most backward nation of Europe, violently shoving it into the role of the vanguard in world history.

In October 1910, women workers in a textile factory went on strike after two of them had died as a result of the working day being lengthened; they gained the support of the 5,000 workers in the plant. In 1913, 2,000 women workers from another textile factory went on strike for almost 50 days calling for wage increases, paid maternity leave, and other demands. Then, 5,000 women workers went on strike in a rubber factory. Others rioted in a textile factory after they were persecuted by their bosses. Another 3,000 women workers paralyzed perfume and pasta factories. In a plywood factory, women workers protested against unsanitary conditions and obscene comments by the foremen. This was the context as Russian socialists attempted to address women workers, promoting their unionization and political organization.

Women in the First Workers' State in History

Since the Revolution of 1905, Alexandra Kollontai, who had joined the Russian Social Democratic Workers' Party (RSDWP) in 1899, dedicated herself to organizing women workers. However, because of the publication of her book *Finland and Socialism*—in which she called for an insurrection against the tsarist regime—and her political work among textile workers, she was put on trial and forced into exile until February 1917. At the time, Kollontai belonged to the Menshevik wing of the RSDWP, which was closer to the positions of the German revisionists who were mentioned earlier. But an editorial in their newspaper, *Golos Sotsial-Demokrata* (*Voice of Social Democracy*), made it clear that they were opposed to Kollontai's policy of independently organizing women workers. The newspaper of the Bolshevik wing of the RSDWP, in contrast, expressed its support for the creation of women's political organizations and unions.

In 1913, International Women's Day was celebrated for the first time in Russia, three years after it had been proposed by Clara Zetkin at the International Socialist Women's Conference in Copenhagen. Events were held in St. Petersburg, Moscow, Kiev, and other cities, despite the well-founded fear of repression by a regime known for its cruelty and despotism. The Bolshevik newspaper *Pravda* (*Truth*) commemorated the day with a special supplement. But as the fervor of women workers grew, the Russian social democrats showed that they had different ways of understanding women's situation. For 1914, the Mensheviks argued that only women should participate in the demonstrations for their international day. The Bolsheviks, in contrast, called on the entire working class to commemorate this date, and began publishing a special column in their newspaper titled "The Life and Labor of Women Workers," with information about the demonstrations, meetings, and preparations for this day. Letters sent by readers were published there as well. Finally, on International Women's Day in 1914, the Central Committee of the RSDWP, on Lenin's initiative, began to publish the newspaper *Rabotnitsa* (*The Woman Worker*) in St. Petersburg, with money collected voluntarily from women workers and members of the editorial board, who took jobs as seamstresses to finance the first issue. Letters, donations, and congratulations reached the editorial board:

> warm greetings to our journal *Rabotnitsa*. We are sure that it will be a true mouthpiece of our needs and interests and we promise you our constant

moral and material encouragement. We are contributing 2 roubles and 74 kopeks to the journal fund.[1]

The editors included the most outstanding women of Bolshevism, such as Inessa Armand, Nadezhda Krupskaya, Anna Yelizarova-Ulyanova, and others. A few days before the first issue hit the streets, all the members of the editorial board except Yelizarova-Ulyanova were arrested and the entire print run was confiscated by the police. Yelizarova-Ulyanova found another printer and the 12,000 copies that had been planned for International Women's Day could finally appear.[2] On that day in 1914, the government prevented meetings from being held in the big workers' districts in St. Petersburg; there was only one event and three of the speakers were arrested. The demonstrators offered to be sent to prison in their place, and as the women workers began to revolt, the police proceeded to make mass arrests.

In the first issue, Krupskaya explained the differences between the Bolsheviks and the bourgeois feminists:

> working women [...] see that contemporary society is divided into classes. Each class has its special interests. The bourgeoisie is in one, and the working class the other. Their interests are counterposed. The division between men and women does not have great importance in the eyes of the working woman. That which unites the working woman with the working man is much stronger than that which divides them.[3]

The impending war revealed the differences between social democrats and feminists: in 1915, the *League for Women's Equality*, recently inflamed by nationalism, called for a mobilization of "the daughters of Russia," claiming "this is our obligation to the fatherland, and this will give us the right to participate as the equals of men in the new life of a victorious Russia";[4] at the same time, Bolshevik women fell in line behind Lenin's position of transforming the imperialist war into a civil war—in other words, the proletariat

---

1. Quoted in Tony Cliff, *Class Struggle and Women's Liberation* (London: Bookmarks, 1984).
2. Only seven issues of *Rabotnitsa* were published, between February and June 1914, when the outbreak of World War One created an obstacle for revolutionary activity.
3. Quoted in Tony Cliff, "Alexandra Kollontai: Russian Marxists and Women Workers," *International Socialism* (London), 2(14) (Autumn 1981).
4. Richard Stites, *The Women's Liberation Movement in Russia: Feminism, Nihilism and Bolshevism 1860–1930* (Princeton, NJ: Princeton University Press, 1978).

of each imperialist country had to be convinced to turn its arms against its own bourgeoisie. This position was presented by the Bolshevik delegates to the Third International Socialist Women's Conference in Berne, in March 1915, which we mentioned earlier. Nadezhda Krupskaya, Lenin's comrade and companion, recalls:

> We submitted our own declaration. It was defended by Inessa [Armand], and supported by Kamenska, the representative of the Polish women. We were not supported by the conference. Everyone criticized our "splitting" policy. Events soon proved the correctness of our position, however. The tame pacifism of the English and the Dutch did not advance international action a single step. A greater role in hastening the end of the war was played by the revolutionary struggle and a clean break with the chauvinists.[5]

Finally, as a compromise between the pacifist positions and those of the Russian delegates, the conference proclaimed the slogan "war against war." Thus, the Third International Socialist Women's Conference, despite its limitations, represented a first step toward the regroupment of internationalists who opposed the betrayal by the Social Democratic Party of Germany.

> Peace! Peace! [...] Proclaim in your millions what your sons cannot yet affirm: Laboring people of all countries are brothers. Only their common will can put an end to the slaughter. Socialism alone will assure the future peace of humankind. [...] Down with the war! Forward to socialism![6]

Between 1914 and 1918 in Russia, while men were sent to the front, women's participation in production increased by 70 percent to 400 percent, depending on the industry. Women became agricultural laborers, eventually accounting for 72 percent of all rural workers. In the factories, they went from 33 percent of the workforce in 1914 to 50 percent in 1917. Throughout

---

5. Nadezhda K. Krupskaya, *Reminiscences of Lenin* (New York: International Publishers, 1970).
6. Quoted in W. Bartel, *Die Linke in der deutschen Sozialdemokratie im Kampf gegen Militarismus und Krieg* (Berlin: Dietz, 1958). Translation by John Riddell, "1915: Socialist Women Unite Against War," *John Riddell*, March 28, 2015, https://johnriddell.com/2015/03/28/1915-socialist-women-unite-against-war/.

Europe, women were obliged to work outside the home, even in industries that had been considered exclusively "male": they manufactured arms and munitions, drove trams and locomotives, and entered heavy industry. The grueling workdays increased the rates of illness and mortality among women. Inflation, scarcity, and misery were compounded by exhaustion, anxiety, uncertainty, and despair in the face of a hitherto unknown world, while their loved ones were enlisted for the war. In the cities, infant mortality reached 50 percent; abortions and stillbirths multiplied.

It was this new "female proletariat" that initiated a revolt in St. Petersburg on April 6, 1915, when the sale of meat was suspended. Similar riots took place in Moscow and other cities.[7] In Kiev, the Bolsheviks distributed a leaflet among women workers:

> Pitiful as the lot of the worker is, the status of the woman is far worse. In the factory, in the workshop, she works for a capitalist boss, at home—for the family. Thousands of women sell their labour to capital; thousands drudge away at hired labour; thousands and hundreds of thousands suffer under the yoke of family and social oppression. And for the enormous majority of working women it seems this is the way it must be. But is it really true that the working woman cannot hope for a better future, and that fate has consigned her to an entire life of work and only work, without rest night and day? Comrades, working women! The men comrades toil along with us. Their fate and ours are one. But they have long since found the only road to a better life—the road of organized labor's struggle with capital, the road of struggle against all oppression, evil, and violence. Women workers, there is no other road for us. The interests of the working men and women are equal, are one. Only in a united struggle together with the men workers, in joint workers' organizations—in the Social Democratic Party, the trade unions, workers' clubs, and cooperatives—shall we obtain our rights and win a better life.[8]

---

7. Riots also took place in the main cities of Europe: the women workers of Berlin organized a massive demonstration to the parliament against the war; in Paris, women stormed warehouses and looted coal depots; in Austria, there was a three-day insurrection after women began to demonstrate against inflation and the war; women workers everywhere would lie down on railway tracks to delay the soldiers' departure.

8. John Riddell (Ed.), *Lenin's Struggle for a Revolutionary International: Documents, 1907–1916, the Preparatory Years* (New York: Pathfinder Press, 1986).

By January 1917, even the tsarist police were taking note of the desperate situation of Russian women, and a secret report warned that women were more open to revolution than the leaders of the party of the liberal bourgeoisie. Women workers posed a greater danger to tsarism than the democrats. They were "the spark that could light the flame."

BREAD, PEACE, FREEDOM, AND WOMEN'S RIGHTS

It was these women workers, especially textile workers, who demonstrated for bread, peace, and freedom on February 23, 1917 (March 8, according to the Western Calendar), and cleared the way for the greatest revolution of the twentieth century, which began on this day and culminated in October when the proletariat seized power under the leadership of the Bolshevik Party. Under the provisional government of Kerensky,[9] which was formed as a result of the February Revolution that overthrew the tsarist regime, Russian women gained the right to vote and to be elected—rights that the most advanced countries of the world, such as England and the USA, only granted in 1918 and 1920, respectively.

With the proletarian revolution in October 1917, Russian women won the right to divorce and abortion, the abolition of the husband's authority over the wife, equality between civil and common law marriage, etc.—before women in the capitalist countries did. The revolutionary Alexandra Kollontai, whom we will encounter later, played a leading role in drafting the new legislation. The most important accomplishment of the revolution, however, was not writing laws, but rather laying the foundation for women to gain full and genuine access to all economic and cultural spheres. The right to vote would have been of little use to women—domestic slaves, according to Lenin's definition—if they had remained solely responsible for the obligations of the family home, with limited access to education and no access to production.[10] The leadership of the Bolshevik Party was convinced that

---

9. Alexander Kerensky (1881–1970) was the head of the provisional government after the Tsar was overthrown, from February to October 1917 (according to the Russian Orthodox calendar). He was toppled by the workers' revolution under the leadership of the Bolshevik Party, which installed a government of workers' councils (soviets).

10.
> The vote does not destroy the prime cause of women's enslavement in the family and society [...] or solve the problem of relationships between the sexes. The real equality of women, as opposed to formal and superficial equality, will be achieved only under Communism,

only a triumphant revolution in the heart of modern Europe would give new impetus to the exhausted forces of the Russian proletariat and to the economy which had been devastated by the war effort. This would allow the cultural level of the masses to be elevated, which for centuries had been held down by tsarism, superstition, and the patriarchs of the Orthodox Church.

But the country, exhausted by its participation in the imperialist war, had to go through an "overt and cruel civil war" in which "economic life was wholly subjected to the needs of the front."[11] Between 1918 and 1921, when the fledgling workers' state experienced the period known as "war communism," all efforts were concentrated on military industry and combatting the hunger that plagued the cities. In the meantime, the revolution was defeated in developed Germany and the conservative forces of the old Europe regained a certain equilibrium. In Russia, industry was producing less than one-fifth of what it had produced before the imperialist war; Moscow's population was just half of what it had been before the conflict, and Petrograd's barely one-third. In early 1919, European reaction encircled the nascent soviet republic. In this situation, the hopes that the Bolshevik leaders placed in the German revolution were no mere fantasy in the heads of worn-out commanders: the fact that the soviet power was able to survive its first months was due to the European proletariat, and especially the heroic German working class; enveloped in the drama of the imperialist war, German workers, wearing soldiers' and sailors' uniforms, had overthrown the Reich. For Lenin and Trotsky, the fate of the Russian Revolution was inextricably linked to the outcome of this monumental class battle in one of the most advanced capitalist countries of the time.

And yet, in the midst of this dramatic situation that clouded the horizon of Soviet Russia, making the revolutionaries fear that they would almost certainly have to retreat from the positions they had conquered, they redoubled

---

when women and all the other members of the labouring class will become co-owners of the means of production and distribution and will take part in administering them, and women will share on an equal footing with all the members of the labour society the duty to work; in other words, it will be achieved by overthrowing the capitalist system [...] and by organising a Communist economy.

See "Methods and Forms of Work among Communist Party Women: Theses," Alix Holt and Barbara Holland (Eds.), *Theses Resolutions and Manifestos of the First Four Congress of the Third International* (London: Ink Links, 1980).
11. Leon Trotsky, *The Revolution Betrayed* (New York: Doubleday, 1937).

their efforts and the first workers' state in history passed especially pioneering legislation.

> The Soviet regime was hardly one month old when it issued a decree that the Provisional Government had proved incapable of issuing throughout its eight months' existence: the law introducing the right to divorce, and in particular, to divorce by mutual consent. (About the same time, civil marriage replaced religious marriage.)[12]

The Bolshevik vision was rooted in a number of fundamental principles. The first was that the emancipation of women was a central task of the revolution and not some *ad hoc* question; the second was that women could only be emancipated through their incorporation into social production, and not through a legal recognition of the value of domestic work, which was underappreciated in capitalist society; and finally, that the abolition of domestic work was essential for women's incorporation into public life.

As Wendy Goldman, the author of *Women, the State and Revolution*, points out,

> From a comparative perspective, the 1918 Code was remarkably ahead of its time. Similar legislation concerning gender equality, divorce, legitimacy, and property has yet to be enacted in America and many European countries. Yet despite the Code's radical innovations, jurists were quick to point out "that this is not socialist legislation, but legislation of the transitional time." As such the Code preserved marriage registration, alimony, child support, and other provisions related to the continuing if temporary need for the family unit. As Marxists, the jurists were in the odd position of creating legislation that they believed would soon become irrelevant.[13]

The discussion and elaboration of new laws sought to express the wide horizon that the revolution had opened, with the conviction that the existence of the workers' state should be transitional, and that equality before the

---

12. Marcel Liebman, *Leninism under Lenin* (London: Merlin Press, 1989).
13. Wendy Goldman, *Women, the State and Revolution: Soviet Family Policy and Social Life, 1917-1936* (Cambridge: Cambridge University Press, 1993). This book has been published in Spanish and Portuguese translations by the women's organization *Pan y Rosas/Pão e Rosas*.

law was not the same as equality in life. Bolshevik policy was based on the idea that:

> women's emancipation depended on the abolition of private property and the creation of a communal domestic economy. Under socialism, relations between the sexes would be based on genuine affection, not property. Relations would become "a purely private affair," concerning "only the persons involved." [...] This commitment to the personal and sexual freedom of the individual constituted a powerful libertarian motif in nineteenth-century socialist ideology.[14]

The economic situation was not easy—on the contrary, it was a great obstacle to the measures that were considered indispensable, beginning with the socialization of domestic work through communal day-care centers, laundries, canteens, and housing. And yet, in the midst of the economic crisis, some of the innovations introduced by the workers' state paved the way for an immense and unprecedented revolution in education: all citizens who knew how to read and write were mobilized in a gigantic literacy campaign; collections of the classics were published and sold at cost; mixed schooling was established; and education was given a polytechnic and collective character. With remarkable historical foresight, the proletarian revolution abolished exams and decreed that schools be governed by councils made up of education workers, representatives of local workers' organizations, and students over the age of 12. There was even extensive debate about the idea—never implemented—of constructing cities for children, which would administer themselves with the help of education and health professionals. A few months of workers' power was enough to proclaim that all university education would be free. One could say that the imagination had taken power!

HARROWING CONTRADICTIONS

But revolutions are very real. In order to transform everything quickly, they have to grapple with the existing material conditions. The revolution struggled to chart its course through harrowing and violent contradictions: cheap

---
14. Ibid.

books intended to teach millions of Russians to read and write ended up being burned to ward off cold, due to the shortage of fuel. Not only the revolution, but also the world war, the civil war, droughts, and plagues had turned the old Russia upside down, exhausting or liquidating the strength of all the social classes that had been fighting each other. Hunger became endemic, and this weakened and demoralized the working class. Added to this was the suffering caused by the cold and the lack of fuel. Epidemics spread easily: between 1918 and 1919, 1.5 million people died of typhus. By the end of 1920, disease, famine, and low temperatures alone killed 7.5 million Russians, while the war had claimed 4 million victims.

Thousands of children roamed the streets looking for a crust of bread to survive. They were orphans of the war, the revolution, and the famines—a social phenomenon that was difficult for the nascent workers' state to resolve. The *besprizornost*, the street children who were accustomed to theft and vagrancy, to a hard life and harsh treatment by the authorities, were sent to the countryside as soon as the agricultural economy began to recover.

In 1921, the economy of the young soviet state was devastated. "We [...] lack enough civilisation to enable us to pass straight on to socialism,"[15] Lenin said, referring to the backwardness of industry, the low urban population, and the preponderance of the countryside in the economy. He therefore proposed the New Economic Policy (NEP), which restored private ownership in some agricultural sectors and loosened restrictions on foreign trade: the goal was to revitalize an economy in ruins through the controlled introduction of certain market mechanisms. At the same time, in Germany, the government brutally repressed a workers' uprising led by the Communist Party, weakening the revolutionary forces in Europe and increasing the isolation of Soviet Russia.

With the NEP, a new middle class emerged that profited from the situation. In 1922, the harvest reached three-quarters of its pre-war level; but as the "NEP men" increased their social and economic power, the industrial working class—the main protagonist of the victorious revolution—was decimated: its politicized and courageous vanguard had fallen in the civil war. Many more had taken on responsibilities as officials of the nascent soviet state, assimilating into the bureaucratic environment; thousands of proletar-

---

15. Vladimir Ilyich Lenin, "Better Fewer, But Better," in Vladimir Ilyich Lenin, *Collected Works*, Vol. 33 (Moscow: Progress Publishers, 1965).

ians abandoned the cities during the famines and returned to their family villages. Industry did not recover at the same pace as agriculture: heavy industry was paralyzed and production in light industry reached barely one-quarter of its pre-war level.

Under these circumstances, the composition of the Bolshevik Party changed as well; before the Revolution, it had about 20,000 members. After the triumph in October, its ranks quadrupled. By the end of the civil war, half a million people had joined, and in 1922, it reached 700,000 members.

> Most of this growth, however, was already spurious. By now the rush to the victors' bandwagon was in full progress. The party had to fill innumerable posts in the government, in industry, in trade unions, and so on; and it was an advantage to fill them with people who accepted party discipline. In this mass of new-comers the authentic Bolsheviks were reduced to a small minority.[16]

All this was happening as Lenin was forced to withdraw from political life due to health problems. In 1922, Stalin was appointed the party's general secretary. Lenin, bedridden and unable to speak, died on January 21, 1924. But in these final months of his life, with his forces decimated by paralysis and aphasia, Lenin waged his final battle: for the restitution of the monopoly of foreign trade, which had been abolished in 1922; against the oppression of the nationalities; and against the bureaucracy that was beginning to gnaw at the organization of the Bolshevik Party and the soviet state.

> Colossal forces had entered into motion: those of the imperialist siege, those of an agrarian bourgeoisie that reemerged again and again, those of a capillary bureaucracy that crept into all the cogs of the administrative apparatus. Nonetheless, Lenin, until his final breath, continues to place his hopes on the consciousness of the vanguard. [...] When the party itself is revealed to be riddled with the virus of bureaucracy, Lenin does not give up. He addresses himself to the vanguard of the vanguard, to that which remains healthy within the party leadership. [...] The year 1923 marks the end of the revolutionary crisis that had shaken Europe for five years. Until then, the young Russian revolution had held out in hope of

---

16. Isaac Deutscher, *The Prophet Unarmed: Trotsky, 1921–1929* (London: Verso, 2003).

a victorious revolution in Germany, without which its own future was theoretically inconceivable. The failure of the German October opens the way for the rise of Nazism and the defeat of the Left Opposition in Russia. The bureaucracy theorizes this enduring isolation and prepares to confine the revolution within the borders of "socialism in one country." To be sure, this trajectory runs counter to the entire history and education of the party. But after the civil war, what has become of the party itself, and of its relations with the masses? Half of the industrial proletariat has melted away. [...] Confronting the unbridled forces of history, Lenin, from his bed, proposes a pact to Trotsky to play a last card against the bureaucracy.[17]

But the bureaucracy had its roots in the defeat of the international revolution and the social, economic, and cultural backwardness of Russia.

For women, this period meant an increase in the unemployment rate and a visibly greater number of urban workers in a situation of prostitution. In the 1920s, 86 percent of women in this situation were workers or self-employed craftswomen (especially dressmakers).[18] These workers had been expelled from production and witnessed drastic reductions in the free services of day-care centers and homes for single mothers; the prevailing hunger and misery forced them into prostitution.

Nonetheless, these difficulties were no impediment to bold thinking by Bolshevik leaders that rose far above the predicaments imposed by reality. As Trotsky wrote in 1923:

> Even in our present economic situation we could introduce much more criticism, initiative, and reason into our morals than we actually do. This is one of the tasks of our time. It is of course obvious that the complete change of morals—the emancipation of woman from household slavery, the social education of children, the emancipation of marriage from all economic compulsion, etc.—will only be able to follow on a long period of development, and will come about in proportion to the extent to which

---

17. Daniel Bensaïd, Preface to Moshe Lewin, *Le Dernier Combat de Lénine* (Paris: Éditions de Minuit, 1978), our translation.
18. Goldman, *Women, the State and Revolution*.

the economic forces of socialism win the upper hand over the forces of capitalism.[19]

Later on, he insisted on the revolutionary role of collective creativity to transform customs:

> Every new form [...] must be recorded in the press and brought to the knowledge of the general public, in order to stimulate imagination and interest, and give the impulse to further collective creation of new customs. Not every invention is successful, not every project takes on. What does it matter? The proper choice will come in due course. The new life will adopt the forms most after its own heart. As a result life will be richer, broader, more full of color and harmony.[20]

The generation that had led the 1917 Revolution had an understanding of the problems of everyday life that was governed by the idea that "the primary task, the one that is most acute and urgent, is to break the silence surrounding the problems relating to daily life."[21] The bureaucracy that took over the workers' state after Lenin's death held exactly the opposite view.

THE PHILOSOPHY OF A PRIEST, THE POWERS OF A GENDARME

The growing inequality between a layer of administrators and party members on the one hand and the entire Soviet working class on the other was also expressed among women.

> The situation of the mother of the family, who is an esteemed communist, has a cook, a telephone for giving orders to the stores, an automobile for errands, etc., has little in common with the situation of the working woman, who is compelled to run to the shops, prepare dinner herself, and carry her children on foot from the kindergarten—if, indeed, a kindergarten is available. No socialist labels can conceal this social contrast,

---

19. Leon Trotsky, *Problems of Everyday Life* (New York: Pathfinder Press, 1973).
20. Ibid.
21. Ibid.

which is no less striking than the contrast between the bourgeois lady and the proletarian woman in any country of the West.[22]

In 1926, under Stalin's bureaucratic regime, civil marriage was reinstituted as the only legal union. The right to abortion would later be abolished and the women's section of the Central Committee dissolved, along with its equivalents at all levels of the party. In 1934, homosexuality was prohibited and prostitution was made a crime. In the eyes of the Thermidorian bureaucracy, not respecting the family became "bourgeois" or "ultra left" behavior. A leading Stalinist declared, in 1936, that:

> Abortions, which destroy life, are unacceptable in our country. A Soviet woman has the same rights as a man, but this does not exempt her from the great and honourable duty imposed on her by nature: she is a mother; she gives life.

The ban on abortion would be part of a broader campaign to discredit and erase the emancipatory ideals that had characterized the social policies of early years of the revolution. Trotsky would refer to the reinstatement of the ban on abortion as the "philosophy of a priest endowed also with the powers of a gendarme."[23]

The reversal of these gains of the revolution was accompanied by the introduction of the death penalty from the age of 12, the authorization of torture, and massive and arbitrary executions that wiped out the generation of old Bolsheviks and everyone who dared to oppose the Stalinist regime. Years later, in 1944, the financial assistance for families was increased and the "Order of Maternal Glory" was created for women who had between seven and nine children, as well the title "Mother Heroine" for those who had ten or more. Illegitimate children were returned to that status, which had been abolished in 1917, and divorce became a costly and difficult procedure.

It is obvious that there is no continuity between the first jubilant decrees of the nascent workers' state in 1917—when laws were seen as something transitory and episodic, just like the state itself and the entire revolutionary society—and the solemn prescriptions of the order established by the bureaucracy for the advancement of the nation. Deportations, forced labor

---

22. Ibid.
23. Leon Trotsky, *The Revolution Betrayed* (New York: Doubleday, 1937).

camps, thousands of tortured and imprisoned people, and thousands of executions were necessary. The revolution needed to be opposed with a counter-revolution.

The Bolsheviks believed that establishing political equality between men and women in the soviet state was the simplest task to be solved, but that achieving this equality in daily life was an infinitely more arduous problem, since it was not dependent on revolutionary decrees. It required a great, conscious effort by the entire proletariat, and it presupposed the existence of a powerful desire for culture and progress. Nothing could be further from the idea that socialism had been "almost achieved"—as Stalin put it—while abortion was prohibited and propaganda was made for women to return to the home and be reduced, again, to household chores.

Trotsky condemned this without circumlocution or illusions:

The October Revolution inscribed on its banner the emancipation of womankind and created the most progressive legislation in history on marriage and the family. This does not mean, of course, that a "happy life" was immediately in store for the Soviet woman. Genuine emancipation of women is inconceivable without a general rise of economy and culture, without the destruction of the petty-bourgeois economic family unit, without the introduction of socialized food preparation, and education. Meanwhile, guided by its conservative instinct, the bureaucracy has taken alarm at the "disintegration" of the family. It began singing panegyrics to the family supper and the family laundry, that is the household slavery of woman.[24]

In *The Revolution Betrayed*, he pointed out:

Unfortunately society proved too poor and little cultured. The real resources of the state did not correspond to the plans and intentions of the Communist Party. You cannot "abolish" the family; you have to replace it. The actual liberation of women is unrealizable on a basis of "generalized want." Experience soon proved this austere truth which Marx had formulated eighty years before.[25]

---

24. Leon Trotsky, "Twenty Years of Stalinist Degeneration," *Fourth International* (New York), 6(3), March 1945.
25. Trotsky, *The Revolution Betrayed*.

Even though these real resources were not sufficient, it is necessary to stress that the ideological reversals of the 1930s, under the iron rule of the bureaucratic apparatus commanded by Stalin, represented "a sharp break with earlier patterns of thought, indeed with a centuries-long tradition of revolutionary ideas and practices."[26]

COMRADE KOLLONTAI

Among the most outstanding women leaders of the Russian Revolution was Alexandra Kollontai, who was born on March 31, 1872 in St. Petersburg into a family of rich landowners. This permitted her to be taught by a private tutor, in a nation where only one in 300 girls had access to secondary education. As a young woman, she studied labor history in Switzerland, and in 1899, she joined the Russian Social Democratic Workers' Party (RSDWP) where, as we mentioned above, she joined the Menshevik faction.[27]

After witnessing the events of Bloody Sunday, when hundreds of workers attempting to present a petition to the Tsar—led by an Orthodox priest, no less—were mowed down by the guns of the autocracy, Kollontai became involved in the revolutionary movement that was rocking Russia, and she focused on organizing women workers. Soon, she was driven into exile. In Europe, she came into contact with the social democratic parties of Germany, Great Britain, and France. Her cultural level and her travels enabled her to speak more than half a dozen languages fluently for the rest of her life.

During World War One, she embraced Bolshevism because she supported Lenin's minority position: that socialists should break off collaboration with bourgeois governments, mobilize the masses against social chauvinism, and transform the war into a revolutionary war. When the revolution broke out

---

26. Goldman, *Women, the State and Revolution*.
27. The Mensheviks represented the moderate wing of the RSDWP, which had split in 1903 as a result of political and ideological disputes with the Bolsheviks, led by Lenin. Although the original split at the Second Congress of the RSDWP appeared to revolve around "organizational" issues, the two factions were fundamentally clashing about what attitude to take toward the liberal bourgeoisie. The Mensheviks believed that a bourgeois-democratic revolution was on the order of the day in Russia, so its leadership would naturally fall to the parties of the liberal bourgeoisie, with whom the proletariat should seek an alliance to fight against the tsarist autocracy. The Bolsheviks, in contrast, called for the political independence of the proletariat from all wings of the bourgeoisie. The party split became definitive in 1912.

in February 1917, she returned to Russia and was elected to the Executive Committee of the Petrograd Soviet. At this time, when Lenin had not yet returned from exile, Stalin argued that the gains of the bourgeois-democratic revolution must be consolidated, and therefore proposed that the Bolshevik Party support Kerensky's provisional government. But a minority made up of metalworkers, supported by Kollontai, opposed Stalin's position, in line with Lenin's view that the soviets were bodies for exercising power and that the bourgeois revolution must be superseded by the proletarian revolution. In July, she was imprisoned along with hundreds of other Bolsheviks after mobilizations were defeated in which thousands of workers and soldiers had called for "all power to the soviets!"

"When I went to Russia, Kollontai was in prison," wrote the American journalist Louise Bryant.

> She had been exiled because of her views against the Tsar's government. She was shut up again for disagreeing with the Provisional Government. She was known to be a Bolshevik and for that "crime" was arrested at the Russian frontier on the outrageous charge of being a German spy. She was let out again because they could not bring her to trial without any evidence whatsoever. She was re-arrested and imprisoned by Kerensky after the July uprising for having openly said that the Soviet government was the only form for Russia.[28]

After the seizure of power, Kollontai was named the People's Commissar of Social Welfare, equivalent to a minister.

> Thursday, November 8th. Day broke on a city in the wildest excitement and confusion, a whole nation heaving up in long hissing swells of storm. [...] Temporary Commissars were appointed to the various Ministries: Foreign Affairs, Vuritsky and Trotsky; Interior and Justice, Rykov; Labor, Shliapnikov; Finance, Menzhinsky; Public Welfare, Madame Kollontai [...] Suddenly, by common impulse, we found ourselves on our feet, mumbling together into the smooth lifting unison of the Internation-

---

28. Louise Bryant, *Six Red Months in Russia: An Observer's Account of Russia Before and During the Proletarian Dictatorship* (New York: George H. Doran Company, 1918), with minor spelling changes for consistency.

ale. A grizzled old soldier was sobbing like a child. Alexandra Kollontai rapidly winked the tears back. [...] The immense sound rolled through the hall, burst windows and doors and seared into the quiet sky. "The war is ended! The war is ended!" said a young workman near me, his face shining.[29]

In the People's Commissariat of Social Welfare, Kollontai will be the author of a large number of the reforms relating to women and the family.

> When I held the position of People's Commissar of Social Welfare, I considered it to be my main task to chart the course that the labour republic should adopt in the sphere of protecting the interests of woman as a labour unit and as a mother. It was at this time that the board which deals with the protection of motherhood was set up and began to organise model "palaces of motherhood."[30]

A few days after the seizure of power, the Bolshevik Party organized the first women's conference, and in the following year, with Alexandra Kollontai in a prominent role, the First All-Russian Congress of Working Women took place and resolved to create commissions for agitation and propaganda. Later, these commissions would become part of the party's Women's Department, called *Zhenotdel* in Russian. The *Zhenotdel* published a monthly magazine, *Kommunistka* (*Communist Woman*), with 30,000 copies printed in 1921. This is same year that Kollontai gave lectures to the women workers in the party, in which she traced the history of women's oppression from its origins to the days of building the revolutionary workers' state. This was also the time of her best-known articles, in which she developed her ideas about the disintegration of the family and proclaimed the new communist relations: free unions, based exclusively on love rather than on necessity.

> There is no escaping the fact: the old type of family has had its day. The family is withering away not because it is being forcibly destroyed by the state, but because the family is ceasing to be a necessity. [...] In place of

---

29. John Reed, *Ten Days that Shook the World* (New York: International Publishers, 1919), with minor spelling changes for consistency.
30. Alexandra Kollontai, "The Labour of Women in the Evolution of the Economy," in Alexandra Kollontai, *Selected Writings of Alexandra Kollontai* (London: Allison & Busby, 1977).

the old relationship between men and women, a new one is developing: a union of affection and comradeship, a union of two equal members of communist society, both of them free, both of them independent and both of them workers. No more domestic bondage for women. No more inequality within the family. No need for women to fear being left without support and with children to bring up. [...] Marriage will be a union of two persons who love and trust each other. Such a union promises to the working men and women who understand themselves and the world around them the most complete happiness and the maximum satisfaction. [...] In place of the individual and egoistic family, a great universal family of workers will develop, in which all the workers, men and women, will above all be comrades. This is what relations between men and women in the communist society will be like. These new relations will ensure for humanity all the joys of a love unknown in the commercial society, of a love that is free and based on the true social equality of the partners.[31]

Kollontai's views about the disintegration of the family were widely shared by other leaders of the Bolshevik Party, and the jurist Alexander Goikhbarg defended them against more conservative positions. They also argued against sectors with even more radical ideas, such as the immediate abolition of marriage and the rejection of any form of state regulation of interpersonal relations. The documents from this time, however, leave no room for doubt that the measures taken by the state were not intended to increase state control at the expense of individual freedoms, but rather to guarantee previously unknown rights, and in this way to fight against church interference in the lives of the working class and the oppressed masses. "While Bolshevik ideology promoted the libertarian freedom of the individual, it also enlarged immeasurably the social role of the state by eliminating intermediary bodies like the family."[32] Ultimately, the Bolsheviks argued, only socialism would be capable of fundamentally resolving the contradiction between work and the family, by completely socializing domestic labor, making institutions like marriage obsolete and unnecessary, transforming them into free relationships based on love and equality, and taking definitive steps toward a society without oppression of any kind.

---

31. Alexandra Kollontai, "Communism and the Family," in Alexandra Kollontai, *Selected Writings of Alexandra Kollontai* (London: Allison & Busby, 1977).
32. Goldman, *Women, the State and Revolution*.

In spite of the debates that he thus provoked, Goikhbarg defended civil marriage against the idea of abolishing it with the stroke of a pen. To support his position in the ensuing discussions, he argued, for example, that the limit to "sexual freedom" was not set by the state, but rather by the reality of a society in which patriarchal behavior was still latent. As long as the development of the productive forces and the possibilities of the workers' state did not make it possible to provide universal contraception or childcare for children born of unwanted pregnancies, then men should not be "liberated" from their legal responsibilities toward women. Goikhbarg was convinced that, in a transitional stage when the most acute prejudices of patriarchal culture endured, "sexual freedom" and free unions would only be a right for men, while the ones who would suffer the consequences of abandonment, separation, unwanted pregnancies, and so on would be women. For this reason, the family code, besides guaranteeing the right to divorce and abolishing the legally inferior status of women, introduced another innovation: It broke the judicial equivalency of "family=marriage" and made family obligations independent of the legal union. It also abolished male privilege over property and inheritance, while eliminating the judicial concept of an "illegitimate child." Under the new law, all children born in or out of wedlock had the same rights, and their parents, regardless of their civil status, had the same responsibilities for them. Without a doubt, this was one of the most progressive legal codes in history, greatly surpassing even the most advanced European legislation.

On November 18, 1920, Alexandra Kollontai presented the decree establishing the right to free abortion on demand with these words:

> During the past decades the number of women resorting to artificial discontinuation of pregnancy has grown both in the West and in this country. The legislation of all countries combats this evil by punishing the woman who chooses to have an abortion and the doctor who makes it. Without leading to favorable results, this method of combating abortions has driven the operation underground and made the woman a victim of mercenary and often ignorant quacks who make a profession of secret operations. As a result, up to 50 per cent of such women are infected in the course of operation, and up to 4 per cent of them die. The Workers' and Peasants' Government is conscious of this serious evil to the community. It combats this evil by propaganda against abortions among working

women. By working for socialism, and by introducing the protection of maternity and infancy on an extensive scale, it feels assured of achieving the gradual disappearance of this evil. But as the moral survivals of the past and the difficult economic conditions of the present still compel many women to resort to this operation, the People's Commissariats of Health and of Justice, anxious to protect the health of the women and considering that the method of repressions in this field fails entirely to achieve this aim, have decided: (1) To permit such operations to be made freely and without any charge in Soviet hospitals, where conditions are assured of minimizing the harm of the operation. (2) Absolutely to forbid anyone but a doctor to carry out this operation. [...] (4) A doctor carrying out an abortion in his private practice with mercenary aims will be called to account by a People's Court.[33]

In this way, the Russian Revolution defended an elementary democratic right of women which was not obtained in the world's most developed countries until many decades later, and must still be won in the majority of semi-colonial countries today.

By the mid-1920s, a feeling of listlessness and apathy was spreading in the Soviet Union, especially after Lenin's death on January 21, 1924. A few months earlier, Kollontai had joined the Soviet Union's diplomatic corps, becoming the first woman ambassador in history, serving in Norway, Sweden, and Mexico. This removed her from the center of political activities in Moscow and Petrograd but, in exchange, she avoided the fate of deportation and execution to which many of her comrades and other oppositionists fell victim under Stalin's iron regime. Until her death on March 9, 1952 in Moscow, Kollontai remained abroad and most of her writings dealt with topics related to women, the family, and sexuality. She also published her autobiography. How much did she know about what was occurring in the workers' state trapped under Stalin's boot? Or was it unease, skepticism, demoralization, and weariness that kept her from waging a new battle for her beliefs? What is certain is that Kollontai, who on numerous occasions had expressed disagreement with Lenin's policies, yet always followed the party's majority decisions and resolutions, this time kept silent. Trotsky, like thousands of left oppositionists to Stalin's Thermidorian regime, did

---

33. Quoted in N.A. Semashko, *Health Protection in the USSR* (London: Gollancz, 1924).

not escape this fate of persecution and banishment. In 1932, the Swedish government denied him a visa at the request of the Soviet ambassador, Alexandra Kollontai, who was following the orders of the Kremlin.

> The Stalinist faction has taken up a shameful position in the struggle of class forces over the question of the visa. It acted with all its power, through its diplomatic agents, to prevent the issuing of the visa to Comrade Trotsky. Kobetsky in Denmark and Kollontai in Sweden threatened economic and other reprisals.[34]

Alexandra Kollontai chose to live the rest of her life in silence and under a false discipline; she saved her skin by not condemning the crimes being committed against revolutionaries—in the name of socialism, paradoxically. However, her political wavering and her silence in the face of Stalin's crimes do not invalidate her audacious thinking about new forms of human relations freed from the yoke of capitalism. Her writings have endured because of their insights about how much love and sexuality are shaped by the social and economic forces of the world we live in. But fundamentally, because of her ability to imagine new, egalitarian bonds between human beings. Kollontai knew that the Bolsheviks' dreams from 1917 were being strangled by the "powers of the gendarme and the philosophy of the priest" imposed by the Stalinist bureaucracy. Beyond her shortcomings, her articles and speeches are paintings that present other forms and colors of love, in the framework of revolutionary commitment and conviction.

OPPOSITIONAL WOMEN

In 1938, Leon Trotsky argued that it was necessary to found a new international in order to raise the revolutionary banner anew. The Third International, strangled by Stalin's policies, was playing a cynical, counter-revolutionary role and openly betraying the world working class. Just as Marx and Engels had fought inside the First International to preserve its revolutionary spirit, and Rosa Luxemburg, Clara Zetkin, Lenin, Trotsky, and others had tried to maintain the thread of continuity with these experi-

---

34. Leon Trotsky, "A Bolshevik–Leninist Declaration on Comrade Trotsky's Journey," in Leon Trotsky, *Writing of Leon Trotsky*, Vol. 4 (New York: Pathfinder Press, 1973).

ences by abandoning the Second International when its majority decided to support the imperialist war, now one of the central leaders of the October Revolution was abandoning the Third International, which had failed the tests of history irredeemably.

Thus, the Fourth International was born, which declared in its program that "a correct policy is composed of two elements: an uncompromising attitude on imperialism and its wars, and the ability to base one's program on the experience of the masses themselves."[35] As it paid special attention to the most exploited sectors of the working class, we do not consider it a coincidence that the Forth International inscribed on its banners: "Open the Road to the Woman Worker! Open the Road to the Youth!" In its program, we read:

> Opportunist organizations by their very nature concentrate their chief attention on the top layers of the working class and therefore ignore both the youth and the women workers. The decay of capitalism, however, deals its heaviest blows to the woman as a wage earner and as a housewife.[36]

Oppositionists to Stalin's regime were already being persecuted, imprisoned, and murdered before the foundation of the Fourth International. At the time of the fraudulent Moscow Trials, which the Stalinist regime staged against the main leaders of the 1917 Revolution and against everyone who opposed its policies, women made up between 12 and 14 percent of the communists sent to labor camps on charges of sabotage, espionage, and "Trotskyism." Among the thousands of oppositionists who were deported, exiled, imprisoned, and shot, we find the distinguished names of Yevgenia Bosch, Nadezhda Joffe, and Tatiana Miagkova—alongside so many other women who bravely continued their struggle against Stalinism under the most difficult conditions.

Yevgenia Bosch was born in 1879, and she joined the Russian Social Democratic Workers' Party in 1900, aligning herself with the Bolshevik left wing from 1903 onwards. In 1913, she was deported because of her revolutionary activities, and two years later she managed to escape and take refuge in the United States. On her return to Russia, after the February Revolution

---

35. Leon Trotsky, *The Transitional Program* (New York: Labor Publications, 1981).
36. Ibid.

of 1917, she played a leading role in the Kiev Uprising and the civil war. Later, she was among the signatories of the "Declaration of the 46," with which 46 members of the Bolshevik Party criticized the position of the Stalinist leadership.[37] Yevgenia committed suicide in 1924, at the age of 45, as a gesture of protest against the bureaucracy.

Nadezhda was the daughter of Adolf Joffe, who until his death was a great friend of Trotsky. She spent her early childhood in Vienna, where her father worked to distribute the newspaper *Pravda* in Russia; she spent time with Trotsky's son Leon Sedov, who was the same age. Back in Russia, in 1917— where her father was one of the most eminent diplomats of the young soviet republic[38]—she joined the Communist Youth League. In 1924, alongside Leon Sedov, she joined the Left Opposition within that organization. After her father's suicide, as a gesture of protest against the Stalinist regime, and the banning of the Left Opposition in 1927, she took part in clandestine activities, and was arrested and deported in 1928. In 1934, convinced by the example of Christian Rakovsky[39]—who had decided to capitulate to the Stalinist regime, invoking the Nazi threat against the Soviet Union—Joffe followed him. But soon she regretted this decision and recanted. Arrested again in 1936, she was not definitively released until 20 years later. Her partner Pavel Kossakovsky was shot in a labor camp in Kolyma[40] in 1938. When she was released in 1956, she devoted herself to the memory of her father and his comrades, founding the association *Memorial*.[41]

---

37. They declared that the country was threatened with economic ruin because the majority of the leadership (the Politburo) had no clear policy and saw no need for industrial planning. They additionally protested against bureaucratism. Trotsky did not sign this declaration, although the signatories supported some of his positions. Among the most well-known signatories were Preobrazhensky, Smirnov, Beloborodov, and Serebriakov.

38. Adolf Joffe was the Soviet ambassador to Germany on the eve of the November Revolution of 1918 and later ambassador to China.

39. Christian Rakovsky (1873–1941) was a Romanian-Bulgarian socialist, a member of the Central Committee of the Bolshevik Party after the 1917 revolution, and Chairman of the Council of People's Commissars of the Ukraine. He was the USSR's ambassador to France in 1925–1927. After Trotsky was sent into exile, he became the main leader of the Left Opposition in Russia, but capitulated in 1934, after years of persecution and interment under inhumane conditions in the Stalinist regime's deportation camps.

40. A region in the far east of Siberia.

41. In 1988, at the Moscow Aviation Institute, she presided over a meeting with more than 1,000 participants dedicated to Leon Trotsky and his people. It was there that Pierre Broué, the director of the *Institut Léon Trotsky* in France and one of the most prominent historians of the Bolshevik Party and the international Trotskyist movement, first met her. On that occasion,

The story of Tatiana Miagkova (1897–1937) is another example of what happened to those who adhered to Trotsky's ideas and opposed the Stalinist bureaucracy. Tatiana was one of the 6,000 Trotskyists who were murdered in the port of Magadan in 1937.[42] When she was still a student, she participated in revolutionary actions and was arrested. The February Revolution of 1917 liberated her, and she joined the Bolshevik Party in 1919. When the troops of the tsarist general Denikin occupied the city of Kiev, she went underground to maintain contact with the retreating units of the Red Army. She published her recollections of this period in the magazine *Letopis' Revolyutsii* in February 1926. After the end of the civil war, she resumed her studies in Moscow and then settled in Ukraine. In 1926, she joined the "United Opposition" formed by Trotsky, Zinoviev, and Kamenev,[43] and she was expelled from the Russian Communist Party in 1927 as a "Trotskyist." In 1928, she was sent into exile in Astrakhan on the Caspian Sea. There, she continued her oppositional activity: together with other exiled members of the opposition, she organized a group that met in her apartment; she recruited young people from the city for the opposition; she reproduced the opposition's documents and distributed them among Communist Party members and young communists in Astrakhan; she proposed to set up a fund to support those in exile. She became the secretary of Christian Rakovsky, the main leader of the opposition inside the Soviet Union after Trotsky's expulsion in February 1929. Accused of having edited and distributed an opposition pamphlet, she was sentenced to three years of exile in Kazakhstan. There, her husband, who was the People's Commissar for Finance in Ukraine, came to visit her, and attempted to convince her to renounce her oppositional opinions and activities.

Joffe arranged for two of Trotsky's grandchildren, the sister and brother Alexandra and Vsevolod (called "Seva"), to meet, after they had been separated for almost half a century. She was very active and took part in numerous congresses and conferences. Together with "Seva" Volkov and Pierre Broué, she did a speaking tour about Trotsky in the United States. She was a great orator, full of passion and humor, trained—as she put it—by the winds of the tundra.

42. A Soviet city and port in Eastern Siberia, an industrial zone of shipyards and goldmines.

43. In June 1926, Zinoviev, Kamenev, and Trotsky formed a united opposition to Stalin's theory of socialism in one country and Bukharin's policy toward the peasants, which called for advancing toward socialism "at a snail's pace." They also demanded a return to workers' democracy within the party. Zinoviev and Kamenev capitulated the following year at the 15th congress of the CP in order to remain in the party.

Tatiana Miagkova was in exile together with two other oppositional women: Sonya Smirnova and Maria Varchavskaia. The latter, who continued to defend her political positions in their totality until her final day, is the one who recounts that Tatiana Miagkova, after long and difficult discussions with her husband, ended up yielding to his arguments and publicly renouncing her political activities. In 1931, she moved to Moscow with her husband, who had become an official in the apparatus of the Central Executive Committee of the USSR. But although Miagkova ceased her political activity, she continued to express her opinions, which had not changed. And on January 12, 1933, she was again arrested and sentenced to three years of prison and isolation. On May 28, 1936, a special conference of the NKVD—the name of the Stalinist secret police, formerly called the GPU and later the KGB—sentenced Miagkova to five years in a labor camp in the Magadan region, which the deportees referred to as the "white crematorium." At the same time, two of Miagkova's old Trotskyist friends, Smirnova and Varchavskaia, arrived in Magadan. Miagkova's daughter writes about these events: "All the Trotskyists, all the oppositionists, all the people capable of defending their point of view and opposing the point of the view of the country's supreme leadership assembled in Magadan."[44] From there, she was sent to another camp further north. One autumn day, in 1937, a convoy stopped near the camp where she was living and she recognized a Trotskyist friend of hers among the prisoners being transported. She wanted to speak to him through the bars, but a guard tried to push her and she protested. According to the testimony of one of her neighbors, she screamed insults at the guards: "Fascists, fascist mercenaries, I know that your power spares neither women nor children, but soon your arbitrary rule will end!" The verdict condemned her for being "an unarmed Trotskyist," for "systematically establishing links with the Trotskyists," and for having gone on a hunger strike for six months; finally, a special conference of the NKVD sentenced her to execution by firing squad. This sentence was carried out immediately. A few days earlier, the special conference had also condemned her friend to death. He was number 49 on a list of Trotskyists who were sentenced to death that day for taking part in a demonstration in protest

---

44. "Une des six mille trotskystes liquidés en 1937 à Magadan: Tatiana Miagkova," *Cahiers du mouvement ouvrier* 1 (April 1998), https://cahiersdumouvementouvrier.org/wp-content/uploads/tous-cmo-pdf/cmo_001.pdf, our translation.

against the treatment of the deportees, for going on a hunger strike, and for carrying out "Trotskyist" activities. The verdict states:

> Poliakov Benjamin Moiseevitch is accused of being a member of the counter-revolutionary Trotskyist committee, of having participated in the counter-revolutionary demonstration in Vladivostok. He is the organizer of a revolt in the course of his transport to Nagaev. He organized the recruitment of participants in the hunger strike and took part in it himself. He has written and signed counter-revolutionary petitions and statements. He refuses to work.[45]

The historian Birioukov, who was in Magadan in 1990 researching the case of Tatiana Miagkova and her comrades, wrote to her daughter:

> The story of how 6,000 Trotskyist prisoners (and not 200, as I wrote to you earlier) were sent to Kolyma, how they tried to obtain justice here (if only by claiming the status of political prisoners), how they attempted to continue their fight against Stalinism, and how they were finally annihilated in those years is a story of greatness, even against the background of the national tragedy of the time. And your mother's fate is a small link in this horrific story.[46]

Nonetheless, this horrific story could not last forever. The bureaucracy that usurped the banner of the October Revolution eventually landed in the dustbin of history. In a process full of contradictions, it collapsed in the face of the corrosion caused by a deep economic crisis and mass mobilizations at the end of the 1980s. Meanwhile, millions of human beings were born and grew up with the idea that the historical abomination of Stalinism was synonymous with socialism. The revolutionary banner was stained for more than half a century by the monstrous crimes of the Thermidorian bureaucracy. Against this backdrop, the ideas of revolution and freedom seemed to follow different paths, or even to oppose each other. However, as the capitalist restoration advanced, the misery of the working people of the former Soviet Union, especially the women, was augmented by new forms

---

45. Ibid.
46. Ibid.

of misery. Unemployment, hunger, and inflation led to the highest rates of alcoholism, violence, criminal mobs, and other hardships ever recorded in Russia. Millions of women were forced out onto the streets with their children, living below the poverty line, leading to a considerable increase in prostitution and trafficking of women to Western countries. Capitalism has proven that it is not the paradise being sold in pro-Western advertisements. The gains of the 1917 Revolution were debased by the Stalinist bureaucracy, but not even Stalin's Thermidorian terror could wipe them out entirely—this only began with the capitalist restoration. But even though the immediate effects of this restoration were devastating, the collapse of the largest counter-revolutionary apparatus of the twentieth century could mean nothing other than the liberation of the energy of millions of exploited and oppressed people in the former USSR and around the world who had been trapped in the straitjacket of this treacherous leadership. The experiences of Soviet women are a source of historical traditions that millions of women around the world—who only know oppression and misery from the hand of capitalism—can draw from.

6

From Vietnam to Paris, Bras to the Bonfire

The personal is political.
—slogan of the second-wave feminist movement

ECONOMIC BOOM AND BABY BOOM

The outcome of World War Two reconfigured the world economy and international politics.[1] At the end of the war, imperialism and Stalinism agreed on a peaceful coexistence—a pact to prevent the revolutionary processes that were emerging in the central countries that had participated in the conflict from questioning the established order. The massive destruction of productive forces during the imperialist war, together with Stalinism's role in the defeat of the revolution in the central countries of Europe in the immediate post-war period, were the conditions that made what became known as "the boom" possible. Although it had to renounce its domination over almost one-third of the globe, since a number of Eastern European countries joined the Soviet sphere of influence, imperialism experienced unprecedented economic growth during these years.[2] This economic growth permitted

---

1.
  American hegemony reached its momentous peak in the aftermath of the Second World War, in what came to be known as the "Potsdam and Yalta Order." It relied upon U.S. military and economic superiority, in the wake of the military defeat of the Axis imperialist powers and the tremendous decline of its allies: France and Britain. But in addition to this, imperialism could count on a key weapon, i.e., the counter-revolutionary collaboration of Moscow and world Stalinism, which acted as a containment of the proletariat and national liberation movements. This agreement laid the conditions for American hegemony in the postwar years.

Juan Chingo and Eduardo Molina, "The War in the Balkans and the International Situation," *Left Voice*, July 1, 1999, available at: www.leftvoice.org/the-war-in-the-balkans-and-the-international-situation; originally published in Spanish as "La guerra de los Balcanes y la situación internacional," in *Estrategia Internacional* (Buenos Aires), No. 13, 1999.

2.
  Thus, not only the wars served to reduce the organic composition of capital, but Stalinism's disciplining of the working class and the subsequent collaboration with US occupation

the co-optation of large, privileged sectors of the proletariat in the central countries—they were given new access to consumption, financed by social benefits and debt, and thus assimilated.

Under the so-called "welfare state," women, particularly in the central countries, won enormous rights in relation to motherhood, and important social legislation was established in this field. Single mothers, working-class women, widows, and abandoned wives benefitted from maternalist policies that included reforms to labor law, health insurance, welfare, family law, tax legislation, and so forth. Women's right to vote was incorporated into the constitutions of the majority of countries in the world. On the other hand, the economic growth of this period allowed for an increasing participation of women in the labor market, which led to their greater inclusion in cultural and political spheres. Women gained access to education and production on a massive scale, which led to a reconfiguration of family relations, gender relations, and the role of housewives.

It was fundamentally also the state that introduced new family policies to increase the birthrate. Maternity allowances and family benefits were part of an important redistribution of the growing national incomes, which made these benefits possible in the first place.

At the end of the war, the birthrate in Europe's central countries had risen considerably. Advances in medicine and improvements in nutrition and hygiene made it possible to reduce the mortality rate for mothers and newborns, resulting in what became known in the USA as the "baby boom." Later, beginning in the late 1950s, this trend was reversed: new options for feeding babies shortened the breastfeeding period and made it possible for people other than the progenitor to perform this task, freeing the mother for activities outside the home such as work or study. Scientific develop-

---

troops permitted an enormous increase in the rate of surplus value. [...] These two factors—the fall of the organic composition of capital and the high rates of surplus value—were, in our opinion, the basis for the enormous increase of the rate of profit that made the boom possible. Similarly, the establishment of the almost absolute hegemony of US imperialism at the end of World War Two was a factor that had obviously not been achieved after the first one, and this became a fundamental element of stabilization of the entire economy. Moreover, one should not overlook the fact that the subsequent development and reconstruction of Germany and Japan (its future competitors) was driven by US imperialism itself, responding in large part to the political necessity of banishing the danger of revolution.

See Paula Bach, "Robert Brenner y la economía de la turbulencia global: algunos elementos para la crítica," *Estrategia Internacional* (Buenos Aires) 13 (1999), our translation.

ment perfected hormonal contraceptives and intrauterine devices (IUDs), granting women greater decision-making power over reproduction. At the same time, the homes of the middle classes and the more affluent sectors of the proletariat underwent an important structural transformation during this period: new homes had kitchens in separate rooms and well-equipped bathrooms, and were connected to running water, natural gas, and electricity, eliminating some of the most burdensome household chores. The burden of others was greatly reduced by the introduction of home appliances. All of this freed women, materially and ideologically, for the production of goods and services—and also made it necessary to increase family incomes. Women's labor, including the incorporation of middle-class women into the workforce, especially in the service sector and administrative jobs, became an additional source of family income that allowed for social advancement and the acquisition of more consumer goods, increasing well-being and quality of life.

But the transformation of women's traditional role in the home eventually led to the "functional devaluation of marriage and the 'destination family,'"[3] characterized by the de-institutionalization and precarization of the marital bond. This profound change in gender relations led to a transformation of feminine subjectivity that became known as "women's discontent." Some authors believe that this change is the "subjective" cause that led to the second-wave feminist movement.

The economic boom and the resulting stability in the class struggle did not last forever.

Toward the end of the 1960s, with the end of the capitalist boom and the ascent of the class struggle in the years 1968–76, the proletariat's struggle in the West against the imperialist governments, in the East against the Stalinist bureaucracy, and in the semi-colonies against the pro-imperialist bourgeoisies re-opens the perspective of a strengthened tendency toward confrontation with the pillars of the Yalta Order. As a result of this, tendencies toward class independence reemerge, expressed

---

3. Nadine Lefaucheur, "Maternity, Family, and the State," in Georges Duby and Michelle Perrot (Eds.), *History of Women in the West*, Vol. 5: Françoise Thébaud (Ed.), *Toward a Cultural Identity in the Twentieth Century* (Cambridge, MA: Belknap Press of Harvard University Press, 1996).

in the *cordones industriales*[4] in Chile, the Popular Assembly[5] in Bolivia, the soldiers' and tenants' councils in the Portuguese Revolution, etc. However, although they were weakened, the Yalta Order and the leaderships that sustained it were not defeated. The revolutionary process was diverted in the central countries and crushed by counter-revolution in Latin America.[6]

During this period of resurgent class struggle in both hemispheres, a new women's liberation movement arose, with a certain mass character in the central countries and an influence on smaller sectors of middle-class women in the peripheral countries.

LIBERTY, EQUALITY, SORORITY

In the midst of economic and political strikes, struggles against national oppression, radicalized demonstrations by students, African-Americans, and gays, and a powerful movement against the imperialist war in Vietnam, women burst onto the international political scene. More and more women began to participate in campaigns for the right to abortion and contraception, for adequate childcare facilities in the workplace, and against all legal restrictions on equality. They denounced sexism in politics, the workplace, education, the media, and everyday life.[7] Although the feminist movement's resurgence took place fundamentally among students and housewives from

---

4. The *cordones industriales* (literally: industrial belts) were council-like structures that the working class built under the government of Salvador Allende. The first *cordón* was formed in 1972 by delegates from 30 factories—one year later, there were 31 such *cordones*. They called on the reformist government to nationalize the factories and to arm the working class in order to prevent a military coup. Allende, however, refused. On September 11, 1973, the government and the *cordones* were simultaneously crushed by the coup under General Pinochet. —translator
5. The *Asamblea Popular* (Popular Assembly) in Bolivia was founded on May 1, 1971, as part of a revolutionary process. Delegates from all the trade unions, but especially from the miners, were represented, as well as peasants. But the assembly had a reformist leadership and did not function regularly. It was dissolved a short time later by a right-wing military coup. —translator
6. Emilio Albamonte and Jorge Sanmartino, "La historia del marxismo y su continuidad leninista-trotskista es la del 'álgebra' de la revolución proletaria," *Estrategia Internacional* (Buenos Aires), 10 (1998), our translation.
7. In 1968, American women at the Miss America pageant crowned a sheep and threw bras, corsets, and false eyelashes into a "Freedom Trash Can." In 1970, a group of French women placed a wreath at the Arc de Triomphe in honor of the unknown wife of the unknown soldier, and another next to it with the following sentence: "One out of every two men is a woman."

the middle class, the demands they raised, combined with the growing contradictions of the capitalist system, allowed them to mobilize broader sectors. One of the main slogans of this mass women's movement was "equal pay for equal work," alongside protests against the double burden for women who had to do household chores after working outside the home.

Since 1945, we have witnessed a proliferation of national and international laws, regulations, and decrees proclaiming, among other things, the right to equal pay for equal work. However, the difference between men's and women's wages remained stable almost everywhere in the world until 1968, the year in which the gap began to narrow, reaching 25–35 percent by 1975, depending on the country. At this time, women working outside the home were doing three times more housework than men. In the labor market, women were particularly represented in the tertiary sector (commerce, banking, services), while they remained a small minority in industry, construction, public works, and transport.

In 1966, Betty Friedan founded the *National Organization for Women* (NOW) in the United States, which mainly organized middle-class, married women with children. By 1971, this organization grew to more than 10,000 members, despite the fact that within a year of its founding it had suffered a split led by young, single women who launched a more radical group, the *Women's Liberation Movement* (WLM). One of the great achievements of the US women's movement, with NOW and WLM both leading the campaign, was that the telephone and telegraph companies were obliged to give their women employees back-pay for the wage difference relative to men, for the entire time since they had been hired—a figure that reached several million dollars. The movement also took aim at questions of reproductive rights, abortion, and sexual violence. In 1971, 374 prominent German women declared on the cover of a magazine that they had had abortions. This inspired a declaration of support signed by 86,500 women who confessed to having done the same, which was then presented to the Federal Ministry of Justice. Finally, in 1974, abortion was decriminalized during the first three months of pregnancy, subject to certain limitations. At the same time in France, 343 famous women publicly stated that they had voluntarily terminated a pregnancy, and in the following year, 345 doctors declared that they had performed abortions. The Movement for the Freedom of Abortion and Contraception (MLAC) in France opened numerous illegal abortion clinics until this right was established in 1975.

In addition to the struggle for democratic rights, second-wave feminism (in contrast to the "first wave" led by the suffragettes at the end of the nineteenth and beginning of the twentieth century) was also interested in the reconstruction of women's history, research on the origins of oppression, and studies on how gender differences affect all areas of knowledge. This opened up a wide field of investigation at the universities, which began to incorporate Gender Studies, Women's Studies, or Feminist Studies in the academic world.[8] Academic feminists questioned the postulates of anthropology, psychoanalysis, sociology, economics, history, and so on. These sciences were accused of being vehicles of traditional prejudices against women. And internationalist links re-emerged as well: In 1976, feminists from various countries gathered in Brussels to hold an International Tribunal on Crimes Against Women.

Influenced by these experiences and by contact with feminist literature from the central countries, many Latin American women—fundamentally from the middle class—also began forming groups for reflection (consciousness-raising) and activism for women's rights. But their movement, as a whole, never reached the mass scale of the feminist movement in the central countries. These groups emerged in the context of an acute radicalization of the class struggle, which manifested itself in an ascent of workers' and mass struggles in Latin America. The most outstanding expressions of this were the *cordones industriales* in Chile, the semi-insurrection of the *Cordobazo*[9] in Argentina, the student mobilizations—of which Tlatelolco[10] in Mexico can be considered the most intense experience—and the rise of numerous urban and peasant guerrilla movements. Latin American feminist groups were therefore quickly caught up in an atmosphere of political radicalization that demanded definitions and commitments. As Leonor Calvera points out in her history of Argentinian feminism:

---

8. Women historians, for example, questioned their discipline for having been written by men (HIStory) and called for a history created by women (HERstory).

9. The *Cordobazo* was an uprising at the end of May 1969 in the Argentinian city of Córdoba. During a general strike, workers and students occupied the city center and erected barricades to protest against the military dictatorship. After two days, the city was recaptured by the military. —translator

10. In the Tlatelolco massacre of October 2, 1968, 300–400 students were murdered in the Plaza de las Tres Culturas in the Tlatelolco district of Mexico City. Ten days before the start of the Olympic Games in Mexico City, some 10,000 students had gathered there for a peaceful rally. In the months before, numerous strikes and occupations had shaken the country. —translator

The confrontations and the wave of partisanship that surrounded us did not cease to deliver hard blows within the group: we reproduced traditional antagonisms and invented new ones. Our analyses revolved less and less around women as an axis, and shifted toward class frameworks.[11]

Later, in the mid-1970s, this ascent of the class struggle was defeated by a bloody counter-revolution in Latin America, opening the way for a new imperialist offensive in the region. The dictatorial regimes that were established in a large part of the continent blocked the development of the feminist movement, not only by imposing a reactionary ideology based on the defense of tradition and the family, but also with political persecution and state terrorism; social, union, and political activists were tortured, forced into exile, imprisoned, disappeared, and murdered. The polarization in these countries was also reflected in differing views on feminism: the Right considered feminists to be subversive and contrarian; the Left, in contrast, called them "petty bourgeois." Even if some groups managed to carry out actions under the dictatorships, and other women met for consciousness-raising and study groups despite the hostile climate, the fact is that the Latin American feminist movement only regained prominence at the beginning of the 1980s with the fall of the dictatorships and the establishment of new bourgeois-democratic regimes in the Southern Cone, and even later in the countries of Central America.

The dictatorships managed to sever, to a great extent, the threads of continuity with the previous stage. Many of the proposals of the feminist movement of the 1970s were discussed once again. In a certain sense, the years of terror forced Latin American feminists to "start over" once the democratic regimes were put in place.

RADICAL AND SOCIALIST FEMINISTS AGAINST PATRIARCHY

The general perspective of the 1970s feminist movement was anti-institutional. It can only be understood in the context of the insurrectional movements developing all over the world, with May 68 in France, the Hot Autumn in Italy, the student and anti-war mobilizations in the USA against the Vietnam War, the Prague Spring, the *Cordobazo* in Argentina, the

---

11. Leonor Calvera, *Mujeres y Feminismo en Argentina* (Buenos Aires: Grupo Editor Latinoamericano, 1990), our translation.

national liberation struggles in Angola and Mozambique, and the revolutions in Portugal, Iran, Nicaragua, among others. It was only in the 1980s that the feminist movement began its reconciliation with institutions like political parties and the state, shifting from street demonstrations to other areas. The different tendencies within the feminist movement defined themselves according to the various ways they understood oppression, and thus the characteristics of the struggle to be waged against it.

The most radicalized tendencies were led by women hailing from other organizations or emancipatory movements, with experience as left-wing political activists. Many of them were Marxists, but they rejected the discrimination they had experienced in their political organizations. They formed autonomous and radical movements because they believed that their struggle was against a patriarchal system that needed to be profoundly transformed, while parties of the Left were simply reproducing it, as was evident in the daily life and public policies of so-called "real socialism" (the Soviet Union and other countries of Eastern Europe under the iron rule of Stalinism) and in the personal experience each of these women had in the guerrilla armies and other left-wing parties and organizations.[12]

Feminists conceptualized gender as a social construct, not determined by anatomy, and rejected the biological determinism of "sex" and "sexual difference" commonly used to justify discrimination against women. For them, there was no excuse for the inequality of rights compared to men that was expressed in all areas of life. In other words, for equality feminists, biology is not destiny. Their goal was to eliminate the hierarchies established around socially constructed gender differences, which reinforced the exclusion and oppression of women. The roots of equality feminism can be found

---

12. Stalinism and the guerrilla movements uncritically reproduced the petty-bourgeois moral values of the peasant masses subjected to cultural and political backwardness, under the influence of religion, prejudices, and traditions. This was alien to the tradition of revolutionary Marxism, which had always fought for women's liberation and, at the beginning of the twentieth century during the Russian Revolution, even removed homosexuality from the list of "perversions" and "crimes." The perpetuation of inherited forms of oppression in the name of socialism ended up reinforcing the embellished view of the imperialist democracies as "realms of freedom." But one of the essential aspects that characterizes a socialist revolution is the metamorphosis that encompasses the entirety of social relations (the economy, technology, science, the family, customs) after the seizure of power, through constant internal struggle, without allowing society to reach an equilibrium. The ruling classes, in contrast, prefer stability in social relations. So do the parasitic Stalinist cliques who usurp the masses' leading role in the name of revolution.

in Enlightenment thought and the concept of universality. This current emphasizes rational abilities common to all subjects and demands that every norm can be universalized. Equality feminism is ultimately a critique that attempts to take the ideals of the revolutionary bourgeoisie of the late eighteenth century to their logical conclusion; the bourgeoisie proclaimed liberty, equality, and fraternity while drafting the *Declaration of the Rights of Man and of the Citizen* and seizing state power. The women of the French Revolution who dared to question the bourgeois ideals that did not recognize their rights as citizens are the "grandmothers" of second-wave equality feminists.

Even with different ideologies, most feminists of the time struggled for their own conceptions of equality. Various authors use the following categorization to understand, schematically, the different tendencies. On the one hand, liberals and socialists advocated a protest feminism that incorporated their analysis of the subordinate position of women in society and their specific demands into more comprehensive ideologies about the functioning of society. Liberals sustained that capitalism must be reformed to improve the situation of women, whereas socialists called for socialist revolution, the destruction of the capitalist system, and the construction of a different social system based on the abolition of private property and thus of exploitation as well. On the other hand, radical feminists held the inverse position: they put their focus on the need to abolish patriarchy, transforming feminism into a political theory for a global understanding of the entire social system.[13] Radical feminists even adapted some elements of Marxist theory to a new conception of women's oppression based on the central idea that women constitute a social class.

The leading representatives of the latter tendency are Kate Millet and Shulamith Firestone. Millet develops a conception using the term sexual politics, in which she shows that patriarchy is a political construct that serves to legitimize the existing social order. She maintains that, in spite of its different historical transformations, patriarchy is the backbone of all political formations in the West. Millet redefines politics as the entirety of power-structured relationships whereby one group of people comes under the control of another group. The radical feminist Millet distinguishes, in turn, between sex and gender, stressing that sexuality is a function molded

---

13. Amalia Valcárcel, *Sexo y filosofía: Sobre "mujer" y "poder"* (Bogotá: Anthropos, 1994).

by culture; she attempts to show that there is no biological necessity or inevitable "correspondence" between the former and the latter term, but rather different cultural modes of relating one to the other. Society organizes the differences between men and women not only via legal mechanisms but also via socializing activities that are more subtle and comprehensive. She defines patriarchy as sexual politics exercised fundamentally by all men over all women, which leads her to affirm that "economic dependency renders [women's] affiliations with any class a tangential, vicarious, and temporary matter."[14] For her part, Shulamith Firestone, the author of *The Dialectic of Sex*, argues that:

> historical materialism is that view of the course of history which seeks the ultimate cause and the great moving power of all historic events in the dialectic of sex: the division of society into two distinct biological classes for procreative reproduction, and the struggles of these classes with one another; in the changes in the modes of marriage, reproduction and child care created by these struggles; in the connected development of other physically-differentiated classes (castes); and in the first division of labour based on sex which developed into the (economic-cultural) class system.[15]

This leads her to formulate the hypothesis that technology will allow women to be liberated from the oppression that is imposed on them by their bodies, thanks to the development of contraceptive methods and extra-uterine reproduction. But by asserting that the central division of society is the division between two sexes (classes), she implies that the specific oppression of women is directly related to their anatomy and their reproductive capacity, thus seeming to understand inequality in biological terms. According to this theory, patriarchy is established as a generalized and ahistorical power structure.

Other authors of radical feminism, known as materialist feminists, start with the premise that women are not a natural group whose oppression is based on their biological nature, but rather that they make up a social category. For these authors, women also constitute a social class, but one

---

14. Kate Millet, *Sexual Politics* (London: Granada Publishing, 1969).
15. Shulamith Firestone, *The Dialectic of Sex* (London: The Women's Press, 1979).

with common interests based on their specific condition of exploitation, that is, as a product of an economic relationship: men's exploitation of the reproductive or domestic labor performed by women.

For its part, socialist feminism attempts to combine the Marxist analysis of classes with an analysis of women's oppression, emphasizing the concept of patriarchy and the historical development of this modality of organizing family relations in the different modes of production. Socialist feminists understand inequality as an absolutely social question: They give priority to the concept of the sexual division of labor—a division that causes the social inequality between both sexes—and define patriarchy as the totality of social relations of human reproduction that are structured as male dominance over women and children. For this current, the subordination of women in the sphere of reproduction is later transferred into the world of production, meaning that women's participation in the productive process takes place under conditions of inferiority. Many of them argue that this oppression was original and a model for all other situations of inequality and domination, such as those of class. Others, following Engels' elaborations, uphold the existence of a matriarchy prior to the existence of societies divided into classes, and conceive of oppression as a relationship that only emerges with the fundamental antagonism created by the possibility of producing a surplus.[16]

These different conceptions of the origin of inequality lead to different political strategies in the struggle for equality. Liberal feminists opt for inclusion in the state apparatus, in places of power, and in regime and government institutions, with the goal of introducing reforms that aim for

---

16. The hypothesis put forward by Engels in *The Origin of the Family, Private Property and the State* proposes an organic relationship between the emergence of the first societies divided into classes (the appearance of private property and therefore the state) and the transformation of family groups (hordes, clans, tribes) into the classical monogamous family, that is, a form of organizing reproduction that forces women into seclusion in the (private) home in order to guarantee the legitimacy of their offspring. Therefore, in the Marxist hypothesis, patriarchy emerges historically in connection with the ruling classes' need to guarantee the perpetuation of their rule. Together with this hypothesis, Engels ventures the idea of a supposed "matriarchal" system that prevailed in social organizations before their division into classes (primitive communism). However, this hypothesis has been questioned by different developments in anthropology and feminist studies. Today, it is preferred to speak of "matrilineal" societies, that is, societies where lineage or kinship structures were based on the maternal bloodline, as a result of ignorance about the role of men in reproduction. Engels' romanticization of pre-class societies is also questioned. He tends to paint an idealized picture of these societies because his

more equality; socialist feminists maintain—strategically and with different nuances—the necessity of an anti-capitalist revolution. A common thread, however, links the different strands: Whether by reformist or revolutionary means, they all agree that the hierarchal differences between the sexes must be eliminated in order to reach equality. This goal, however, will be challenged not much later. By the mid-1970s, a new tendency, known as difference feminism, was entering the movement.

---

focus is on showing the brutal opposition that exists between them and the class societies that came afterwards; additionally, he aims to show, sharply, that the subordinate position of women in class societies is a historical product and not a role that corresponds to their nature. See Friedrich Engels, *The Origin of the Family, Private Property and the State*, in Friedrich Engels, *Selected Works*, Vol. 3 (Moscow: Progress Publishers, 1970).

7
Difference of Women, Differences Between Women

Being women together was not enough. We were different.
Being gay-girls together was not enough. We were different.
Being Black together was not enough. We were different.
Being Black women together was not enough. We were different.
Being Black dykes together was not enough. We were different.
Each of us had our own needs and pursuits, and many different alliances.
   Self-preservation warned some of us that we could not afford to settle for one easy definition, one narrow individuation of self. [...]
It was a while before we came to realize that our place was the very house of difference rather than the security of any one particular difference.
—Audre Lorde

THE IMPERIALIST OFFENSIVE SWEEPS EVERYTHING AWAY

The extended process of radicalization that we mentioned in Chapter 6 was the context of a radical questioning of daily life. The feminist movement recreated itself under new conditions in this "second wave"; the movement for sexual liberation came out of the closet imposed by repression, bursting onto the world scene with the barricades of Stonewall and the visibility of "Pride"; the African-American population also proclaimed its rebellion and raised the flag of Black Power; college campuses became sites of political and philosophical debates, musical experimentation, and LSD; and the traditional family, the monogamous heterosexual couple, and all intersubjective relations were challenged by free love and communal life.

This period of social and political radicalization that shook the East and the West simultaneously, between the late 1960s and the early 1980s, was brought to an end via reforms and concessions to the masses in the central countries, and via bloody counter-revolutionary coups in a number of countries in the periphery. The imperialist counter-offensive—known as "neoliberalism"—was unleashed on the masses, inflicting not only a political but also a cultural defeat. In this period of Reaganism-Thatcherism,[1] the bourgeoisie attempted to escape from an intensifying structural crisis. But the partial recovery that capitalism was able to achieve at this time was not, in contrast to the periods of the world wars of 1914–1918 and 1939–1945, based on the destruction of productive forces by the machinery of war. Although there were some physical defeats, the basis of this "new order" was, essentially, the colossal fragmentation of the working class. The defeat of Argentina in the Malvinas War[2] of 1982 served to discipline the Latin American continent and the entire semi-colonial world, a situation that continued with the defeat of Iraq in the Gulf War of 1991. The lesson learned was that imperialism was not to be opposed—that it was invincible. Further, the dirty war of the Contras in Nicaragua, armed by the USA, followed by the capitulation and co-optation of the leaderships of other guerrilla armies in the region, with pacts and agreements that dismantled the revolution in Central America, completed this imperialist offensive that fragmented the working class and put mass movements on the defensive. In Europe, in the 1980s, the recently elected "social democratic" governments, like that of François Mitterrand in France or Felipe González in Spain, became fierce agents of capital, initiating the attacks on the conquests of the workers' movement and the masses that continued and intensified in the 1990s. For its part, the bureaucracy of the Soviet Union and the Eastern Bloc handed their countries over to imperialism, facilitating the opening of their markets and the restoration of capitalism in the face of the economic debacle provoked

---

1. Ronald Reagan of the Republican Party was the US president at this time, and Margaret Thatcher of the Conservative Party was the British prime minister.
2. The *Guerra de las Malvinas* (also known as the Falklands War) was a war between the United Kingdom and Argentina in 1982. The Falkland Islands (Islas Malvinas in Spanish) off the coast of Argentina are a British colony with several thousand inhabitants and a large military base. They are also claimed by Argentina. In April 1982, the Argentinian military dictatorship under Leopoldo Galtieri invaded the islands by surprise. British imperialism under the government of Margaret Thatcher was able to quickly recapture the islands with the support of US imperialism. This also gave Thatcher momentum for new attacks on the working class in the UK. The Argentinian Left supported the anti-imperialist demand to expel the British from the South Atlantic, without supporting the dictatorship. Within the framework of the mass mobilizations in support of the war, the Argentinian Left was also able to reappear in public for the first time since the beginning of the dictatorship. Immediately afterwards, the dictatorship collapsed. –Translator

by the suffocating foreign debts. The following decade was a period in which the transfer of wealth from Latin America to the USA and Europe reached scandalously astronomical levels.[3]

The free market model and the ideology "there is no alternative" dominated this period of bourgeois restoration, as the ascent of mass struggles was diverted and channeled via the extension of the democratic capitalist regimes, opening the way for economic, social, and political measures that liquidated a large part of the conquests obtained during the previous period. This process extended in time and space to a degree that had never been seen before.

> While expanded geographically, it was a degraded democracy, one based fundamentally on the urban middle classes and some privileged sectors of the working class (especially in the advanced economies), on those who had the door of expanded consumption opened to them. The deideologization of political discourse, through a combination of the glorification of the individual and their realization through consumption ("consumerism") was the basis of this "new pact," one which was far more elitist than that of the postwar period, and which coexisted with the increasing exploitation and social degradation of the majority of the working class, together with high unemployment, and the exponential growth of poverty.[4]

While the upper layers of the working class and the middle classes were incorporated into the consumerist bonanza, the big majority was condemned to chronic unemployment, overcrowding in slums, and social, political, and cultural marginalization. Individualism also permeated mass culture.

---

[3]. About a trillion dollars in profits, interest payments on the debt, trade surpluses, and royalty payments were taken out of the region, combined with the sale of the assets of the most lucrative companies and the transfer of control of important swathes of the domestic market. This brought us to the current situation, in which the 200 largest multinational corporations control no less than one-quarter of the world's production. And just the 200 most powerful magnates have a personal fortune that exceeds the annual income of the poorest 2.5 billion people on the planet.

[4]. Emilio Albamonte and Matías Maiello, "At the Limits of the 'Bourgeois Restoration,'" *Left Voice*, December 24, 2019, www.leftvoice.org/at-the-limits-of-the-bourgeois-restoration. First published in Spanish in *Estrategia Internacional* (Buenos Aires) 27 (March 2011).

To make this happen, the ruling class counted on the collaboration of the Stalinist, social democratic, and bourgeois-nationalist political leaderships, which diverted the processes of radicalization and betrayed the mass mobilizations, leading them to defeat. In the face of this imperialist attack on the masses and their conquests, the organizations created by the working class (from the social democratic and communist parties and unions to the bureaucratized workers' states) acted as agents for implementing these measures that reconfigured the rule of capital.

This "integration" that established a "new pact" between the classes was made possible by the incorporation, albeit in a degraded form, of many of the democratic demands put forward by social movements, including feminism. An ideological offensive, summarized in the idea of the "end of history and ideologies," provided the context for the transformation of the feminist movement: from insubordination to institutionalization. After a long history of shared barricades, the divorce was finally completed: between the working class on the one hand—with its traitorous leaderships surrendering the workers' conquests or, in the best of cases, offering purely trade unionist resistance to the neoliberal attacks—and the social movements on the other hand—which, in the face of the historical defeat, abandoned the perspective of a radical transformation of the global system.

Feminism was incorporated into battles for "recognition" waged within the framework of the "democratic state," or trapped in self-imposed marginalization, and thus it abandoned the struggle against the social and moral order established by capital, which inflicts great suffering and misery on women. During these decades of profound bourgeois restoration, the countries that made up so-called "real socialism" provided no model for feminism to follow, as had been the case at the beginning of the twentieth century. On the contrary, they only seemed to confirm that any attempt to oppose the existing system of domination would only lead to new and monstrous forms of domination and exclusion: Stalinism had tarnished the emancipatory banners of Bolshevism for women's liberation and transformed them into their opposite, re-establishing the family order in which women can only be wives, mothers, or homemakers; repealing the right to abortion; criminalizing prostitution, as in tsarist times; drastically reducing or completely eliminating public policies for the creation of communal laundries, canteens, and housing; and finally, abolishing all women's party organizations.

The radicality of feminism was finally devoured by the system. Its subversive approach was reversed, setting out on a path "from the streets to the palace" and from radical social transformation to symbolic transgression. Amid the unprecedented expansion of consumption for broad sectors of the masses, the exaltation of individualism as a social value, and the transformation of social movements into recruiting grounds for technocrats to provide expert personnel for development agencies, feminism lost its critical character. Later on, we will see how—far from returning to the most radical critique that feminism had used to target the alliance of capital and patriarchy—the idea of an individual emancipation became preponderant, deceptively integrated into the possibilities of consumption and the appropriation and subjective transformation of one's own body.

AUTONOMOUS AND INSTITUTIONALIZED FEMINISTS IN LATIN AMERICA

Beginning in 1981, the *Encuentros Feministas Latinoamericanos y del Caribe* (*Latin American and Caribbean Feminist Meetings*) brought together feminists every two to three years for political reflection about the situation of the movement and the elaboration of new lines of action. However, the most important trends shaping the feminist movement in this period were academization, incorporation into the institutions of the political regimes and into different levels of government, and NGO-ization, which alongside a multiplicity of new experiences, actions, and knowledge, led to the movement's incipient fragmentation and growing co-optation. Critiques and differences about theoretical concepts, political foundations, and practices within the movement itself did not take long to appear. The division between "autonomous" and "institutionalized" feminists was one of the most acute expressions of this internal critique.[5]

For Latin American and Caribbean women, the 1980s culminated in the fourth meeting in Taxco, Mexico, where a group of women produced

---

5. Initially, one of the fundamental debates was about "double militancy," understood as the commitment to feminism on the one hand and to political organizations or movements that were not specifically feminist on the other hand. The meetings that took place in the 1980s were marked by this discussion, and also by discussions about: the adherence to different currents within feminism that expressed different ideological and political traditions; the practice of consciousness-raising groups or of "bringing" consciousness to other groups of working-class and poor women; and so on.

a document in which they sharply criticized the "myths" of the feminist movement, which, according to the signatories, were preventing it from developing. This document had a great impact. It states that:

> feminism has a long way to go because what it really aspires to is a radical transformation of society, politics, and culture. Today, the development of the feminist movement leads us to rethink certain analytical categories and political practices we have been using.

Later on, in the same document, they enunciated the "myths" that prevented an assessment of the differences within the movement and hindered the construction of a feminist political project. These are:

1. We feminists are not interested in power;
2. We feminists engage in politics in a different way;
3. We feminists are all equal;
4. There is a natural unity that comes from the sole fact of being women;
5. Feminism only exists as a politics of women with women;
6. The small group is the movement;
7. By their very existence, women's spaces guarantee a positive process;
8. Because, as a woman, I feel something, it's right;
9. The personal is automatically political; and
10. Consensus is democracy.

They concluded that: "These ten myths have generated a situation of frustration, self-satisfaction, exhaustion, inefficiency, and confusion that many feminists detect and recognize, and is present in the immense majority of groups engaged in feminist politics in Latin America today."[6] Finally, they proposed to Latin American feminists:

---

6. The document "From Love to Necessity" was produced collectively during the workshop on Feminist Politics in Latin America Today at the Fourth Latin American and Caribbean Feminist Meeting in Taxco, Mexico on October 21, 1987. The participants were Haydée Birgin (Argentina), Celeste Cambría (Peru), Fresia Carrasco (Peru), Viviana Erazo (Chile), Marta Lamas (Mexico), Margarita Pisano (Chile), Adriana Santa Cruz (Chile), Estela Suárez (Mexico), Virginia Vargas (Peru) and Victoria Villanueva (Peru). It was signed by: Elena Tapia (Mexico), Virginia Haurie (Argentina), Verónica Matus (Chile), Ximena Bedregal (Bolivia), Cecilia Torres (Ecuador) and Dolores Padilla (Ecuador). [English translation of the ten points from: Marta Lamas, *Feminism: Transmissions and Retransmissions* (New York: Palgrave Macmillan, 2011). The rest of the translation is by the translator.]

> Let us not deny the conflicts, contradictions, and differences. Let us be capable of establishing an ethics of feminism's rules of the game, reaching a pact among ourselves which will allow us to advance in our utopia of developing feminism in Latin America in both breadth and depth.[7]

The myths that were condemned in the Taxco document were preventing the development of deeper political discussions, while the movement was reshaping itself in a way that did not include everyone—but this very fact could not be criticized. Despite the document's impact, these myths persist in a large part of the movement, even to this day, while the movement itself, with its meetings, forums, and other spaces for international regroupment, became increasingly elitist, due to the growing pauperization of the masses in Latin America.

By the end of the 1980s, the problems that were preventing the feminist movement from advancing in the spirit of a "radical transformation of society, politics, and culture," at least in the eyes of some activists, had become visible. Despite attempts at homogenization, the stifling of criticism, and "romantic sisterhood," the emerging disagreements were impossible to ignore in the heat of an apparently inevitable wave of lay-offs, privatizations, and attacks on the masses' standard of living across Latin America, which intensified during the 1990s. For many feminists, this acute process of institutionalization that swept through feminism in the central countries and later reached our continent, represented the co-optation of the movement by patriarchy, proving that the struggle for equality did not question the foundations of the system that oppressed women. This critique led many women to positions that were later called difference feminism.

If the pursuit of equality had led to the co-optation of the feminist movement, now difference feminists aimed to highlight and revalue the aspects in which women differed profoundly from men, who had built this world of oppression and injustice.

> With the bankruptcy of the hopes for peace and moral progress, we are witnessing the emergence of women as an Other, but now with a positive connotation. This conceptualization of women acquires a different character according to the essentialist or constructivist assumptions of the

---

7. Ibid.

thought behind it: woman as the biological Other, as a nourishing mother and a fertile nature in contrast to man, who is genetically destined to aggression; the feminine as the pre-logical and inexpressible in everyday language, versus masculine reason; woman as a cultural construction of the patriarchy, with values that are positive despite having been derived from marginalization etc.[8]

REVALUING THE FEMININE

The Italian activist Carla Lonza and the *Rivolta Femminile* collective had criticized that: "Equality is an ideological attempt to subject woman even further. [...] Liberation for woman does not mean accepting the life man leads, because it is unlivable; on the contrary, it means expressing her own sense of existence."[9] Feminism that placed demands on the state, which had emerged from the radicalization of the late 1960s and early 1970s, was accused of calling for assimilation into a social and symbolic order that made women invisible. In contrast, a new current called for the creation of a different symbolic order, based on the idea of sexual difference and the materiality of the feminine condition. The question underlying this controversy was the incorporation of the feminist agenda into the public policies of states, governments, and international financial organizations. By obtaining recognition in exchange for integration, as we have seen, feminism had gone from questioning the basis of the capitalist system to legitimizing bourgeois democracy as the only regime in which greater gender equality could be gradually achieved, through partial reforms that do not question its foundations.

This new difference feminism would attempt to show that morphological sex differences are symbolically charged, with a hierarchical gaze that favors the male body to the detriment of the female body. From this perspective, every struggle for equality is an attempt at assimilation into an androcentric order that only considers that which concerns men to be valuable and respectable. In other words, egalitarianism only reproduces the devaluation

---

8. Alicia H. Puleo, "En torno a la polémica igualdad/diferencia," Cátedra de Estudios de Género, Universidad de Valladolid, 1999, online at: www.nodo50.org/mujeresred/feminismo-a_puleo-igualdad-diferencia.html, our translation.
9. Manifesto of *Rivolta Femminile*, 1970, in Carla Lonzi, *Let's Spit on Hegel* (New York: Secunda, 2010).

of femininity, in its aspiration to win equality with the rights that patriarchy grants exclusively to men. Difference feminism accuses equality feminism of being trapped in the discourse of the Self and the Other of phallogocentric thinking. If the patriarchal system establishes man as the model of the universal (human being = man), then being a woman means being the Other, that is, something different and inferior to the Self that functions as the norm. The specific critique of equality feminism is that it aspires for women to constitute themselves as the Same (as the Self) and that this aspiration forms part of domination, and is functional to it. It is a concession the patriarchal system would grant to women; a trap of phallogocentric logic, since the patriarchal system is constituted by the Self that exercises domination and an inferior Other that eternally fights to be the Same as the One, without ever obtaining it.

Adapting the slogan *Black is Beautiful* from the anti-racist movements in the USA, and the term *"Pride,"* difference feminists advocate a new, positive, and revalued interpretation of femininity. Difference feminism aims to think about sexual difference philosophically, which is seen as a concealed basis of the discourses of philosophy, science, psychoanalysis, and religion—all discourses of phallogocentric thought. This concealment serves to cover up the fact that all human beings are born from women, and that the feminine is the negated primordial; the subject constitutes itself through this negation, constrained by the laws of language. The political conclusion of this is that it is necessary to exalt difference instead of fighting to achieve "Sameness," which would only lead women to "chase after" men. In summary, we could say that—despite nuances from different authors and tendencies—difference feminism posits the existence of an idealized and laudable femininity that is intrinsic to being a woman. They highlight motherhood as something that belongs to women—associating it with supposedly positive qualities such as non-violence—and emphasize women's relation to nature in opposition to the world of male culture, even calling for a women's world uncontaminated by the masculine—including separatism as a political-sexual option. Difference feminists agree that women's liberation depends on the creation and development of a women's counter-culture.[10]

---

10. Celia Amorós, a prominent philosopher of equality, refers to this voluntaristic valuation as a "stoic valuation" and considers it a trap of the naivety of the oppressed. In one of her lectures

Difference of Women, Differences Between Women

One of the fundamental critiques that the proponents of equality feminism have directed against difference feminism is that by rejecting the existence of something that can be classified as "generically human," it leads to an irreducible ontological dualism. If there is nothing human without sexual differentiation, it leads to the logical and ontological impossibility of the "human" itself, that is to say, the negation of the universal that could transcend sexual difference. The most important theoretical consequence of this denial is a return to the biological essentialism that equality feminists had fought against. They argue that difference feminism does nothing but ontologize the socially constructed differences that are used to subject women to gender discrimination. From another point of view, difference feminism is accused of condemning women irremissibly to marginalization.

INTEGRATED OR MARGINALIZED

Systems of domination present the oppressed with a dilemma: integration into the system through its acceptance of their demands for equality, or marginalization in subcultures or ghettos based on differences. Equality feminism inevitably leads to the former, and difference feminism inexorably condemns women to the latter. And so it came to pass that this new feminism, which had emerged as a reaction to equality feminism's assimilation into the system, dismissed political struggle, retreating to the creation of a counter-culture based on new values arising from sexual difference. And alongside its rejection of egalitarian feminism, it ended up challenging the project of an egalitarian society liberated from exploitation and oppression.

If equality feminism had the merit of conceptualizing gender as a social and relational category linked to the concept of power, making visible the fact that women's oppression has a historical character and is not a "natural" result of anatomical differences, difference feminism, on the other hand,

---

in Buenos Aires, she remarked with notable irony, "What has historically been recognized as valuable will be recognized as valuable, even if women now decide that it is valuable to wash pots or dishes." She later added,

> If we want to console ourselves for all the frustrations we experience in social life by making roast chickens, thinking that making roast chickens is the very essence of self-realization and creativity, as certain magazines and certain feminists claim, you are naturally within your rights; but you have to know that this is not the way things are transformed.

Celia Amorós, *Mujer: participación, cultura política y estado* (Buenos Aires: De la Flor, 1990), our translation.

resisted assimilation into a system based on subordination, discrimination, and oppression of everything that differs from the "universal" model forged under patriarchal domination. But the steps toward political equality achieved in capitalist democracies do not dissolve social inequality, nor do the shared burdens of the exploited social class dissolve the inequalities created by oppression.

How can we imagine an equality that is not just the rule of the identical and uniform? How can we imagine a difference that is not constituted as identity and hierarchy? Far from taking a simple position in favor of equality, Marxism posits a materialist and dialectical interpretation of differences: it questions the metaphysical abstraction of formal equality that confines concrete differences within an empty universalism. In others words, under capitalism, equality can only exist formally, by means of abstracting the specific elements of social existence. The capitalist state achieves this fetishized division of politics and economics, and as a result presents us with a divided human being: on the one hand, either a proprietor or a dispossessed person, that is, with differences; but on the other hand, an equal citizen. For Marxism, it is a question of equal attention to diverse needs: this is the only way that difference is not hierarchy and equality is not uniformity, which is something that an "expansion of citizenship" granted by capitalist democracies will never be able to offer. Only a society of free producers can be a society in which equality is not based on a despotic norm that seeks to conceal differences, but rather on equal respect for the differences that determine the particular elements of social existence.

As the bourgeois restoration advanced, neither equality feminism's integration into capitalist democracy nor difference feminism's resistant counter-culture could prevent the further reproduction—and growth at an unconceivable global scale—of violence and oppression for millions of women around the world. Understanding the struggle for women's emancipation as nothing more than a quest for inclusive equality within the system leads to sterile reformism: it presupposes the existence of a system that can be perfected for women, while the heart of this system—which remains deeply hierarchical—is not to be questioned. But difference feminists did not present any alternative: by turning their backs on the state and taking solace in relations between women and the creation of a new women's culture that was counter-hegemonic to the traditional values of patriarchy, they collaborated in the depoliticization of the feminist movement and its separation from social struggles. Saying that we do not want to be integrated into the capitalist and patriarchal state is not enough to do away with it. For this, it is essential to confront and destroy it. Along this path, the search for better, more egalitarian forms of existence is important for millions of women around the world, even within the narrow framework of a society based on exploitation. But it is not enough, as long as our bodies, our desires, our very lives remain subjected to exploitation, discrimination, and submission, which result from property relations and are safeguarded by the state—we cannot escape them by willpower alone.

Difference feminists accuse equality feminists of having been co-opted by patriarchy in exchange for a few perks and minuscule privileges, as a very few were granted access to limited positions of power. But difference feminists also support the capitalist system—by omission—because they decide to not confront it, choosing an autonomous life on the "margins," emphasizing solidarity networks and personal experiences in place of active politics against it. Even though solidarity among some women can seem like an impregnable space where life can be almost as in our dreams, the system remains in place, subjecting millions of fellow women to super-exploitation, forcing them into a life full of indignities, insults, and humiliations, making women—by no coincidence—the poorest of the planet's poor.

INTERSECTION OF DIFFERENCES

Before long, lesbians, Black women, and women from the so-called "Third World" began to question this "celebration" of feminine values because it made the existing differences between women themselves invisible, and these were also established as oppressive hierarchies. They condemned the fact that these supposedly feminine values were nothing more than the universalist—and therefore normative—form of expressing the particular idiosyncrasies of white, Anglo-Saxon, middle-class women from the central countries. Sexual difference thus erupted into different, intersecting differences between women, opening the way for varied identities and a fragmented political subject. Black and lesbian women accused feminism of being an imperialist discourse that claimed to represent all women from an exclusive and particular position: their experiences did not coincide with those of other women, their situations of oppression were not identical, and their links with men were also different; often these links were more important to them than relations with women of other ethnicities, classes, or nationalities. Feminist discourse was criticized for its essentialism: under the unambiguous term "woman," it claimed to have found a unifying experience for all women. The discussion thus shifted from gender difference to differences between women themselves. This opened up an enormous controversy within the feminist movement about different topics: heterosexism, racism, colonialism, political alliances with other social movements, among others.

With this eruption of multiple differences, emphasis was placed on localized studies, to the detriment of comprehensive social theories. Multiculturalism took hold in gender studies and in the feminist movement itself, with its respect for diversity but also dragging along its rejection of any "horizon of universality." The new cultural studies loosened the bonds of social structures and historical and economic processes, so that differences were no longer understood from the point of view of a theory capable of showing that the bearers of "disrespected identities" were victims of an ideology to which they were subjected because of its repressive power. Multiculturalism, escaping from economic reductionism, stripped identities of their roots in specific, necessary relations of social collaboration: it transformed cultural "producers" into cultural "consumers"; it turned identities into merely textual, discursive differences; it exalted the values, experiences, and opinions of subordinate groups, presuming that they were progressive in and of themselves and stemmed directly from the experience of subordination. Studies about everyday life were the academic expression of the concept of "giving a voice" to the oppressed, since this voice, having been silenced by the mechanisms of oppression, subordination, and exclusion from dominant discourses, was, by definition, seen as authentic.

In the course of the feminist movement's second wave, we can observe how difference went from being a social construction to rebel against, to a biological nature to be pondered. Later, with the eruption of differences within the feminist movement itself, difference was re-categorized and made absolute as identity. The critique of the mode of production and the patriarchal system became a critique of the legal system; the questioning of exploitation became a questioning of generalized alienation.[11] This space

---

11. Exploitation is seen as just another form of alienation in the turn-of-the-century capitalist system, and thus the question of social reappropriation is no longer at the center of emancipatory political programs. See Daniel Bensaïd, *Les irréductibles* (Paris: Textuel, 2001).

was now occupied by the demand for an ever-greater acceptance of alienated differences in social marginalization, as if there could be a gradual process of smooth and therefore peaceful evolution toward the liberation of every individual who makes up society. In the words of Slavoj Žižek, "So we are fighting our pc battles for the rights of ethnic minorities, of gays and lesbians, of different life-styles, and so on, while capitalism pursues its triumphant march."[12]

The phenomenon of the eruption of differences within feminism led to the reappearance of the concept of social class, but now considered to be one variable among many (sex, race, etc.) that define identity. By placing differences of gender, sexual orientation, ethnicity, and so on, on the same level as class differences, multiculturalism undertakes the task—according to the author just cited—of making the inalterable presence of capitalism invisible. Situating class differences on an equal plane with others is equivalent to hiding the key role the economy plays in structuring society; that is, it blurs capitalism's primordial utilization of differences to maintain the *status quo* of systematic domination.

> The very domain of the multitude of particular struggles with their continuously shifting displacements and condensations is sustained by the "repression" of the key role of economic struggle—the leftist politics of the "chains of equivalences" among the plurality of struggles is strictly correlative to the silent abandonment of the analysis of capitalism as a global economic system and to the acceptance of capitalist economic relations as the unquestionable framework.[13]

In Marxist thought, class cannot simply be added to other multiple and diverse identities, as it forms the nucleus around which all other identities are articulated and acquire their concrete definition. The identities that the system considers subordinate (woman, Black, homosexual, etc.) only acquire their concrete social significance in relation to their connection with a social class, where class is the axis that determines how each subject experiences their own identity-based subordination. The articulation of the diverse identities of gender, sexuality, ethnicity, and so on is based on

---

12. Slavoj Žižek, "Multiculturalism, or, the Cultural Logic of Multinational Capitalism," *New Left Review* 1(225) (September–October 1997).
13. Ibid.

the close connection between exploitation and oppression under the rule of capital. It is true that each subject is a specific combination of multiple affiliations to diverse places of identity; but only a liberal reading could lead us to the interpretation that existing society is the result of a sum of individuals with different identities. The refusal to understand the totality of the capitalist system as a structure necessarily implies the impossibility of profoundly questioning it—and therefore of overthrowing it.[14] As Marxists, we do not question the notion of difference, but rather its supposedly biological or absolute nature—as well as the relativism with which different identities are approached and treated as equally respectable. As the English Marxist Terry Eagleton points out, no one has a certain skin pigmentation because someone else has another, and no one has one sex because there are others who possess a different one, but there are in fact millions of people who find themselves in the "position" of wage earners because there are a few families in the world who concentrate the means of production in their hands. Both categories (bourgeois/proletarian or exploiter/exploited) are related to each other in such a way that only the abolition of this specific relationship (capital/labor) can lead to the abolition of the subordinate "identity," which does not apply to other identities.[15] In a society without oppression of any kind, we can imagine women in the same hierarchical position as men, just like Black and white or heterosexual and homosexual. But there will still be women and men, different skin colors, and diverse sexual orientations, coexisting in harmony. In other words, the elimination of one identity or the other is not necessary for the elimination of oppression (this is precisely the point!). There is no possibility, however, of thinking in similar terms about equal "recognition" for bourgeois and proletarians. These identity categories are mutually dependent and mutually exclusive. Liberating humanity from wage slavery inevitably means fighting the system at its roots and revolution-

---

14. If marriage, for example, is an institution that subordinates women to men through the sexual contract, it is also true that a woman's marriage to a man from the class that owns the means of production exempts her from the possibility of being exploited. In contrast, those women who have to sell their labor power bear double chains, since the capitalist system subjugates them as women and as workers. In the latter case, oppression and exploitation are dramatically intertwined; in the former, on the contrary, the relationship of oppression relieves that of exploitation.

15. As Eagleton explains: "nobody has one sort of skin pigmentation because someone else has another, or is male because someone else is female, in the sense that some people are only landless labourers because others are gentlemen farmers." See Terry Eagleton, *The Illusions of Postmodernism* (Oxford: Blackwell Publishers, 1996).

izing it. Striving for "recognition" for the exploited class means abolishing private property, and therefore the exploiting class itself.

Only a social revolution that questions this relationship can create the conditions for the abolition of all hierarchies and valuations that are associated with differences. This will allow people to pursue their maximum potential, freed from the metaphysical prisons of bourgeois law and the dark dungeons of rotting relations of exploitation, which are imposed on the majority of humanity by a parasitic minority.

8
Postmodernity, Postmarxism, Postfeminism

Is there another normative point of departure for feminist theory that does not require the reconstruction or rendering visible of a female subject who fails to represent, much less emancipate, the array of embodied beings culturally positioned as women?

—Judith Butler

THE 1990S: NGO-IZATION AND GENDER TECHNOCRACY

The 1990s began with the defeat of Iraq in the first Gulf War (August 1990–February 1991) at the hands of an enormous military coalition of imperialist powers, which in turn allowed for an intensification of the attacks on the rest of the semi-colonial world in order to force the opening of their economies for international monopolies. In the face of this imperialist plunder, international financial institutions recognized the unavoidable: the attacks would likely provoke a response from those who were set to lose everything. "Governance" was the name that technocrats found for the looming problem; it could be translated as the entirety of the conditions necessary to maintain the process of "reforms" and avoid an eruption of mass movements. (This also included the necessity to establish "fruitful" relationships with social movements and their organizations for sustainable development.) Thus, as state services were being privatized and unemployment and precarious work were growing, the World Bank and other international financial institutions began to consider reforms of their funding objectives and their relationships with social organizations. When most of the "neoliberal" program had already been implemented, the World Bank prioritized financing social programs under the slogans of participation and transparency, appropriating critical discourses that were originally directed against them. Non-governmental organizations (NGOs) were the favored agents of these targeted aid projects.[1] According to information from the OECD, in 1970, NGOs in Latin America received $914 million; in 1980, the figure rose to more than $2.3 billion; and in 1992, it reached $5.2 billion. In other words, in 20 years, the money destined to NGO's increased by more than 500 percent. These numbers would need to be combined with those of subsidies paid by the governments of the "North," which went from $270 million in the mid-1970s to $2.5 billion by the early 1990s. In summary, OECD statistics inform us of state and private contributions to NGOs of around $10 billion, which represents one-quarter of global bilateral aid.[2]

Many feminists with a certain prestige in the movement, with specific knowledge and a political trajectory in the struggle for women's rights, became part of this technocracy that joined the international organizations, the financial institutions, the World Bank, and the thousands of NGOs, which also became platforms for launching personal careers. Others remained on the sidelines of funding and criticized these trends harshly, but their voices remained a minority and their struggle—although exemplary—only echoed in the void that surrounded them. The autonomous feminists of ATEM[3] in Argentina condemned the process of NGO-ization that permeated the movement with the following words:

> Most of these NGOs, made up of technocrats and experts, work with women from the "popular sectors," from the poor neighborhoods. They present themselves as mediators between financial institutions and women's movements, and they formulate programs for them, offering services that range from all kinds of workshops and classes to food distribution, the organization of soup kitchens, family planning (birth control), etc. This relationship, which involves differences in class, power, and access to resource management, generates hierarchical relationships and

---

[1]. The World Bank and the rest of the financial institutions played a very important political and ideological role in this period in relation to social control. Formerly leftist intellectuals transformed themselves into progressive technocrats who assumed the responsibility of collaborating in these projects of governance, sustainable development, and so on. The "postmarxists" running NGOs did not collaborate in reducing the economic impact of these projects in a substantial way, but they did help enormously in diverting the population away from the struggle for their rights.

[2]. These figures are from 1992.

[3]. ATEM: *Asociación de Trabajo y Estudio de la Mujer* (*Association for the Work and Study of Women*), founded in 1982 in Buenos Aires.

tensions between the women from the NGOs and those from the movements they work with, as well as competition among the technocrats for funding.[4]

As many autonomous feminists pointed out, the NGOs ended up being confused with the movement itself, and their financed projects and their paid positions were confused with "actions," as if they were the same as the mobilizations and struggles that the movements carry out for their own demands and grievances. In summary, neoliberal policies fragmented and privatized the feminist movement as well. As individualism reigned supreme, hand in hand with economic policies that drove millions into unemployment, fragmenting and delocalizing the working class, feminism was moving further and further away from a project of collective emancipation, withdrawing to an increasingly solipsistic discourse that was limited to rousing an elite that demanded its right to be recognized in its diversity, tolerated, and integrated into consumer culture. As we argued previously, the dominant paradigm of self-styled postfeminism called for the utopia of individual liberation based on the deconstruction of hegemonic discourses and confrontation with gendered representations of heteronormativity, essentially linked to the reappropriation of desire and the transformation of one's own body.

PERFORMATIVITY, PARODY, AND RADICAL DEMOCRACY

Capital's counter-offensive against the masses in the 1990s was accompanied by the growing influence of post-structuralist or postmodernist tendencies. In feminism, postfeminism entered the scene, with Judith Butler as one of its most lucid and controversial representatives.[5] Her aim is to criticize feminism's heterosexual assumptions from a post-structuralist perspective, that is, by deconstructing the categories of sex, gender, desire, and so on. She asks how non-normative sexual practices call the stability of gender as an analytical category into question. According to Butler, minorities would be

---

[4]. Marta Fontenla and Magui Bellotti, "ONGs, financiamiento y feminismo," *Hojas de Warmi* (Barcelona), 10 (1999), our translation.
[5]. Judith Butler is a Professor for Comparative Literature and Critical Theory at the University of California, Berkeley. The book that generated the most debate was *Gender Trouble*, first published in English in 1990 and translated into Spanish almost a decade later.

respected if the cultural value structures underlying the normative dichotomy of homosexual–heterosexual were transformed. The resolution of this binary—in which homosexuality is the devalued correlate of the construction of heterosexuality—would therefore lie in the negative practice of deconstruction, which means unmasking the foundational and exclusionary repression that is the basis of all identity. For this reason, she will present the general outline of her *Theory of Gender Performativity* as a conclusion, postulating that only practices of parody can disrupt the categories of body, sex, gender, and sexuality.

Butler's theory is rooted in contemporary philosophical irrationalism (starting with Nietzsche and Heidegger as critics of the metaphysics of substance, and continued by Derrida with deconstructionist post-structuralism) and incorporates different aspects of the linguistic turn fostered by Wittgenstein and Austin. In her work, she sketches a genealogical critique of identity categories, inspired by Foucault, investigating the political interests in designating them as origin and cause, while she considers them the effect of institutions, practices, and discourses. Her goal is to respond to the following question: "I asked, what configuration of power constructs the subject and the Other, that binary relation between 'men' and 'women,' and the internal stability of those terms?"[6] Her search for a strategy of deconstructing the binary principle of sexual intelligibility attempts to respond to the need for multiple axes in the struggle against oppression.

While multiculturalism advocated a positive conception of identity differences in order to promote their inclusion, Butler's new conceptualization defines identities as repressive and exclusionary discursive constructions. For Butler, the category "woman," as a representation of determined values and characteristics, is normative and therefore exclusionary. She declares that every identity is absolutely dispensable. In her article "Gender Trouble, Feminist Theory, and Psychoanalytic Discourse," she argues: "Is there another normative point of departure for feminist theory that does not require the reconstruction or rendering visible of a female subject who fails to represent, much less emancipate, the array of embodied beings culturally positioned as women?"[7] The question is rhetorical because Butler has

---

6. Judith Butler, *Gender Trouble: Feminism and the Subversion of Identity* (New York, Routledge, 1990).

7. Judith Butler, "Gender Trouble, Feminist Theory, and Psychoanalytic Discourse," in Linda J. Nicholson (Ed.), *Feminism/Postmodernism* (New York: Routledge, 1990).

already taken a position on the matter. Her answer is that the critique of the subject—as formulated by post-structuralism—should not be limited to the rehabilitation of its multiple, interrelated identities, in the sense of the pluralist, coalitional subject that multiculturalism promotes: identity is a fiction. The gendered has no ontological status beyond the acts that constitute it. Social discourses about the surface of the body create a false belief in an identity, in an inner essence, *a posteriori*. This constant repetition ultimately creates the appearance of substance, converting gender into an apparently natural expression of the body. This repetition institutionalizes gender, leaving it rigid. For Butler, "acts and gestures articulate and enacted desires create the illusion of an interior and organizing gender core, an illusion discursively maintained for the purposes of the regulation of sexuality within the obligatory frame of reproductive heterosexuality."[8] Social existence is understood as the symbolic order that is reproduced in constantly repeated, ritualized gestures, through which the subjects assume their place in this order. This leaves open the possibility of modifying the symbolic contours of existence through the performance of acts of parodic displacement. It is clear that when she speaks of "parody," Butler does not assume the existence of an original to be imitated. On the contrary, parody is an expression of the fact that this original does not exist—it is the parody of the notion of an original identity. The figures of the drag queen, the transvestite, of transsexuality and transgenderism, and so on, are imitations of a gender identity that never existed. The very displacement of these meanings, according to Butler, creates openings for the resignification and recontextualization of gender identities.[9] In the words of the feminist theorist Rosi Braidotti: "Attacking the normative fiction of heterosexual coherence, Butler calls for feminists to produce a whole array of new, noncoherence genders."[10]

---

8. Butler, *Gender Trouble*.
9. In an interview with Regina Michalik in the feminist magazine *Lola Press*, the American philosopher said:

> My understanding of queer is a term that desires that you don't have to present an identity card before entering a meeting. Heterosexuals can join the queer movement. Bisexuals can join the queer movement. Queer is not being lesbian. Queer is not being gay. It is an argument against lesbian specificity: that if I am a lesbian I have to desire in a certain way. Or if I am a gay I have to desire in a certain way. Queer is an argument against certain normativity, what a proper lesbian or gay identity is.

10. Rosi Braidotti, *Nomadic Subjects: Embodiment and Sexual Difference in Contemporary Feminist Theory* (New York: Columbia University Press, 1994).

In summary, for postfeminism, all identity is normative and exclusionary, because the same act that establishes the limits of identity—enunciating what it defines—also establishes what is excluded. Gender does not constitute an essence; it is not "natural," nor can it have pretensions to be a universalizing classification. Behaviors have a constitutive power over our bodies; gender is an unstable "position," acts of speech, a self-produced performance, a performative statement. Failure to comply with the cultural "script" imposed on us by language would deprive us of the status of subject, exclude us from hegemonic conventions instituted by power, dehumanize us, and transform us into "the abject." Normative heterosexuality can therefore be challenged through various forms of parody of gender and sexuality. "Imitations" of the feminine and masculine can transgress gender norms and stereotypes in their instability and failure, becoming subversive political practices. Resignifying normative discourse through parody is a form of politics that can undermine hegemony and open up new horizons of meanings. In the words of Judith Butler,

> parodic proliferation deprives hegemonic culture and its critics of the claim to naturalized or essentialist gender identities. Although the gender meanings taken up in these parodic styles are clearly part of hegemonic, misogynist culture, they are nevertheless denaturalized and mobilized through their parodic recontextualization. As imitations which effectively displace the meaning of the original, they imitate the myth of originality itself.[11]

Butler's deconstructionist anti-essentialism, in its zeal to abolish identities, places an equal sign between all of them, without asking which are rooted in the maintenance of the *status quo* of a determined system of domination and which are in opposition to existing social relations of oppression. This is because Butler, following Foucault, argues that subjects are constituted through exclusion; in other words, politics of subjectification necessarily include practices of exclusion. Whenever a subject is constituted, the abject will be constituted as the normative exclusion that is necessary for the existence of the former. And all resistance to power will always, inevitably be a new discourse of power, in the full Foucauldian sense. In this

---

11. Butler, *Gender Trouble*.

new postmodern theory, women's liberation could be better interpreted as the liberation from one's own identity, which is genuine oppression. If we women must emancipate ourselves from anything, then for Butler, it is this burdensome, repressive, and exclusionary ontological definition of the identity of "woman."[12]

Judith Butler's radical conclusions and her strange proposal for political subversion caused profound controversies in the feminist movement and in other areas. For her, the result of parodic practices is what she calls "subversive laughter." The author overestimates the subversive potential of performance in relation to the constitution of gendered subjects or gender identities to the extent that she does not propose the complete restructuring of this hegemonic symbolic order, which has its basis in a historically determined social order of exclusions, appropriations, and material oppressions. This is where Butlerian thought intersects with the politics of pluralist democracy, whose objective, according to Chantal Mouffe, is not "to eliminate power" but "to constitute forms of power more compatible with democratic values."[13] Ambiguity, non-acceptance of fixed identities, and "nomadism" are what would supposedly compel power to create new and mobile exclusionary definitions, thus destabilizing it. This model of "radical democracy" therefore does not consist in the total inclusion of differences, which would be impossible. Even though there will always be discriminated identities and groups, the political goal is to not allow this discrimination to become structurally fixed or a discursive space of discrimination to be set *a priori*. The highest ideal to which democratic society can aspire is that no social actor can claim the right to represent the whole; on the contrary, everyone should be willing to accept the particular and limited character of their own demands. Politics would then consist in the precarity and permanent displacement of identities, questioning today's restricted democratic inclusion and creating a radical and pluralist regime. But in order to achieve

---

12. For Butler, the political signifier is politically effective precisely because of its inability to describe or represent that which it names in a complete way. Following the work of the post-Marxists Ernesto Laclau and Chantal Mouffe, she argues that, to the extent that such signifiers are always incomplete in themselves, they can and must be perpetually rearticulated among themselves, allowing for the production of new subjective positions and new signifiers. Herein lies the political and theoretical potential of "radical democracy." When the category of "women" is left open, without fixed or determined reference points, the American philosopher sees the possibility for feminism to permanently transform and resignify this category.

13. Chantal Mouffe, *The Democratic Paradox* (London: Verso, 2000).

this radical and pluralist democracy to which Butler adheres, it is first necessary to renounce any pretension of radically eliminating power.

CONSUMERISM, INDIVIDUALISM, AND SKEPTICISM

For Judith Butler, hegemony consists "in the possibilities for expanding the democratic possibilities for the key terms of liberalism, rendering them more inclusive, more dynamic and more concrete."[14] The infinite semiosis that Butler postulates as the ideal to be achieved with radical and plural democracy already exists. It is none other than the fetishized image presented by civil society: the market, that form with which eminently human practice manifests itself; a free market where free men exchange goods in uninterrupted (infinite?) circulation. Its appearance hinders the comprehension of the mechanisms of surplus value extraction.[15] Butler's political considerations operate within the never-mentioned framework of the capitalist system, where exploitation is unspeakable and production is merely symbolic. This capitalism whose name cannot be spoken is the unquestionable limit of Butler's political imagination, the "not said" that is therefore impossible to deconstruct. It is a system, moreover, where any attempt at opposition will be limited to a mere rearticulation of the horizon of what is included—which, in the same act, will be constrained to serve as a new regulatory discourse.

We share the struggle against the hegemonic universalist conception of the abstract human, and against the absolute values and the metaphysics of the citizen. But this is only one aspect. In the capitalist system, every uniqueness of use values is subsumed into the universal abstraction of exchange values; every individuality of subjects—whether they be exploited or, on the

---

14. Judith Butler, Ernesto Laclau, and Slavoj Žižek, *Contingency, Hegemony, Universality: Contemporary Dialogues on the Left* (London: Verso, 2000).

15. The free and infinite circulation of goods is the reverse side of exploitation. A democracy of free, fraternal, and equal citizens must necessarily include, as a counterpart of its implementation, the existence of a class that has historically expropriated humanity from the means of production. The labor contract between free and equal men conceals exploitation, and at the same time is the necessary form that the capitalist mode of production acquires in "modern" bourgeois states. But judges and policemen cancel the infinite semiosis of civil equality as soon as private property and the freedom of the labor contract are threatened by the action of the subaltern classes. The apparently voluntary nature of the contract conceals the violence of the original expropriation; democracy, meanwhile, with its seemingly free election of representatives, also masks domination as voluntary acceptance.

contrary, exploiters—is subsumed into the formality of equality before the law in the figure of the free citizen. The arbitrariness of universalization on the legal or political plane is only the reverse side of a society fragmented into classes. Questioning the former without condemning the latter means upholding—by omission—the material basis of class society, anchored in the economic structures of the social relations of production. This is why Terry Eagleton defined postmodernism as "politically oppositional but economically complicit."[16] As different authors point out, postmodern cultural criticism, in its attempt to not fall into essentialism, makes the existence of the capitalist system invisible.

While difference feminism ultimately succumbed to biological essentialism, these postfeminist theories had the merit of rejecting the idea that difference be transformed into fixed, immobile identities, opening a powerful path in culture and the construction of subjectivity. Politically, however, postfeminist theory is absolutely useless for building up a movement of struggle for the emancipation of all those oppressed by compulsory heteronormativity. Postmodern theories, which aim for differences to dissolve as identity categories (or for us to have no need of them), refer to the excluded. Yet because they do not regard the capitalist relations of production that form the basis of these exclusions, they end up in a struggle for "inclusion" (made possible by radical and plural democracy) that, instead of subverting capitalism, eventually clears the way for new, market-based "tolerance" for diversity. A radical questioning of the stability of sexual identities and heteronormativity loses its subversive potential if it does not point out the inextricable relationship between the capitalist mode of production and the multiple fragmentations that contribute to domination. Because what happens instead is that capital integrates, reabsorbs, includes, and neutralizes differences, commodifying them as objects of desire for new, diverse consumers. Rather than subverting established conventions, "nomadism" becomes the basis of a permanent insatiability that adequately feeds back into the consumerism of the included. Performance and permanent displacement of identity positions, instead of becoming tools to disrupt hegemonic discourse, create consumers for new market niches; diversity becomes a constellation of fetishized uniqueness.

---

16. Terry Eagleton, *The Illusions of Postmodernism* (Oxford: Blackwell Publishers, 1996).

Postmodern theories that uphold an abstract political model of radical/liberal democracy, without contemplating class rule, also do not consider the "cultural" impossibility of conquering hegemony among the oppressed in issues that are so deeply ingrained in the masses' consciousness, such as gender domination/subordination. Ultimately, the most severe limit of postfeminism is its notable lack of mass appeal. Proclaiming the elimination of binary identities in a world where such differences are the source of brutal wrongs and injustices ends up looking more like a self-satisfying discourse for a small, enlightened, progressive minority than a critique from a powerful movement fighting for radical transformation.

By Way of Conclusion

I see that women are capable. We can do more than wash and iron and cook at home for the kids. I believe this is real. I am feeling it now, and I am living it. I have discovered a side of myself that had been asleep, and now that it is awake, I can't even think of stopping.[1]

—Celia Martínez

The economic, social, and political crisis that is sweeping the world is the result of capitalism's inability to survive, except at the cost of greater suffering for the masses, and degradation and political erosion of the democratic regimes. As we pointed out in the Introduction, the period of bourgeois restoration, which led to this new capitalist crisis, offers up a contradictory scenario: co-optation and integration of broad sectors of the middle classes and fringes of the working class, alongside the exclusion—including the most extreme marginalization—of the broad masses; an unprecedented fragmentation of the working class but, at the same time, the imposition of wage slavery for millions of human beings driven into the urban centers, and the incorporation of entire countries into the world market.

But while the world situation drives women and the most oppressed sectors to develop their subversive potential—as demonstrated in each and every historical moment of great social, economic, and political crises and cataclysms—feminism finds itself separated from the masses, and its majority is far removed from the perspective of a collective emancipatory project. If feminism does not aspire to transform the reality of millions of women who face hunger, exploitation, violence, abuse, and humiliations on a daily basis, often without understanding the reasons for this, then it will remain limited to academic elaborations, political lobbying, and providing "cadres" for government bodies and international organizations.

Recovering feminism's perspective of insubordination requires us—given the current configuration of the highly feminized world working class—to

---

1. Interview with Celia Martínez, worker at the Brukman factory in Buenos Aires, occupied by its workers and set in motion on December 18, 2001.

recognize the need to fight capitalism, which is dragging us toward barbarism. The ruling class has declared war on us, and a program for women's liberation is vital in order to awaken the will to fight among the broadest masses, who are driven into a miserable life and exploited by big capital which has patriarchal oppression inscribed on its forehead. At the same time, while the working class has the (potential) power to bring the gears of the capitalist economy to a halt, this strategic position is not enough to revolutionize the prevailing order, unless it attempts to forge and lead an alliance with other classes and sectors that are ruined by capital, condemned to discrimination and marginalization, and made "the abject" by a dominant culture that denies them recognition.[2] This is why—while we accompany all struggles to wrest better living conditions from the capitalists, for millions of people subjected to the most unimaginable indignities—our goal remains the conquest of a society without a state and without social classes; a society liberated from the chains of exploitation and all forms of oppression that make human beings "wolves" to their fellows.

We know that communism does not arise from the mere desire for it, even if that desire is shared by a few thousand or a few million exploited people. It is not enough to yearn for another order—we need to overthrow the existing one. Hence the need for any partial victory, won within the narrow confines of degraded democracies, to be placed in the context of this ultimate strategy. This is the only realistic antidote to the postfeminist utopia of "radical democracy" and the dystopia of bureaucratic totalitarianism, which betrayed the revolution and transformed it into its antithesis.

---

2. Faced with this situation, most currents of the Left have adapted to the *status quo* of the last few decades of bourgeois restoration. Skeptical about the possibility of reversing the defeats imposed by the imperialist counter-offensive, they adopted a strategy of expanding rights within bourgeois democracy. If the ruling classes were at times forced to incorporate these demands in order to deactivate radicalization and co-opt and integrate broad sectors into the regime, these left-wing currents, instead of seeing these partial victories as a starting point for further struggles, proclaimed them to be the ultimate horizon. They exchanged their anti-capitalist program for an anti-neoliberal one, with a minimum, defensive goal of limiting the most perfidious effects of bourgeois restoration. At the opposite pole, other currents of the Left dismissed the need for a program and politics for women's liberation based on the democratic rights that had already be won, and this was another form of adaptation: by omission, the "issues" of oppression were left to the multi-class social movements, while trade unionism and sectoral demands became entrenched in the workers' movement. In the last analysis, this meant abandoning the strategy of proletarian hegemony by way of sectarian abstentionism.

Our daily struggle has this final goal: the emancipation of women in order to fight for social revolution on an equal footing with the rest of the oppressed and exploited; social revolution to open the path toward the definitive liberation of women and all of humanity from the chains that bind us today.

Appendix

Bread and Roses: International Manifesto (June 19, 2020)

Women on the Front Lines of the Health Crisis and the Fight Against Patriarchal and Racist Capitalism!

One hundred days of the Covid-19 Pandemic: International Manifesto of the Feminist, Socialist, and Revolutionary Group *Pan y Rosas* (Bread and Roses)

One hundred days ago, on March 11, 2020, the World Health Organization (WHO) recognized that Covid-19 had become a global pandemic. Since then, the coronavirus—which had jumped from China and other Asian countries to Europe—has spread to every continent, leaving half a million people dead and several million infected. Today, 100 days after the pandemic's start, the number of deaths in Europe has been surpassed by those in Latin America, where the curve of infections and deaths is only approaching its peak. In addition, the closures of factories, shops, and schools, as well as travel and entertainment restrictions, have an immediate impact on the lives of millions of working people and their families. In just three months, according to estimates, nearly 300 million jobs were lost, and 60 million people fell below the extreme poverty line, adding to the 700 million who were already surviving on less than $2 a day before the pandemic.

Meanwhile, during the pandemic, the capitalist states have strengthened their repressive powers, with increased surveillance and social control, and have also increased repression against the working class and oppressed sectors, particularly the Black community. The murder of George Floyd in Minneapolis comes against this backdrop of growing violence against Black people by police and white supremacist groups supported by Donald Trump, as well as the murder of Breonna Taylor, an EMT killed by police in May while sleeping in her Kentucky home. Trump's racism, xenophobia, sexism, and transphobia have already provoked massive mobilizations that now defy "curfews" and face repression ordered by governors and mayors, both Republicans and Democrats. The cry of "Black Lives Matter!" and, during Pride Month, "Black Trans Lives Matter!" have ignited anger and solidarity that have spread like wildfire from Brazil to Germany, from Britain to Argentina. In France, at the call of Assa Traoré—sister of Adama, who was killed inside a police station in 2016—thousands mobilized against racism and police crimes. In Brazil, women have denounced the killing of their children inside their homes, demanding justice for Miguel and João Pedro.

The racist hatred emanating from the Trump administration is an extreme example of the deep and structural segregation of the Black population in the United States. This is also evident in the pandemic, where victims are disproportionately Black and poor. In Chicago, where the Black population represents only one-third of the city total, they account for 73 percent of coronavirus deaths. In Milwaukee, Black people make up 26 percent of the population but account for 81 percent of the dead. Likewise in the state of Michigan, where people of African descent make up 14 percent of the population but account for 40 percent of Covid deaths. This situation is not just a phenomenon in states governed by the Republican Party; it is the same where Democrats are in power.

It is people of African descent, along with the Latinx and immigrant communities, who are putting their lives at risk in essential service work, in precarious jobs without health protections. And they are a significant part of the 40 million workers who became unemployed overnight during this pandemic. If the anti-racist rebellion against police violence in the United States has found an echo worldwide, it is because Black people, like the immigrant population, have become special victims of the coronavirus worldwide—with a risk of death closely linked to precariousness and conditions of super-exploitation, aggravated by racism. Black women in Brazil—which has the largest Black population outside the countries of Africa—are paid up to 60 percent less than white men. They are the ones who lose their children to one of the world's most murderous police forces. It is Black women who hold the worst, most precarious jobs, and who suffer the worst consequences of clandestine abortions.

For women, there have been other specific consequences of the pandemic: the closure of schools, childcare, and recreation centers, as well as the conditions of quarantine itself, increase the burden of care-related tasks women take on at home. This has been even worse for women who are the sole support for their families, for those forced to continue working, for those who lost their jobs, and for women from the poorest sectors of society. In addition, an estimated 18 million women who had access to contraception may have lost that access during the pandemic, as contraceptives became scarce in many countries and impossible to acquire because of the restrictions. Meanwhile, budget cuts in healthcare systems before the pandemic limited their capacities, with many consequences. These include restricted access to safe abortion services: one estimate states that a reduction of only 10 percent in such access in the most impoverished countries will have produced 3 million clandestine abortions, leading to around 28,000 women dying and another 15 million having to endure unwanted pregnancies. Further, during government-imposed quarantines around the world, reports of gender-based violence increased by 30 percent.

Today, 100 days after the declaration of a global pandemic, health workers—more than 70 percent of whom are women—continue to struggle with overcrowding in intensive care units in some countries, and in other places they are already beginning to sound the alarm about the lack of resources to deal with the aftermath of anxiety, fear, and stress from pandemic-related job insecurity, loss of pay, and lack of resources for entire families. They are also denouncing governments for their lack of investment and preparation for possible further waves of the virus, and demanding greater resources for public health.

A few days before the WHO declared the global pandemic, millions of us had mobilized in the streets of hundreds of cities around the world, as we have done every March 8 in recent years, to commemorate International Women's Day and to fight for our rights, against sexist violence and femicide, for the legalization of abortion, against the precarization of labor, and so on. Now the signers of this manifesto address ourselves to all those whom the capitalists put on the front lines of super-exploitation and precarity, who work on the front lines of family social reproduction without pay, as well as those who work on the front lines of the different services and industries that are essential to making social life possible. We address ourselves to all those who are paid less than our male colleagues and do not have access to the same labor rights but nevertheless are on the front lines producing more and more profits for a handful of capitalists; to those of us who occupy the front lines in the fight against misery and hunger, surviving at the expense of our own work under the worst conditions. Today, we address all those women, organized in unions and without the right to organize, Black women, immigrant women, racialized women, indigenous women, peasants, mothers of the tortured, imprisoned, disappeared, and murdered by the violence of the state's repressive apparatus, women defenders of the land, young students, and lesbian and transgender activists.

We want to organize ourselves on the front lines of the economic, social, and political struggle against the bosses, against the governments and the parties that represent their interests, against the trade union bureaucracies that divide us and limit our strength. Again, as so often in history, we are willing to put ourselves on the front lines of the class struggle, to take heaven by storm.

1. THE CORONAVIRUS PANDEMIC IS NOT "NATURAL": IT HAS DEEP ROOTS AND SERIOUS ECONOMIC AND SOCIAL CONSEQUENCES

The origin of this pandemic lies in the abrupt rupture of ecological equilibrium caused by the unbridled advance of agribusiness. Its rapid spread, all over the planet, went hand in hand with the global value chains that, in recent decades, have tremendously expanded the frontiers of capital in its search for greater profitability. But the pandemic also broke out particularly brutally in countries whose healthcare systems have been depleted by decades of austerity plans, budget adjustments, and lay-offs—at the same time that the pharmaceutical industry has focused its investments in research and development on "profitable" diseases, while governments underfunded or altogether ignored research programs on epidemics.

Nor can it be said that the tens of thousands of deaths caused by Covid-19 are the inevitable consequence of the spread of the virus. Governments were slow to respond to the warnings and slow to shut down nonessential activities because they wanted to give the greatest protection to capitalist profits. Then they imposed drastic global quarantines, without providing for mass testing or an expansion of hospital capacity in time. And then they rushed to send us back to work, without clear information or adequate prevention and hygiene measures, for the same reason. Most countries avoided taking over the private healthcare system and other fundamental measures so as not to negatively affect capitalist interests.

As we approach 500,000 deaths, we also declare that it is not "natural" that in some US cities in which people of African descent make up 30 percent of the population, Black people make up 70 percent of coronavirus deaths. The same is true of the Latinx communities in the United States, and is repeated in the poor neighborhoods of all the large imperialist metropolises, where mostly immigrant families live. In the dependent countries, the situation is far worse. The infection and mortality rates of different sectors of the population show that confronting the pandemic when one has adequate housing, running water, a sewage system, a balanced diet, and access to prevention and hygiene products is not the same as doing so with none of that. The conclusion is that while anyone can contract the coronavirus, the exposure of people to the disease and the distribution of resources to deal with it is deeply uneven, affecting the exploited classes and the oppressed especially severely. Those who are most exposed to contagion and death are precarious workers, Black and indigenous people, peasants, immigrants, the poor in overcrowded and marginalized urban neighborhoods, and the homeless.

The virus has only accelerated, strengthened, and further exposed the brutal contradictions of the capitalist system, which is in its historic decline. While debates continue about how the coronavirus originated and about the true number of deaths resulting from the disastrous management of the pandemic, one thing is clear to millions worldwide: in capitalism, profit—profit for the few—comes before our lives.

2. THE CORONAVIRUS IS NOT RESPONSIBLE FOR THE CAPITALIST CRISIS THEY WANT US TO SHOULDER

The capitalists and their governments are taking advantage of the coronavirus pandemic to increase lay-offs, company closures, and furloughs with wage cuts, which will be followed by greater precariousness and worsening working conditions. The figures are as brutal and scandalous as the contagion the capitalists could not prevent: in the United States, nearly 40 million people have applied for unemployment, and there were historic drops in production in China and almost all of Europe. Throughout the world, bailouts have primarily benefitted the big capitalists, with the imperialist countries giving some insufficient financial aid to the people, but only to avoid further economic paralysis and, above all, to prevent social uprisings.

In the dependent countries, priority has been given to paying the foreign debt and rescuing businesses, with pitiable aid for the millions of working and poor families facing catastrophe.

But the coronavirus is not to blame for this crisis, which is rooted in the trends that developed after the previous economic crisis in 2008: low investment and productivity growth, high government and corporate debt, and stock market bubbles, which already heralded the possibility of a recession before the pandemic. The responses that governments are testing have only exacerbated the situation, especially since many sectors of the economy remain shut down, there will likely be new outbreaks of the virus, and a vaccine thus far remains elusive.

The capitalists will seek to save themselves with new attacks on the working class and poor masses even greater than those we saw during these first 100 days: they bring only misery and hunger to billions, wage cuts and worsening working conditions, more flexible working hours, and higher rates of unemployment. Therefore, we will have to fight for every demand—for jobs, wages, and working conditions, for quality universal health care, and against environmental destruction. Make the capitalists pay for the crisis!

3. THE CAPITALIST SYSTEM CANNOT FUNCTION WITHOUT WOMEN WORKERS AND WITHOUT THE BENEFITS IT GETS FROM WOMEN'S UNPAID LABOR

During the long decades of neoliberalism around the globe, the working class was dislocated, fragmented, and attacked. The pandemic, though, has revealed that it is workers—both formal and informal—who truly make the world function and ensure the survival of millions. This is true of workers on the front lines of the healthcare system, as well as agricultural workers, sanitation workers, and textile workers; workers in logistics, transport workers on land, sea, rivers, and in the air; home delivery workers, telecommunications workers, workers in the energy sector, at water treatment plants, and so many others.

With our protests and strikes demanding the shutdown of factories and businesses in nonessential sectors during the pandemic, we also demonstrated capitalism's enormous dependence on human labor. The fact is that despite great advances in robotics and artificial intelligence, it is workers who generate the profits that go into the capitalists' pockets.

Meanwhile, life continues to be reproduced in the home, thanks primarily to the women who, for the most part, do the work involved in the social reproduction of the workforce without payment. All that unpaid work is on top of what we already have to do at our paid jobs, where we represent a majority or at least a very large component of the front lines, as healthcare personnel, eldercare and childcare workers, in cleaning, in the production and sale of food and other basic goods, and in paid domestic work in the homes of the wealthy. And we go beyond that—because women now represent 40 percent of salaried workers in general, worldwide, for the first time in history!

In short, the pandemic has shown that both the economy and the reproductive work that sustains the capitalist system and the lives of millions every day depend on the work of the class that makes up the majority of society. Not only has it been demonstrated that our work is essential for social reproduction—something that no one could deny—but also that we occupy strategic positions for the reproduction of capital. And by occupying these "vulnerable points" in global supply chains, we and our co-workers collectively constitute a social force that can have an impact on the functioning of capitalism.

4. LET'S ORGANIZE AND EXPAND OUR FRONT LINE IN THE WORKING-CLASS STRUGGLE!

Working and poor women—as so often in history—are also on the front lines of the struggle against those who want to take away our bread and our future. That is why the scribes of the bourgeoisie are already warning their leaders and bosses about the potential for insurrections and revolutions that could occur when the pandemic is over and the austerity plans and cuts being made by capitalist governments load the costs of the crisis onto our shoulders with even greater brutality.

The Italian nurses were among the first to call all workers out for a general strike in March, which they could not do themselves because of their lifesaving work. Today, in Spain, healthcare workers are demanding a return of the portion of their salaries that was stolen with the austerity measures that followed the 2008 economic crisis, and demanding the defense of public health care. In the United States, healthcare workers have had to face police repression and arrests as they have joined the "Justice for George Floyd!" mobilizations as street medics. In all countries, the anger of healthcare workers, as well as teachers, caregivers, and social workers, continues to mount against the governments responsible for disaster and for helping the rich, whose incomes and property are the first things to be "rescued."

Thousands of workers at fast-food companies, in supermarkets, and in warehouses, sweatshops, and nonessential factories have, along with their colleagues, rebelled against the criminal bosses in Italy, France, and particularly in the heart of US imperialism, as well as in several Latin American countries. In many places, these protests—some of them genuine revolts against hunger, food shortages, and famine—have been led by poor families. They are a preview of what could happen if millions of workers return to their jobs in unsafe conditions, if new and worse hiring conditions, lower wages, and longer working hours are imposed on them, or if more families remain on the streets.

The union bureaucracies have, however, closed ranks with the bosses and governments, quarantining our demands and our plans to fight to defend our rights. Where there have been struggles, they try to keep them isolated and limit them to sectoral demands. In contrast, we call for a workers' united front. We demand that the leaders of all existing working-class organizations make agreements that allow us to strike together, even if we march separately. But our larger goal is to drive them out and take back the unions for our class.

That is why we want to organize and expand that front line of fighters, against the bureaucracies that divide us and seek only reconciliation with governments and capitalist states, because we must triumph in today's struggles and prepare to win in those to come, which will surely multiply.

5. FOR POLITICAL INDEPENDENCE FROM THE PARTIES THAT REPRESENT THE INTERESTS OF THE CAPITALISTS

We know that the working class, increasingly feminized and racialized, can disrupt the functioning of the economy and impair capitalist profits, establish alliances with other poor and oppressed people, and build a new social order based on meeting the needs of the great majority of people and not on the profit motives of a parasitic class. But when that potential is put into action, when we confront the bosses, we confront not only the agents of the bosses within the labor movement—the union bureaucrats who are always ready to negotiate the rate of exploitation, but never rip it out at the roots—but also the states and the political parties that represent the capitalists' interests.

These politicians go beyond Donald Trump, Giuseppe Conte, Boris Johnson, Jair Bolsonaro, Sebastian Piñera, and Emmanuel Macron. There are also women such as Angela Merkel, who with a motherly smile and imperialist firmness is proposing a program for rebuilding Europe that will salvage states and big businesses with bailouts that the working class will have to pay for; the terms of this are being worked out behind our backs. There's Jeanine Áñez in Bolivia, who now calls for prayer and fasting to confront the pandemic, and who did not hesitate to order military massacres to consummate last November's *coup d'état*. There are other extreme right-wing forces that were already growing before the pandemic, deploying their reactionary crusades against the women's movement, LGBTQ+ people, and immigrants. Together with the Vatican and fundamentalist evangelical churches, they attack feminism and what they call "gender ideology," combining the conservative aim of subordinating women to traditional family roles with their hatred of foreigners. Now, in the face of the crisis, they are once again trying to capitalize—in a reactionary way—on the social discontent with governments.

In response to the growth of these extreme right-wing forces, the reformist Left in Europe, the United States, and Latin America is pushing the idea that we should resign ourselves to the "lesser evil," be it the old social-liberal parties in Europe, the Democratic Party in the United States, or "progressives" in Latin America. But "lesser-evilism" has always meant accepting the same neoliberal policies combined with just a few very limited social measures that are purely cosmetic given the magnitude of the current crisis. In order to fight the extreme Right, "lesser-evil" governments do not represent an alternative; they leave capitalist profits intact and continue to rely on the most reactionary institutions of their states, such as the police, the courts, and the church hierarchies. The capitalist regimes do not dare to put the brakes on these messages of hate; only the feminist mobilizations and today's anti-racist mobilizations have taken that up.

That is why we must also find a way around the old and new reformists who, using the language of the Left, administer or offer to administer capitalism in decline. They are the ones who today haggle with their countries' big capitalists over crumbs, with the illusion that after the pandemic everything will return to how it was before: tremendous profits for the capitalists and more precarious wages for working families. That is the scandalous role Unidos Podemos is playing in the imperialist Spanish State, governing together with the neoliberal PSOE, paying tribute to the parasitic Bourbon monarchy, and sticking to the 1978 constitution inherited from Franco.

These parties, such as the *Frente de Todos* (*Front for All*) in Argentina, speak of "inclusion," while the government continues to pay the fraudulent foreign debt and young women in the slums around the nation's capital die after two weeks of complaining that they have no access to clean water in the middle of a pandemic. Likewise in Mexico, the government of Andrés Manuel López Obrador (AMLO)—which came to power on the hopes of change from millions of people, including broad sectors of women who trusted his promise to govern "for rich and poor people alike"—now favors policies that benefit big business. Meanwhile, militarization continues in Mexico—with femicide increasing for the last 12 years—as part of AMLO's subordination to imperialism and Trump's demands. And in Bolivia, Evo Morales's MAS has engaged in systematic negotiations with the coup leaders who now control the state, using as a bargaining chip the blood spilled during the brave and spontaneous popular resistance to the coup, in which the brave "*pollera* women"[1] played a leading role.

They are the same ones who, like Bernie Sanders, play the sad and tragic role of trying to rehabilitate a bloodthirsty political formation like the US Democratic Party, promising some minor social reforms with fiery speeches, only to end up withdrawing from the race and endorsing Joe Biden, an establishment politician whom, no matter how hard they try, they cannot dress up as a progressive insurgent. In the face of the crisis of the Trump administration and the emergence of anti-racist protests, the Democratic Party has been called on once again to play its historic role of pacifying social movements and assimilating them into the imperialist bourgeois regime. It remains to be seen if the Democrats will succeed with a candidate who spoke at a memorial for George Floyd but then said that police should

---

1. A pollera is a traditional dress worn by indigenous women in Bolivia.

be trained to shoot people "in the leg instead of the heart" as a way to avoid killing civilians. Biden also stands accused of sexual harassment and other markedly misogynistic behavior.

And they all play the same calamitous role we saw with Syriza in Greece, which came to power as the "hope of the Left" and ended up applying the brutal austerity plans imposed by the troika in the context of the last great crisis that began in 2008.

While the representatives of the conservative parties, the Right, and extreme right-wing populism vie for the top spot in the tournament of misogynists, xenophobes, racists, homophobes, and transphobes, the old and new reformists employ a "politically correct" discourse but they largely lack concrete policies to substantially change the lives of millions of women, lesbians, and transgender people, immigrants, racialized people, and precarious workers. In many countries, with a few minor measures and quite a lot of talk, they have assimilated and co-opted a good part of the feminist and women's movement. While millions of women workers and young students have embraced the anti-patriarchal struggle in recent years, some of the most recognized activists have been integrated into government institutions or have become spokespersons, candidates, or campaigners for reformist parties.

In opposition to this, we fight for the complete independence of the women's movement from all political representatives of the regimes who, in different ways, represent the interests of various capitalist sectors—but do not represent our interests, those of working people. And we fight for a working-class solution to this enormous crisis. Not in our name!

6. OUR LIVES ARE WORTH MORE THAN THEIR PROFITS!

The capitalists, the governments and political parties that represent their interests, and the trade union bureaucracy as their agents in the labor movement, have a program of measures to make us pay for the crisis. We raise an opposing program that challenges the interests of the capitalists so that working people will not have to pay for the crisis again.

All over the world, to deal with the pandemic and provide quality health care, we continue to demand the centralization and nationalization of healthcare systems—including private health care, with investments and appropriate wages—under workers' control.

The pandemic is no excuse for closing or cutting back on sexual and reproductive health programs, public services for safe abortions, or any other service for women and LGBTQ+ people. Nor is it an excuse for continuing to condemn pregnant women to serious health consequences or death from unsafe, clandestine abortions in countries where that right has not yet been established. That is why we continue to fight for the right to legal, safe, and free abortion, as demanded by the women's movement in Argentina, Mexico, Chile, and other countries.

We call for organizing those who must continue to work and we demand that they have control over safety and hygiene conditions. At the same time, we fight against lay-offs and against furloughs with wage cuts—in fact, we demand that lay-offs be prohibited. We pay special attention to precarious workers, those lacking labor rights, and we demand subsidies and quarantine wages so they will have an income that allows them to meet their basic needs.

We fight for equal pay for equal work. Racism and sexism are mechanisms of domination that reinforce super-exploitation, which is why we fight to eliminate the wage gap between men and women, and why we fight against racial, ethnic, and xenophobic discrimination.

We confront racism with the cry "Black Lives Matter!" We demand justice for Marielle Franco. We defend the rights of immigrant women who, in the face of indiscriminate border closures, have been forced into overcrowded camps for temporary agricultural workers, with inhumane conditions, without health care and other essential services. We defend the rights of women who have been forced to quarantine in their employers' homes, suddenly separated from their families and living like inmates. We demand the closure of all immigration detention centers.

Against the demagogy of the Right, we fight for working-class organizations to demand state subsidies, debt forgiveness, and cheap credit for small businesses, self-employed people, and freelancers who have lost income during periods of quarantine.

We fight for progressive taxes on large fortunes, because it is obscene that the richest 1 percent of the planet holds 82 percent of global wealth. Tax-exempt church properties, as well as the huge number of empty properties owned by large real estate groups that speculate on rents and tourism, must be put at the service of the needs of working people, beginning with the homeless, families living in overcrowded and unhealthy conditions in slums and temporary structures, and women and children who are victims of male violence and abuse.

In the dependent countries, we call for the cancellation of foreign debts, because we cannot allow banks and financial capital to continue to sink entire countries and regions, nor saddle states with debts they cannot pay. That is why we also call for the nationalization of banks under workers' control in order to centralize national savings according to the needs of the people.

A state monopoly on foreign trade is necessary in all countries. In countries that export raw materials, this would prevent a handful of multinational corporations in agribusiness, mining, and fishing from seizing all the revenues.

We reject the strengthening of state repressive apparatuses—security forces, armed forces, and the police. They murdered George Floyd, just as every day they kill young people of African descent and the children of poor families around the world. They are repressing our protests. They are responsible for torture, extortion, drug trafficking, and trafficking women. They enforce the quarantines. We also reject police and state spying and control with the supposed objective of stopping the spread of the virus. We stand for broad self-organization so we can use the self-control and self-discipline of the working class to confront the pandemic.

In the imperialist countries, we fight reactionary patriotism, racism, and all forms of discrimination against immigrants. It is essential to raise the banner of anti-imperialism in these countries, whose monopoly companies and governments brutally plunder the oppressed nations of the world. We demand an end to sanctions against Venezuela, Cuba, and Iran.

Just as women have mobilized every March 8 in massive numbers around the world to fight for our rights, so we call for working-class internationalism, to unite across borders against our common class enemies. With our voices burning with anger, we call on women workers around the world to organize and fight for this program. Our lives are worth more than their profits!

7. FOR BREAD AND ROSES!

Working-class women have never passively accepted attacks on our living conditions, nor have we stood by and watched our families starve. We did not remain silent when our rights and freedoms were violated, nor have we hesitated when we have set out to achieve what we think is right. That is the story of the poor women of France in 1789, the Black women at the forefront of the revolution that abolished slavery in Haiti in 1804, and the Russian textile workers who in 1917 kicked off the revolutionary process that brought the working class to power. There are many other examples throughout history of women providing the spark that launched a revolution.

In the same way, working-class women will confront the attacks that are now being prepared amidst the pandemic—a crisis that will allow new ways of thinking to emerge. Will our current and coming struggles for bread set the prairie ablaze? Our goal is to break the backs of the capitalists once and for all, so we can stop always having to fight back and instead achieve victory. As the great revolutionary Rosa Luxemburg said, we "take a stand for the establishment of a new society," not "for surface modifications of the old society" that has enslaved us.

We are fighting for a society in which reproduction and production develop in harmony with nature—a society freed from all the forms of exploitation and oppression that are now forced on the vast majority of people. But we are aware that such a society will not emerge spontaneously from the current crisis, even if rebuilding the capitalist system becomes increasingly difficult and any recovery will be more short-lived than the previous one. We know that although the contradictions of capitalism are increasingly unresolvable under its normal rules of operation, capitalism's decline will not automatically lead to the dawn of a triumphant global insurrection. It is necessary to prepare that, beginning now.

Women workers, anti-capitalist feminists, and revolutionary socialists are counting on women being on the front lines of the political and class struggle to defeat the capitalists, their governments, and their states. We are aware that as we struggle for a program that offers an independent workers' solution to the crisis that is afflicting humanity right now, we must also prepare for future struggles. We are aware that we need to establish a revolutionary working-class political organization or we will be powerless in the next battles of the class struggle, which the capitalists—who have declared a real war against us, made more intense by the pandemic—are preparing.

Let's get to work! Let's build an international revolutionary political organization of the working class that creates a real perspective for defeating capitalism and establishing a new socialist order—one in which bread and roses abound.

June 19, 2020

SIGNERS

ARGENTINA: Myriam Bregman, lawyer, member of the Workers Left Front (FIT), Buenos Aires; Andrea Lopez, general practitioner at the Hospital José Ingenieros, member of the Board of Directors of the healthcare workers' union CICOP, La Plata; Natalia Aguilera, nurse at the Hospital San Martín, La Plata; Pamela Galina, resident at the Hospital Noel Sbarra, CICOP delegate, La Plata; Natalia Paez, resident at the Hospital San Martin, CICOP delegate, La Plata; Lucía Rotelle, psychologist at the Hospital José Ingenieros, delegate of the public sector workers' union ATE, La Plata; Laura Cano, resident at the Hospital José Ingenieros, CICOP delegate, La Plata; Julieta Katcoff, nurse at the Hospital Castro Rendón, ATE delegate, Neuquén; Florencia Peralta, nurse at the Hospital Castro Rendón, ATE delegate, Neuquén; Barbara Acevedo, nurse at the Hospital Garrahan, Buenos Aires; Carina Manrique, nurse at the Garrahan Hospital, Buenos Aires; Florencia Vargas, administrative assistant at the Garrahan Hospital, Buenos Aires; Florencia Claramonte, administrative assistant at the Garrahan Hospital, Buenos Aires; Laura Magnaghi, medical technician, member of the board of directors of ATE Sur, Alende Hospital, Lomas de Zamora; Claudia Ferreyra, nurse at the Hospital Rivadavia, Buenos Aires; Melina Michniuk, psychologist at the Hospital Piñero, Buenos Aires; Andrea D'Atri, founder of the women's group *Pan y Rosas*, Buenos Aires.

BOLIVIA: Fabiola Quispe, lawyer and member of PRODHCRE (Professionals for Human Rights and Against State Repression), La Paz; Gabriela Ruesgas, economist and professor of sociology at the Higher University of San Andrés (UMSA), La Paz; Daniela Castro, PhD student in anthropology at the UMSA, La Paz; Gabriela Alfred, bachelor of philosophy, researcher, Tarija; Violeta Tamayo, political scientist and researcher, La Paz.

BRAZIL: Letícia Parks, member of the Black revolutionary group *Quilombo Vermelho*; Fernanda Peluci, leading member of the São Paulo subway workers union; Carolina Cacau, teacher of the Rio de Janeiro State Network; Silvana Araújo, front-line strike activist for outsourced workers at the University of São Paulo; Diana Assunção, leader of the non-academic workers' union at the University of São Paulo; Maíra Machado, leader of Apeoesp (São Paulo State Teachers' Union); Flávia Telles, coordinator of the Academic Center of Human Sciences of the State University of Campinas; Flavia Valle, teacher of the State Network of Minas Gerais; Val Muller, student at the UFRGS and activist of the youth group *Juventude Faísca*, Rio Grande do Sul; Virgínia Guitzel, trans activist and student at the UFABC, São Paulo.

CHILE: Natalia Sánchez, doctor of the Emergency and Protection Committee, Antofagasta; Silvana González, worker at the Antofagasta Hospital and leader of the trade union No. 1 Siglo XXI, Antofagasta; Carolina Toledo, nurse and member of the Health Brigades in the revolt of October 18, 2019, Santiago; Carolina Rodriguez, paramedic technician at the Sotero del Río Hospital, Santiago; Isabel Cobo, industrial worker and laboratory union leader, Santiago; Joseffe Cáceres, cleaning worker and union leader at the Pedagogical University, Santiago; María Isabel Martínez, leader of the local teachers' association in Lo Espejo, Santiago; Patricia Romo, president of the local teachers' association, Antofagasta; Pamela Contreras Mendoza, education assistant and former spokesperson of the March 8 Coordinating Committee, Valparaiso; Nataly Flores, retail worker, the leader of the Easy union, Antofagasta; Camila Delgado, retail union leader, Temuco.

COSTA RICA: Stephanie Macluf Vargas, student, University of Costa Rica; Fernanda Quirós, president of the Philosophy Students' Association at the University of Costa Rica; Paola Zeledón, call center worker, host of the program "Perspectiva de Izquierda" at *La Izquierda Diario CR*.

FRANCE: Laura Varlet, railway worker at the SNCF in Seine-Saint Denis, Paris region; Nadia Belhoum, trash collector at the RATP (Paris urban transport company); Marion Dujardin, arts teacher in the Paris region; Elise Lecoq, history teacher in the Paris region; Diane Perrey, teacher, Toulouse.

GERMANY: Charlotte Ruga, midwife at the München Klinik, Munich; Lisa Sternberg, ICU nurse at the München Klinik, Munich; Lilly Schön, economist and employee at the University of Applied Sciences for Engineering and Economics (HTW), Berlin; Tabea Winter, student of social work, Alice Salomon University of Applied Sciences, Berlin.

ITALY: Scilla Di Pietro, restaurant worker; Ilaria Canale, nursing student.

MEXICO: Sandra Romero, paramedic in the front line of the fight against Covid-19; Úrsula Leduc, laboratory worker at the Mexican Social Security Institute (IMSS) and the Secretariat of Health; Lucy González, precarious worker in the healthcare sector; Sulem Estrada Saldaña, grade school teacher; Flora Aco González, reinstated public sector worker and defender of labor rights; Yara Villaseñor, precarious service worker; Alejandra Sepúlveda, reinstated public sector worker and defender of labor rights; Miriam Hernández, administrative worker, non-academic workers' union of the National Autonomous University of Mexico (UNAM); Claudia Martínez, medical intern.

PERU: Zelma Guarino, agronomy student; Cecilia Quiroz, leader of the women's group *Pan y Rosas*; Melisa Ascuña, teacher; Fiorela Luyo, university student.

SPANISH STATE: Josefina L. Martínez, journalist and historian, Madrid; Cynthia Burgueño, historian and education worker, Barcelona; Raquel Sanz, domestic worker, Madrid; Àngels Vilaseca, social services worker, Barcelona; Soledad Pino, communications worker, Madrid; Rita Benegas, immigrant domestic worker, Barcelona; Neris Medina, immigrant worker in a fast food chain, Madrid; Lucía Nistal, researcher at the Autonomous University of Madrid (UAM), Madrid; Verónica Landa, journalist at *Esquerra Diari*, Barcelona.

UNITED STATES: Tre Kwon, nurse, New York City; Julia Wallace, Black Lives Matter activist, member of Local 721 of the Southern California Public Service Workers Union, Los Angeles; Tatiana Cozzarelli, PhD student in Urban Education at CUNY, New York City; Jimena Vergara, Mexican immigrant, correspondent for *Left Voice*, New York City.

VENEZUELA: Suhey Ochoa, student at the Central University of Venezuela (UCV).

And more signatures from the workers, students, housewives, and activists that make up *Brot und Rosen*, Germany; *Pan y Rosas*, Argentina; *Pan y Rosas*, Bolivia; *Pão e Rosas*, Brazil; *Pan y Rosas "Teresa Flores,"* Chile; *Pan y Rosas*, Costa Rica; *Pan y Rosas*, Spanish State; *Bread & Roses*, United States; *Du pain et des roses*, France; *Il pane e le rose*, Italy; *Pan y Rosas*, Mexico; *Pan y Rosas*, Peru; *Pan y Rosas*, Uruguay; *Pan y Rosas*, Venezuela.

Translation: Scott Cooper and Nathaniel Flakin

Bibliography

Albamonte, Emilio and Maiello, Matías (2019) "At the Limits of the 'Bourgeois Restoration.'" *Left Voice*, December 24, www.leftvoice.org/at-the-limits-of-the-bourgeois-restoration.

Albamonte, Emilio and Sanmartino, Jorge (1998) "La historia del marxismo y su continuidad leninista-trotskista es la del 'álgebra' de la revolución proletaria." *Estrategia Internacional* (Buenos Aires), 10.

Álvarez González, Ana (2010) *As Origens e a comemoraçao do Dia Internacional das Mulheres*. São Paulo: Expressão Popular.

Amorós, Celia (1990) *Mujer: participación, cultura política y estado*. Buenos Aires: De la Flor.

Amorós, Celia (1991) *Hacia una crítica de la razón patriarcal*. Barcelona: Anthropos.

Amorós, Celia (2007) *La gran diferencia y sus pequeñas consecuencias ... para las luchas de las mujeres*. Madrid: Cátedra.

Amorós, Celia (2008) *Mujeres e imaginarios de la globalización*. Rosario: Homo Sapiens.

Astelarra, Judith (2003) *¿Libres e iguales? Sociedad y política desde el feminismo*. Santiago de Chile: CEM.

Badia, Gilbert (1993) *Clara Zetkin: féministe sans frontières*. Paris: Les Éditions Ouvrières.

Bach, Paula (1999) "Robert Brenner y la economía de la turbulencia global: algunos elementos para la crítica." *Estrategia Internacional* (Buenos Aires) 13.

Bartel, W. (1958) *Die Linke in der deutschen Sozialdemokratie im Kampf gegen Militarismus und Krieg*. Berlin: Dietz.

Bax, E. Belfort (1914) "Socialism and the Feminist Movement." *The New Review* (New York, May), 2(5).

Bebel, August (1897) *Woman in the Past, Present and Future*. San Francisco, CA: G.B. Benham.

Bebel, August (1910) *Woman and Socialism*. New York: Socialist Literature Co.

Bensaïd, Daniel (1978) "Preface." In Moshe Lewin, *Le Dernier Combat de Lénine*. Paris: Éditions de Minuit.

Bensaïd, Daniel (2001) *Les irréductibles*. Paris: Textuel.

Bock, Gisela (1996) "Nazi Gender Policies and Women's History." In Georges Duby and Michelle Perrot (Eds.), *History of Women in the West*, Vol. 5: Françoise Thébaud (Ed.), *Toward a Cultural Identity in the Twentieth Century*. Cambridge, MA: Belknap Press of Harvard University Press.

Braidotti, Rosi (1994) *Nomadic Subjects: Embodiment and Sexual Difference in Contemporary Feminist Theory*. New York: Columbia University Press.

Bibliography

Bryant, Louise (1918) *Six Red Months in Russia: An Observers Account of Russia Before and During the Proletarian Dictatorship*. New York: George H. Doran Company.

Butler, Judith (1990) *Gender Trouble: Feminism and the Subversion of Identity*. New York: Routledge.

Butler, Judith (1990) "Gender Trouble, Feminist Theory, and Psychoanalytic Discourse." In Linda J. Nicholson (Ed.), *Feminism/Postmodernism*. New York: Routledge.

Butler, Judith (1993) *Bodies that Matter: On the Discursive Limits of "Sex."* New York: Routledge.

Butler, Judith, Laclau, Ernesto, and Žižek, Slavoj (2000) *Contingency, Hegemony, Universality: Contemporary Dialogues on the Left*. London: Verso.

Calvera, Leonor (1990) *Mujeres y Feminismo en Argentina*. Buenos Aires: Grupo Editor Latinoamericano.

Careaga, Gloria (Ed.) (2002) *Feminismos latinoamericanos: Retos y perspectivas*. Mexico City: PUEG.

Casale, Rolando and Chiachio, Cecilia (2009) *Máscaras del deseo: Una lectura del deseo en Judith Butler*. Buenos Aires: Catálogos.

Chingo, Juan and Molina, Eduardo (1999) "The War in the Balkans and the International Situation." *Left Voice*, July, 1, www.leftvoice.org/the-war-in-the-balkans-and-the-international-situation

Cliff, Tony (1981) "Alexandra Kollontai: Russian Marxists and Women Workers." *International Socialism* (London) 2(14) (Autumn).

Cliff, Tony (1984) *Class Struggle and Women's Liberation*. London: Bookmarks.

Cornell, Drucilla (1998) *At the Heart of Freedom: Feminism, Sex, and Equality*. Princeton, NJ: Princeton University Press.

Costa, Silvio (1998) *Comuna de París: o proletariado toma o céu de assalto*. São Paulo: Anita Garibaldi.

Curiel, Ochy and Falquet, Jules (Eds.) (2005) *El patriarcado al desnudo. Tres feministas materialistas*. Buenos Aires: Brecha Lésbica.

D'Atri, Andrea (Ed.) (2006) *Luchadoras: Historias de mujeres que hicieron historia*. Buenos Aires: Ediciones IPS.

de Beauvoir, Simone (2009) *The Second Sex*. London: Jonathan Cape.

de Lauretis, Teresa (2000) *Diferencias: Etapas de un camino a través del feminismo*. Barcelona: Horas y Horas.

Delphy, Christine (1977) *The Main Enemy: A Materialist Analysis Of Women's Oppression*. London: Women's Research and Resources Centre Publications.

del Rosal, Amaro (Ed.) (1963) *Los Congresos Obreros Internacionales en el siglo XX*. Mexico City: Grijalbo.

Deutscher, Isaac (2003) *The Prophet Unarmed: Trotsky, 1921–1929*. London: Verso.

Draper, Hal (2011) *Women and Class: Toward a Socialist Feminism*. Alameda, CA: Center for Socialist History.

Duby, Georges and Perrot, Michelle (Eds.) (1994–1996) *History of Women in the West*, 5 volumes. Cambridge, MA: Belknap Press of Harvard University Press.

Duhet, Paule-Marie (1971) *Les femmes et la Révolution 1789–1794*. Paris: Julliard.

Durany Vives, Carlota (1937) "El doble papel de la mujer." *Emancipación*, May 29.

Dunayevskaya, Raya (1991) *Rosa Luxemburg, Women's Liberation, and Marx's Philosophy of Revolution*. Champaign, IL: University of Illinois Press.

Eagleton, Terry (1996) *The Illusions of Postmodernism*. Oxford: Blackwell Publishers.

Engels, Friedrich (1993) *The Condition of the Working Class in England*. Oxford: Oxford University Press.

Engels, Friedrich (2015) *The Peasant War in Germany*. Abingdon: Routledge.

Engels, Friedrich (1970) *The Origin of the Family, Private Property and the State*. In Karl Marx and Friedrich Engels, *Selected Works*, Vol. 3. Moscow: Progress Publishers.

Espinosa Miñoso, Yuderkys (2007) *Escritos de una lesbiana oscura: Reflexiones críticas sobre feminismo y política de identidad en América Latina*. Buenos Aires: En la Frontera.

Etchebéhère, Mika (1987) *Mi guerra de España*. Barcelona: Plaza & Janés.

Femenías, María Luisa (2000) *Sobre sujeto y género: Lecturas feministas desde Beauvoir a Butler*. Buenos Aires: Catálogos.

Femenías, María Luisa (2003) *Judith Butler: Introducción a su lectura*. Buenos Aires: Catálogos.

Femenías, María Luisa (2007) *El género del multiculturalismo*. Bernal: Universidad Nacional de Quilmes.

Firestone, Shulamith (1979) *The Dialectic of Sex*. London: The Women's Press.

Fischer, Edmund (1919) "Die Frauenfrage." In Wally Zepler (Ed.), *Sozialismus und Frauenfrage*. Berlin: Cassirer.

Fontenla, Marta and Bellotti, Magui (1999) "ONGs, financiamiento y feminism." *Hojas de Warmi* (Barcelona), 10.

Fraser, Nancy (1997) *Justice Interruptus: Critical Reflections on the "Postsocialist" Condition*. New York: Routledge.

Gargallo, Francesca (2006) *Ideas feministas latinoamericanas*. Caracas: El Perro y la Rana.

Goldman, Wendy (1993) *Women, the State and Revolution: Soviet Family Policy and Social Life, 1917–1936*. Cambridge: Cambridge University Press.

Grogan, Susan (2002) *Flora Tristán: Life Stories*. London: Routledge.

Heinen, Jacqueline (1978) *De la Iª a la IIIª internacional: la cuestión de la mujer*. Barcelona: Fontamara.

Hollander, Nancy (1974) *La Mujer ¿esclava de la historia o historia de esclava?* Buenos Aires: La Pléyade.

International Socialist Conference (1904) "Resolution über das Frauen-Stimmrecht." In *Internationaler Sozialisten-Kongreß zu Amsterdam 1904*. Berlin: Expedition der Buchhandlung Vorwärts.

International Socialist Conference (1910) *Report of the Socialist Party Delegation and Proceedings of the International Socialist Congress at Copenhagen, 1910*. Chicago, IL: H.G. Adair.

Jelin, Elizabeth (Ed.) (1987) *Ciudadanía e identidad: las mujeres en los movimientos sociales latinoamericanos*. Geneva: UNRISD.

Käppeli, Anne-Marie (1993) "Feminist Scenes." In Georges Duby and Michelle Perrot (Eds.), *History of Women in the West*, Vol. 4: Geneviève Fraisse (Ed.), *Emerging Feminism from Revolution to World War*. Cambridge, MA: Belknap Press of Harvard University Press.

Kirkwood, Julieta (1990) *Ser política en Chile: Los nudos de la sabiduría feminist*. Santiago de Chile: Cuarto Propio.

Kollontai, Alexandra (1971) *The Autobiography of a Sexually Emancipated Communist Woman*. New York: Herder and Herder.

Kollontai, Alexandra (1975) *Die Situation der Frau in der gesellschaftlichen Entwicklung: vierzehn Vorlesungen vor Arbeiterinnen und Bäuerinnen an der Sverdlov-Universität 1921*. Frankfurt: Neue Kritik.

Kollontai, Alexandra (1977) *Selected Writings of Alexandra Kollontai*. London: Allison & Busby.

Krupskaya, Nadezhda K. (1970) *Reminiscences of Lenin*. New York: International Publishers.

Lamas, Marta (2011) *Feminism: Transmissions and Retransmissions*. New York: Palgrave Macmillan.

Lefaucheur, Nadine (1996) "Maternity, Family, and the State." In Georges Duby and Michelle Perrot (Eds.), *History of Women in the West*, Vol. 5: Françoise Thébaud (Ed.), *Toward a Cultural Identity in the Twentieth Century*. Cambridge, MA: Belknap Press of Harvard University Press.

Lenin, Vladimir (1965) "Better Fewer, But Better." In Vladimir Ilyich Lenin, *Collected Works*, Vol. 33. Moscow: Progress Publishers.

Lenin, Vladimir (1972) "Lessons of the Commune." In Vladimir Ilyich Lenin, *Collected Works*, Vol. 13. Moscow: Progress Publishers.

León, Magdalena (Ed.) (1982) *Sociedad, subordinación y feminismo: Debate sobre la mujer en América Latina y el Caribe*. Bogotá: ACEP.

León, Magdalena (1994) *Mujeres y participación política: avances y desafíos en América Latina*. Bogotá, Tercer Mundo.

Lewin, Moshe (1967) *Le Dernier Combat de Lénine*. Paris: Éditions de Minuit. (English: 1968: Lenin's Last Struggle. New York: Random House.)

Lewis, Jane (1984) *Women in England 1870–1950: Sexual Divisions and Social Change*. London: Wheatsheaf.

Liebman, Marcel (1989) *Leninism under Lenin*. London: Merlin Press.

Lonzi, Carla (2010) *Let's Spit on Hegel*. New York: Secunda.

Luna, Lola (Ed.) (1991) *Mujeres y Sociedad: Nuevos enfoques teóricos y metodológicos*. Barcelona: Universitat de Barcelona.

Luna, Lola (2003) *Los movimientos de mujeres en América Latina y la renovación de la historia política*. Cali: La Manzana de la Discordia.
Luxemburg, Rosa (2004) *The Rosa Luxemburg Reader*. New York: Monthly Review Press.
Marx, Karl (1990–1992) *Capital*, 3 volumes. London: Penguin.
Marx, Karl (1970) *Critique of the Gotha Programme*. In Karl Marx and Friedrich Engels, *Selected Works*, Vol. 3. Moscow: Progress Publishers.
Marx, Karl (2010) *The Civil War in France*. In Karl Marx and Friedrich Engels, *Collected Works*, Vol. 22. London: Lawrence & Wishart.
Marx, Karl (2010) *On The Jewish Question*. In Karl Marx and Friedrich Engels, *Collected Works*, Vol. 3. London: Lawrence & Wishart.
Marx, Karl and Engels, Friedrich (1956) *The Holy Family*. Moscow: Foreign Languages Publishing House.
Marx, Karl and Engels, Friedrich (1969) *The Communist Manifesto*. In Karl Marx and Friedrich Engels, *Selected Works*, Vol. 1. Moscow: Progress Publishers.
Meiksins Wood, Ellen (1986) *The Retreat from Class: A New 'True' Socialism*. London: Verso.
Michel, Andrée (1979) *Le féminisme*. Paris: Presses Universitaires de France. (Spanish: 1983: *El feminismo*. México: Fondo de Cultura Económica-GREA.)
Michel, Louise (1981) *The Red Virgin: Memoirs of Louise Michel*. Tuscaloosa, AL: University of Alabama Press.
Millet, Kate (1969) *Sexual Politics*. London: Granada Publishing.
Molina Petit, Cristina (1994) *Dialéctica feminista de la Ilustración*. Madrid: Anthropos.
Mouffe, Chantal (1993) *The Return of the Political*. London: Verso.
Mouffe, Chantal (2000) *The Democratic Paradox*. London: Verso.
Nash, Mary (Ed.) (1984) *Presencia y protagonismo: aspectos de la historia de la mujer*. Barcelona: Serbal.
Nicholson, Linda J. (Ed.) (1990) *Feminism/Postmodernism*. New York: Routledge.
Pankhurst, E. Sylvia (1977 [1931]) *The Suffragette Movement: An Intimate Account of Persons and Ideals*. London: Virago Press.
Pérez, Inés (2012) *El hogar tecnificado: Familias, género y vida cotidiana 1940–1970*. Buenos Aires: Biblos.
Pla, Alberto (Ed.) (1986) *Historia del movimiento obrero*. Buenos Aires, CEAL.
Proudhon, Pierre-Joseph (1995) *La pornocracia o la mujer en nuestros tiempos*. Madrid: Huerga y Fierro Editores.
Puleo, Alicia H. (1999) "En torno a la polémica igualdad/diferencia," Cátedra de Estudios de Género, Universidad de Valladolid, www.nodo50.org/mujeresred/feminismo-a_puleo-igualdad-diferencia.html.
Reed, Evelyn (1969) *Problems of Women's Liberation*. New York: Merit Publishers.
Reed, John (1919) *Ten Days that Shook the World*. New York: International Publishers.
Riddell, John (Ed.) (1986) *Lenin's Struggle for a Revolutionary International: Documents, 1907–1916, the Preparatory Years*. New York: Pathfinder Press.

Riddell, John (2015) "1915: Socialist Women Unite Against War." Translation, *John Riddell*, March 28. https://johnriddell.com/2015/03/28/1915-socialist-women-unite-against-war/.
Rivera Garretas, María Milagros (2002) *El fraude de la igualdad*. Buenos Aires: Librería de Mujeres.
Sánchez, Luis Alberto (2004) *Una mujer sola contra el mundo: Flora Tristán*. Lima: UNMSM.
Sazbón, José (2007) *Cuatro mujeres en la Revolución Francesa*. Buenos Aires: Biblos.
Scott, Joan Wallach (1993) "The Woman Worker in the Nineteenth Century." In Georges Duby and Michelle Perrot (Eds.), *History of Women in the West*, Vol. 4: Geneviève Fraisse (Ed.), *Emerging Feminism from Revolution to World War*. Cambridge, MA: Belknap Press of Harvard University Press.
Semashko, N.A. (1924) *Health Protection in the USSR*. London: Gollancz.
Stites, Richard (1978) *The Women's Liberation Movement in Russia: Feminism, Nihilism and Bolshevism 1860–1930*. Princeton, NJ: Princeton University Press.
Stürtze, Alizia (n.d.) "Feminismo de clase." *Lahaine*. At: www.lahaine.org/sturtze/feminismo_clase.htm.
Third International (1980) "Methods and Forms of Work among Communist Party Women: Theses." In Alix Holt and Barbara Holland (Eds.), *Theses Resolutions and Manifestos of the First Four Congress of the Third International*. London: Ink Links.
Thompson, E.P. (1980) *The Making of the English Working Class*. London: Penguin.
Thönessen, Werner (1976) *The Emancipation of Women: The Rise and Decline of the Women's Movement in German Social Democracy, 1863–1933*. London: Pluto Press.
Todd, Allan (1998) *Revolutions 1789–1917*. Cambridge: Cambridge University Press.
Tristán, Flora (1980) *Lettres*. Paris: Du Seuil.
Tristán, Flora (1983) *The Workers' Union*. Urbana, IL: University of Illinois Press.
Tristán, Flora (1985) *Peregrinations of a Pariah*. London: Virago Press.
Tristán, Flora (1993) *Feminismo y Utopia*. Mexico City: Fontamara.
Tristán, Flora (1993) *Utopian Feminist: Her Travel Diaries and Personal Crusade*. Bloomington, IN: Indiana University Press.
Tristán, Flora (2003) *Peregrinaciones de una Paria*. Lima: UNMSM.
Tristán, Flora (2007) *El tour de Francia*. Lima: UNMSM.
Trotsky, Leon (1937) *The Revolution Betrayed*. New York: Doubleday.
Trotsky, Leon (1945) "Twenty Years of Stalinist Degeneration." *Fourth International* (New York), 6(3) (March).
Trotsky, Leon (1962) *The Permanent Revolution and Results and Prospects*. London: New Park Publications.
Trotsky, Leon (1973) "A Bolshevik–Leninist Declaration on Comrade Trotsky's Journey." In Leon Trotsky, *Writing of Leon Trotsky*, Vol. 4. New York: Pathfinder.
Trotsky, Leon (1973) *Problems of Everyday Life*. New York: Pathfinder Press.
Trotsky, Leon (1981) *The Transitional Program*. New York: Labor Publications.
Trotsky, Leon (2008) *History of the Russian Revolution*. Chicago, IL: Haymarket.

Trotsky, Leon (2012) *Where Is Britain Going?* Abingdon: Routledge.
Valcárcel, Amalia (1994) *Sexo y filosofía: Sobre "mujer" y "poder."* Bogotá: Anthropos.
Vargas Valente, Virginia (2008) *Feminismos en América Latina: Su aporte a la política y a la democracia.* Lima: UNMSM.
Waters, Mary-Alice (1989) *Marxismo y Feminismo.* Mexico City: Fontamara.
Weinbaum, Batya (1978) *Curious Courtship of Women's Liberation and Socialism.* Boston: South End Press.
Wollstonecraft, Mary (2004) *Vindication of the Rights of Woman.* London: Penguin.
Zetkin, Clara (1934) *Reminiscences of Lenin.* New York: International Publishers.
Zetkin, Clara (2015) *Selected Writings.* Chicago, IL: Haymarket.
Žižek, Slavoj (1997) "Multiculturalism, or, the Cultural Logic of Multinational Capitalism." *New Left Review*, 1(225) (September–October).

Index

Abortion xi, 4, 5, 7, 77, 86, 87, 95–6, 101–2, 113–4, 125, 152–3, 162
AIDS 6
Anthony, Susan B. 33 n.3
Argentina ix–xii, 6, 78, 115–6, 123, 139–40, 160, 162
Armand, Inessa 70 n.15, 75, 84–5
Auclert, Hubertine 33

Bastille 11, 13, 45
Bax, Ernest Belfort 66
Bebel, August 39 n.9, 63–4, 68
Bensaïd, Daniel 92–3
Bernstein, Eduard 68
Besant, Annie 24
Black feminism / Black women x, xii, xiii, 6, 31 n.1, 122, 130, 133, 151–5, 162, 164
Black Lives Matter 152, 162
Bolívar, Simón 40, 52
Bolivia xi–xii, 113, 159, 160
Bonaparte, Napoleon 15, 40, 46
— Louis Napoleon (Napoleon III) 24 n.8
Bosch, Yevgenia 104–5
Brazil ix, xii, 26, 152
Bread and Roses Strike (in Lawrence, Massachusetts in 1912) 1–2, 25 n.10
Brussels 33, 70 n.15, 115
Bryant, Louise 98
Butler, Judith 138, 140–5

Chazal, André 42–52
Chile xi, 113, 115, 162
de Condorcet, Marquis 13, 71
Considerant, Victor 44

Contraception 7, 101, 112, 114, 119, 153
Copenhagen 2, 70, 83
Coronavirus / Covid-19 ix, xii–xiii, 151–67

Deroin, Jeanne 24
Difference Feminism 121, 128–33, 146
Divorce 40, 42–6, 49–52, 87, 89, 95, 101, 125
Dmitrieff, Elisabeth 26, 38
Durany Vives, Carlota 78–9

Eagleton, Terry 136, 145
Engels, Friedrich 35–8, 41, 52–3 n.27, 54, 62, 103
Equality Feminism 117–8, 129–33

Falklands War—see Malvinas War
Firestone, Shulamith 118–9
Floyd, George x, 151, 158, 160, 163
Flynn, Elizabeth Gurley 25
Fourier, Charles 34–5, 42, 44, 47, 50
France xii, 9–17, 19, 22, 24 n.8, 25–30, 33, 38, 39–62, 71, 74, 76, 78, 80, 86 n.7, 105 n.39 and 41, 110 n.1, 114, 116, 123, 152, 158, 164
  French Revolution 9–17, 26, 29, 40, 51, 54, 56–7, 164
Franco, Francisco 77, 79, 160
Franco, Marielle 162

Germany ix, xi, 2, 39, 42, 52 n.17, 63–71, 74, 79, 85, 86 n.7, 88, 91, 93, 97–8, 105 n.38, 111 n.2, 114, 152
Gleichheit (Equality) 2 n.1, 65, 71
de Gouge, Olympe 9, 13

Homosexuality, including gay liberation and LGBTQ+ 95, 112, 113, 117 n.12, 122, 141–2, 152, 159, 162
Hugo, Victor 39

imperialism x, 64–81, 104, 110–1, 123, 158, 160, 163
Industrial Workers of the World 1, 24 n.5, 25 n.10
International
 First International 26, 38, 48
 Second (Socialist) International 63–70, 103
 Communist (Third) International 70 n.15, 71, 103–4
 Fourth International 103–4
International Socialist Women's Conference
 Stuttgart (1907) 70
 Copenhagen (1910) 2, 83
 Berne (1915) 69–70, 85
International Council of Women 33
International Women's Strike xi
Intersectionality 133–7
Italy ix, xi, 40, 42, 69, 80, 116, 157–8

Jackson, Aunt Molly 24
Jews / Judaism 52 n.27, 74, 79
Joffe, Adolf 105
 Nadezhda 104–5
Jones, Mother (Mary G. Harris Jones) 24

Kiev 83, 86, 105, 106
Kollontai, Alexandra 10–1, 83, 97–103
Krupskaya, Nadezhda 75, 84–5
Kuliscioff, Anna 66

Lacombe, Rose 11, 15
Lassalle, Ferdinand 38–9, 64
Lemlich, Clara 23
Lenin, V.I. 69–71, 73, 83–8, 91–4, 97–8, 102–3

London 14, 20, 22, 24 n.7 and 8, 33, 40, 43, 52, 71–2
Lonza, Carla 129
López Obrador, Andrés Manuel 160
Lorde, Audre 122
Luxemburg, Rosa 68–9, 70 n.15, 71, 75, 103, 164

Malvinas War 123
Marx, Karl 20–1, 35–8, 41, 52–3 n.27, 54, 60, 103, 120
de Méricourt, Théroigne 13
Mexico ix, xii, 6, 26 n.6, 102, 115, 126–7, 160, 162
Miagkova, Tatiana 104, 106–8
Michel, Louise 25–8
Mill, John Stuart 33
Millet, Kate 118–9
Morales, Evo 160
Moscow 69, 83, 86, 88, 102, 104, 105 n.41, 106–7
Mouffe, Chantal 144
Movement for the Freedom of Abortion and Contraception (MLAC, France)

Napoleonic Code (Civil Code) 15, 40, 42, 51–2
National Organization for Women 114
NATO 6
Nazis 74, 79–80, 93, 105
New York 1, 23–4, 77
NGO (Non-Governmental Organization) 126, 138–40
Niboyet, Eugénie 44
Nicaragua 117, 123
Nin, Andreu 78

Owen, Robert 34, 50

Pankhurst, Emmeline 67, 72–5
 Sylvia 72–4

Index

Paris xii, 9–15, 19, 25–30, 38, 40, 42–6, 48, 50, 52 n.27, 60, 66, 69, 71, 86 n.7
  Paris Commune 25–30, 38
Petrograd (St. Petersburg) 3, 69, 83–4, 88, 97–8, 102
Peru xi, 40–1, 43–6, 56
Poland 68, 85
Portugal 113, 117
Postmodernism 138–57
POUM (Workers Party of Marxist Unification) 78–9
Prague 116
Proudhon, Pierre-Joseph 38–9, 61

Radical Feminism 116–21
Rabotnitsa (The Woman Worker) 83–4
Rakovsky, Christian 105–6
Reagan, Ronald 123
Reed, Evelyn 8
Reed, John 98–9
Rodríguez, Simón 40
Roland, Madame 12
Roland, Pauline 24
Russia 2–3, 69–71, 73–4, 76, 80, 82–109, 164

Sand, George (Amantine Lucile Aurore Dupin) 24 n.8, 60
Sanders, Bernie 160
Second Wave Feminism 34, 74, 110, 115–22, 135
Sedov, Leon 105
Seneca Falls Convention 32
Social Democratic Party of Germany (SPD), including Socialist Workers' Party of Germany (SAPD) 39, 63–71
Soviet Union 73, 77, 80, 87–109, 110, 117, 123
Spain xi–xii, 40, 74, 77–9, 123, 157, 160
Stalin, Joseph 92, 96, 97, 98

Stalinism 74, 78–9, 94–7, 102–9, 110, 112, 117, 125
Stonewall Riot 122
Suffragettes 1, 33, 67, 71–3, 115
Switzerland 42, 69–70, 85, 97

Taylor, Breonna 151
Thatcher, Margaret 123
Tristán, Flora 31, 39–62
Trotsky, Leon 8 n.6, 16, 29, 69, 76–7, 78 n 21, 88, 93–6, 98, 102–6
Trump, Donald 151–2, 159, 160
Truth, Sojourner 25

United Kingdom (including England, Britain) 6, 9, 14, 17, 20–3, 33, 42, 69, 72–7, 80, 87, 97, 110 n.1, 123, 152
United States of America ix, x, xii, xiii, 1, 23–4, 31 n.1, 33, 77, 80–1, 87, 104, 106 n.41 111, 114, 116, 123–4, 130, 151–60

Vietnam 113, 116
Voilquin, Suzanne 44

Washington, D.C. 33
Wilkes, John 14
Wollstonecraft, Mary 14, 42
Women's Liberation Movement 114
Women's Social and Political Union 72–3
World War
  One 2 n.1, 67, 69–75, 84–6, 97
  Two 79–81, 110–1

Yelizarova-Ulyanova, Anna 84
Young Women's Christian Association 32

Zetkin, Clara 2, 64–69, 70 n.15, 71, 75, 83, 103
Žižek, Slavoj 135

The Pluto Press Newsletter

Hello friend of Pluto!

Want to stay on top of the best radical books we publish?

Then sign up to be the first to hear about our new books, as well as special events, podcasts and videos.

You'll also get 50% off your first order with us when you sign up.

Come and join us!

Go to bit.ly/PlutoNewsletter

Thanks to our Patreon Subscribers:

Abdul Alkalimat
Andrew Perry

Who have shown their generosity and comradeship in difficult times.

Check out the other perks you get by subscribing to our Patreon – visit patreon.com/plutopress. Subscriptions start from £3 a month.